DOING HISTORICAL ARCHAEOLOGY

EXERCISES USING DOCUMENTARY, ORAL, AND MATERIAL EVIDENCE

D0162004

Russell J. Barber
California State University, San Bernardino

Prentice Hall, Englewood Cliffs, New Jersey 07632

Library of Congress Cataloging-in-Publication Data

BARBER, RUSSELL J.
    Doing historical archaeology : exercises using documentary, oral,
and material evidence / Russell J. Barber.
        p. cm.
    Includes bibliographical references.
    ISBN 0-13-176033-5
    1. Archaeology and history.   I. Title
CC77.H5B37   1994
930.1—dc20   93-39035

Acquisitions editor: *Nancy Roberts*
Editorial/production supervision and interior design: *Joanne Riker*
Cover design: *DeLuca Design*
Cover photo: *USDA—SCS photo by B.C. McLean*
Production Coordinator: *Mary Ann Gloriande*
Editorial assistant: *Pat Naturale*

Printed in the United States of America

10 9 8 7 6 5 4 3 2 1

ISBN 0-13-176033-5

Prentice-Hall International (UK) Limited, *London*
Prentice-Hall of Australia Pty. Limited, *Sydney*
Prentice-Hall Canada Inc., *Toronto*
Prentice-Hall Hispanoamericana, S.A., *Mexico*
Prentice-Hall of India Private Limited, *New Delhi*
Prentice-Hall of Japan, Inc., *Tokyo*
Simon & Schuster Asia Pte. Ltd., *Singapore*
Editora Prentice-Hall do Brasil, Ltda., *Rio de Janeiro*

CONTENTS

ACKNOWLEDGMENTS

This book never could have been written on a desert island, since comments and criticisms from many people have helped shape it. Lois Aguilar has discussed strategies and tactics with me for hours and has read each draft of the manuscript; her comments have been invaluable. Several of my colleagues at California State University, San Bernardino, have read and commented on specific chapters, particularly Frances Berdan, Peter Robertshaw, and Ward McAfee. Students in several of my courses have been willing and thoughtful guinea pigs, using generations of these exercises in some of my courses and freely commenting on their strengths and weaknesses. All of these individuals have earned my sincere gratitude. Finally, of course, I owe a special debt to Professor Leslie Squarkmuffin and his colleagues, a small part of whose massive—though fictional—scholarly contributions are used here as the basis for many of the exercises.

— INTRODUCTION —

THE NATURE OF THIS MANUAL

First as a graduate student and later as an archaeologist and professor, I have had to slog through volumes devoted to the nature of archaeology. Some authors have decided that archaeology is a set of methods that can be applied equally well to anthropology, history, classics, or art; others have decided that there is a core of theory that is distinctly archaeological and that archaeology is a discrete discipline in the fullest sense. Some authors have decided that archaeology is a portion of a single academic discipline (usually that of the writer), leading to the various characterizations of archaeology as "anthropology or nothing," "the handmaiden of history," or "the study of art and architecture of the ancient world." I have read and considered these various claims, and the disappointingly thin conclusion that I have drawn from my investment is that archaeology is what archaeologists do.

Perhaps I shouldn't be so disappointed with this conclusion. After all, archaeologists are a pretty diverse lot, and this definition provides a very broad umbrella under which they all can be sheltered. Some archaeologists study the remains of very ancient species ancestral to our own, while others deal with recent—even living—peoples. Some archaeologists are affiliated with academic departments of anthropology, history, art, classics, and even geography; a few are affiliated with distinct departments of archaeology. Still others work for governments or private consulting firms, carrying out the legal mandate to examine archaeological sites of potential significance before their destruction by public development projects, such as roads or reservoirs.

Within this diversity of archaeologists are the historical archaeologists, archaeologists who specialize in the archaeology of peoples recent enough to have left behind written records of themselves. Historical archaeology is sometimes called "text-assisted archaeology" "documentary archaeology," or (in Great Britain) "post-medieval archaeology" and in practice it focuses on the period following about 1500 A.D. The Society for Historical Archaeology, the main professional association in North America, lists over 2,000 members, and similar organizations in Great Britain and elsewhere would greatly expand that number.

While historical archaeologists are unified by a common period of interest, they vary greatly in their approaches to its study. Some are primarily concerned with reconstructing historical events and conditions; others try to understand the processes of history on a case-by-case basis; still others search for systematic patterns that cut across many cases. These different goals and approaches, often termed "paradigms," call for different types of analysis.

Most historical archaeological research falls into one of three paradigms. Historical particularism focuses on the individuality of a single case, emphasizing the specifics that characterize it. Historical particularist archaeology might aim at determining the style of the Norbridge House, the pattern of change in the popularity of different kinds of smoking pipes in Alexandria, or the extent of George Washington's gardens at Mount Vernon. Whatever the exact research, historical particularism's goals include exploring the details of a specific case as an end in itself. Historical particularism is rooted in the humanist academic tradition that characterizes much research in history and has been a part of historical archaeology since the origin of the discipline.

Processualism, on the other hand, is an outgrowth of the social sciences, particularly in the 1960s. Processualist studies focus on the regularities of human behavior, trying to recognize patterns of behavior that occur consistently in response to cultural and other forces ("culture process"). Causal explanations are an important part of most processual archaeology. Many processual studies utilize elements of the scientific method, such as hypothesis testing, models, quantification, and systems analysis; processual studies sometimes examine several cases in an effort to assure that a truly generalizable pattern has been established. Historical archaeological research in the processual paradigm might include isolating and explaining different patterns of trash disposal among the social classes of colonial Georgia, producing a model to explain the population density of Welsh towns before and after the industrial revolution, or explaining the willingness of French-American colonists to adopt native foods in colonial North America.

Processual archaeology raised the hopes of many that a true explanation of human behavior would be forthcoming, that scientific understanding comparable to that in chemistry or physics was around the corner. But far more factors complicate human behavior than the behavior of molecules and masses, and the sweeping successes of processualist archaeology have been few. To be sure, there are excellent examples of processual research, examples that truly help explain behavior, but the pace of progress has been slower than some of the more avid advocates of processualism had predicted, and there was a backlash in the late 1970s. This backlash, collectively termed post-processualism, included a variety of loosely related viewpoints, united in their conviction that processualism as it was practiced was neither the only nor the best way to conduct research. Many post-processual studies try to incorporate the rigor and some of the methods of processual archaeology, while focusing on the specifics of a particular case. Some archaeologists view post-processualism as a break from processualism, but others see it as simply a refinement, permitting the use of powerful methods over a broader range of subjects.

These three paradigms are all part of historical archaeology today. While some historical archaeologists hotly defend one or another as the only proper way to conduct research, most are more comfortable drawing on the wisdom of all three paradigms. Indeed, it is not uncommon for a single historical archaeologist to produce some research that is squarely particularist, while other research is clearly processualist and still other research is post-processualist. The data of historical archaeology are rich enough to support a variety of different styles in their interpretation.

This exercise book was assembled to provide you with a cross-section of the diverse sorts of things historical archaeologists do. I have consciously tried to include exercises that illustrate the different paradigms current in historical archaeology today. And, working from the premise that better understanding is gained from doing something than from reading about someone else having done it, I have created exercises that draw on and develop the sorts of skills and concepts that historical archaeologists use in their research. While some of the exercises include field or laboratory work, none requires highly technical or equipment-intensive activities, and they include no excavation or other destructive fieldwork.

The data sets included with most of the exercises are fictitious but realistic. In many cases they are modeled after data from real archaeological studies. Many of these exercises are based on the research of Prof. Leslie Squarkmuffin and his colleagues, some of the most productive fictional archaeologists of all time. While the archaeologists providing the data sets have been invented for this manual, the methods and theories discussed are real, as are the archaeologists who devised them.

At the end of this set of exercises, a student should have a tolerable understanding of what a historical archaeologist does, and that is the true nature of historical archaeology.

THE ORGANIZATION OF THIS MANUAL

The exercises in this manual are divided into five parts, each treating a major division of historical archaeological study. Part I deals with documents and oral histories, rich data sources that distinguish historical archaeology from its prehistoric sibling. Part II treats spatial analysis and stratigraphy, ranging from the level of the region down to the individual house and even the individual deposit. Part III considers the analysis of foodways, the complex of behavior surrounding what people eat and drink. In Part IV, exercises deal with various ways of analyzing artifacts. Finally, Part V provides exercises dealing with the study of historic cemeteries; these exercises call upon you to collect data in the field, as well as to analyze and interpret them. The appendices provide information that may assist you in completion of the exercises.

PART ONE

Written and Oral Sources

O NE OF THE GREAT ADVANTAGES of historical archaeology is that the archaeological record can be enriched with other data sources. The most important of these are written and oral sources.

The written record is enticing to the archaeologist, with its wealth of detail and coverage of issues about which the archaeological record is largely mute. A written description of a slave cabin may tell how many people lived there, who they were, what their ages were, what they ate for dinner, and what their religious beliefs were. It may describe what was stored on shelves and how often the cabin was cleaned. It may elaborate on the relationships between these people, other slaves, and their owners. Any of this information might be critical to an interpretation of the slave cabin, but much of it would be unknowable or ambiguous without these accounts. In a few words, a document may resolve many points about which archaeologists using only physical remains could argue for years.

Archaeology students learning about historical archaeology for the first time tend to be overawed by the wealth of information in documents and sometimes see the written record as a fountain of truth against which the archaeological record can be measured. Curiously, history students often see archaeological remains in a similar light, as an independent and unbiased set of data against which their documentary evidence can be weighed. Each set of students, recognizing the problems inherent in the set of data with which they are most familiar, hopes for fewer ambiguities and distortions in their newly discovered class of evidence. In truth, however, neither set of data is the yardstick of truth, and both must be considered in historical archaeology.

Especially in earlier times, the writers of documents in America have tended to be literate, well-to-do, politically active, urban, white males. Not surprisingly, these authors were most interested in and knowledgeable about issues that bore directly on their lives, and the documents they wrote are usually sketchy (at best) in their treatment of other issues. Consequently, the poor, illiterates, women, recent immigrants, and ruralites generally are represented poorly in documents. Even when writing about themselves or topics close to them, the authors of documents may have distorted facts, either purposefully (perhaps to assure a favorable place in history) or not. In colonial New England, for example, privies (outdoor toilets) are almost never mentioned in documents, presumably because potential readers already were aware of their existence and because mentioning them might have violated propriety; it would be poor history, however, to assume on the basis of these documents that colonial New Englanders had no privies. Documents certainly are valuable, but they have flaws, gaps, and distortions that demand that they be assessed, rather than simply accepted uncritically.

Archaeological remains, on the other hand, predominantly are simple refuse, and it is difficult to conceive of most archaeological remains having been purposefully manipulated by their makers. But the remains, nonetheless, have been affected by a host of processes that have modified, reshuffled, and partially destroyed them; uncritical interpretation of them will lead to distorted pictures of the past. The absence of a specific class of remains, for example, may or may not be meaningful. Fish bones might be absent from an archaeological site either as the result of post-depositional processes (the fine bones rotted away in acidic soil or were eaten by dogs before they made their way into the soil) or as the result of meaningful cultural and behavioral patterns (the people didn't eat fish, or perhaps they scrupulously discarded fish bones away from the site). Further, archaeological remains usually are anonymous and cannot be attributed to a particular individual on the basis of material evidence alone. Coupled with the limited level of detail usually attainable through the analysis of only physical remains, the archaeological record clearly has as many limitations as the documentary record.

Fortunately, documentary and archaeological evidence often are complementary. The wise historical archaeologist will assess the strengths and weaknesses of each set of evidence, compare them to find areas of substantial agreement or disagreement, and, if warranted, use one set of information to fill in gaps in the other.

Other exercises will explore the virtues and weaknesses of archaeological evidence, but the exercises in Part I deal particularly with written and oral sources. Exercises 1 through 4 provide experience in evaluating documents, using place names as clues to the past, collecting and evaluating oral information, and interpreting probate inventories (a particular class of document). Exercise 5 gives you practice in integrating the evidence of documents and archaeological fieldwork.

— EXERCISE 1 —
SOURCE ANALYSIS

OVERVIEW

Documents must be evaluated in terms of the likelihood of them being true. This exercise asks you to use the methods of source analysis to evaluate the probable truth value of a document from Vermont at the time of the Revolutionary War.

BACKGROUND ON SOURCE ANALYSIS

Source analysis is the examination of documents to try to determine their potential usefulness to the historian (and historical archaeologist). Source analysis is divided for convenience into two types:

1. *external analysis*: the examination of a document for authenticity—whether it was produced at the date and by the author claimed; and
2. *internal analysis*: the evaluation of a document for credibility—whether (and to what degree) the historian should believe the claims made in the document.

There are many factors to take into consideration when conducting the external analysis of a document. Several of these factors relate to the physical properties of the document itself, but others relate to its content. Some of the more important of these factors are targeted by the following questions:

- Is the paper or other writing material consistent with the date claimed?
- Is the pen or other writing implement consistent with the date claimed?
- Is the ink or other writing medium consistent with the date claimed?
- Is the penmanship consistent with the date, language, and country claimed?
- Is the penmanship consistent with the educational background of the author claimed?
- Are the vocabulary, communication skills, and knowledge evidenced consistent with those of the author claimed?
- Do technical methods of dating (*e.g.*, radiocarbon dating) substantiate the date claimed?
- Is there consistency of style and usage throughout the document (or do different parts of the document appear to have been written by different authors at different dates)?

- Are there telltale anachronisms (words, information, or concepts that would not have been available or current at the claimed time of writing)?

If a document clearly fails to pass any of these tests, it must be considered either suspect or false. At its most ludicrous, a seventeenth-century document might mention a helicopter, revealing its nature as a forgery. Equally bizarre true examples have occurred, however, such as a counterfeit coin with the stamped date of "34 B.C." and a supposedly Civil War era document written with ink that would not be invented until the 1920s. Most cases, however, are less clear-cut and are more difficult to evaluate.

Even if a document is determined to be a forgery, it still may provide valuable historical information. A forgery produced at the date claimed but by a different author, for example, may reveal an issue volatile enough to have inspired the author to lie. Those lies, in turn, may disclose areas of the author's knowledge or ignorance that otherwise would have remained hidden. Great care must be used in the interpretation of forgeries, of course, but even they may have usefulness.

Internal analysis aims to assess how likely it is that a document presents accurate information. Some factors important in this task are targeted by the following questions:

- Was the author in a position (educational, intellectual, social, and physical) to know and understand the things that he or she reported?
- Was the report made at the time of the event or later, after memory might have faded?
- Did the author have a bias that might have slanted his or her perceptions or reporting?
- Did the author have a vested interest in presenting one viewpoint at the expense of others?
- Are there internal contradictions in the document, suggesting fabrication or confusion?
- Is the statement inherently plausible? (This can be a highly subjective criterion, yet one that you have to address.)
- Does the statement fit in with or run counter to the bulk of historical documentation on a subject? (Running counter to prevailing evidence, of course, does not mean that a source is wrong, but it does mean that it must be a very reliable source to warrant trusting it rather than the other, well-established sources that contradict it.)

In the same way that Sherlock Holmes never simply accepted a witness's testimony, the historian always must assess historical testimony with an eye toward factors that might make it unreliable. The memoirs of a convicted traitor may well present a portrait of a patriot, if the writer selects and slants evidence to craft a false impression. A report of conditions in a black community during Reconstruction by a Ku Klux Klansman probably should be viewed with considerable skepticism, since prejudice can condition what a

writer observes or selects to report. A spectator who speaks only English may
have attended a speech given by Mussolini in Italian, but any description of
the speech—no matter how well intentioned—is limited by the spectator's lack
of linguistic skills in Italian. The role of internal analysis is easy to see in these
drastic examples, but the same sorts of factors can be manifested in more subtle
forms in cases where they are much less obvious.

In any particular application of source analysis, some of these factors
become more important than others; it is part of the critical process to decide
which areas require the most thorough examination. Some factors, particularly those regarding the physical characteristics of the document, may be
either inapplicable because the original document is unavailable for study or
irrelevant because it already has been investigated. In such cases, your analysis
obviously must rely on the other factors.

External analysis typically comes up with a conclusion that a document
is either legitimate or not. Internal analysis, on the other hand, typically comes
up with a more complex assessment of a document's credibility. An author
may have distorted or lied about one issue but been completely truthful about
another; he or she may have been competent to judge one issue and not
another. Consequently, internal analysis often leads to conclusions that certain
parts of a document are highly reliable regarding certain issues, while other
parts may be more suspect.

YOUR ASSIGNMENT

You have decided on the topic for your doctoral dissertation in historical
archaeology: a study of ironworking techniques in New England during the
American Revolution. As one way of gathering information for the dissertation, you will be conducting excavations at the Shields Furnace, a colonial
iron-smelting and casting furnace in Woodbridge, Vermont. You are ecstatic,
because you have located the Nathan Harrington document, which claims to
describe the furnace at the period in which you are most interested. You are
now ready to write a proposal to the National Science Foundation requesting
funding for the excavation and analysis, but you have to evaluate the likely
usefulness of the Harrington document for that proposal. Your dissertation
advisor at Miskatonic University, Prof. Leslie Squarkmuffin, has asked you to
undertake a source analysis and submit a report to him for review before you
write the all-important grant proposal.

Your task in this exercise is to complete your source analysis and write
your report for Squarkmuffin. You will want to divide your report into two
parts.

The first part should be the external analysis. Obviously, you won't be
able to do technical analysis on the paper or ink or anything like that, since
you don't have access to the original document in this exercise. Therefore, you

will have to focus your attention on the content of the document, particularly possible anachronisms and hints about whether it could have been written by Harrington or could have been written at the date claimed. Part of the process of source analysis is deciding which issues and evidence warrant the greatest attention, so think about what you want to focus on. Be sure that you conclude whether the document is legitimate or not; this part of your report should include the level of confidence you have in your conclusion and your arguments for it.

The second part of your report should focus on the internal analysis. (Even if you decide the document is a forgery, you should complete the second part of the exercise as if it were legitimate.) In this second part of your report, examine how reliable the information given in the document probably is. To do this, ask yourself how likely it is that Harrington would have been able to know the things recorded in the document, given what you know about him, his background, and his position in the community. Referring back to the questions on the previous pages should help you focus your analysis. As with the external analysis, you will have to decide what areas to explore more deeply, and you will have to present your conclusions and their justifications. There is no need to write a third part to the report summarizing your conclusions unless you wish to.

Since the document and its author are fictitious, there is no point in trying to research either. Instead, consider the information provided in this exercise as the complete set of information that will ever be available. You will, of course, have to consult outside sources to assess whether particular words used in the document would have been available to Harrington in 1778. The most useful of these sources will be the *Oxford English Dictionary*, a massive compilation of words and definitions in English, along with many historical notes and quotations that indicate the period when each word was in common usage. Other sources you may wish to consult are listed in the "Bibliography on Word Usage Sources" at the end of this exercise.

Background Information on Nathan Harrington

Nathan Harrington was born in Eelbourne, East Anglia, in the southeastern part of England in 1711. His parents immigrated to the American colonies in 1719 or 1720, settling initially in Greenwich, Connecticut. The family was of modest means upon arriving in America, and Nathan's father, Jonathan, became a woodcutter for a charcoal company, a position he held until his death in 1741. The details of Nathan's youth are unclear. He was raised in the Church of England, although he does not appear to have been particularly devout. He apparently was educated in the home with an expectation that he would follow in his father's woodcutting footsteps. Indeed, he was a woodcutter for a few years (1728-1731), but he reportedly tired of this dull job and left for the frontier in 1742. The years between woodcutting and departure for the frontier are undocumented, except for his marriage to Consistency Hoyt in 1738.

In 1742, Harrington and his wife arrived in Pownell, a small village in the Grants, the disputed area between New York and Massachusetts, in what is now Benningboro County in southern Vermont. Harrington set up a small farm on a large claim of land that was granted by the Massachusetts government but disputed by the New York legislature (which had granted the land to another party, Joshua Van Orman, who apparently never made any attempt to occupy or otherwise use the land). Around 1751, Harrington constructed a lime kiln and produced lime for agricultural and other purposes for the surrounding area by burning local limestone, quarried from portions of his property. At various times from 1750 to 1775, Harrington added to his commercial interests, accumulating a saw mill, a grist mill, a fulling mill, and an ill-fated flax-pressing operation (for pressing linseed oil from flax). The flax-pressing operation burned to the ground the night after its third day of operation in 1774, and there were suspicions of arson, since many of Harrington's neighbors were opposed to his pro-Tory politics and increasingly determined support of the British Crown. (On the other hand, it is perfectly possible that the flammable flax oil was improperly cleaned from the press and took fire from the residual heat held in the machinery or from heat produced by slow oxidation of the oil.) Harrington also opened a general store in North Pownell in 1763. His commercial operations were supported by the provisioning needs occasioned by the French and Indian War but were not disrupted by military actions, since none occurred in the area of Pownell.

Nathan and Consistency had four children: Elise (1743), Marten (1745), Margaret (1746), and Mary (1752). Consistency died in childbirth for Mary, though the child survived; Nathan never remarried. Elise died in the influenza epidemic of 1754; Marten and Margaret lived into old age; Mary died in childbirth in her early thirties. Margaret married Seth Schuyler in 1762 and moved to Tareytown, New York; Mary married Otto Kresge in 1771, and they lived in nearby Sage, Vermont; Marten married Rachel Bourne, daughter of Matthew Bourne (an outspoken and early supporter of a break with the British Crown) in 1767, and she came to live with him in Pownell. Marten was a Revolutionary soldier in the First Vermont Volunteers and later was a successful businessman.

During the American Revolution, Nathan Harrington was outspoken about his support for the British, although he claimed that his support did not go so far as military or financial support; he claimed an intellectual allegiance to Britain, coupled with a neutrality of action. This stance was neither understood nor appreciated by his predominantly rebellious neighbors, and his popularity and financial success diminished with the outbreak of hostilities. After the Revolution, he remained in Pownell and gave control of most of his holdings to his son, Marten. Marten's service in the Revolution sat well with the townspeople, and the company's prosperity returned. Nathan died of pneumonia in 1788.

Background Information on the Shields Furnace

The Shields Furnace was a combination iron-smelting furnace (for converting locally mined iron ore into iron) and casting operation (for pouring molten iron into molds to produce cast objects). The operation began in 1761 under the direction and ownership of Abel Shields and continued as a family operation through 1797, when it closed. The operation reopened briefly in 1812 but was abandoned as commercially unprofitable so far from easy lines of transportation to the markets in major cities.

The Shields Furnace was located in Woodbridge (now Vermont), about 11 miles north and slightly east of Pownell. The furnace was on the grounds of the Shields home and was clearly visible from the main road passing over Woodbridge Mountain to Dummerville, a major settlement.

The Shields Furnace produced a variety of cast-iron products, especially household goods, but with the war effort for the Revolution, it became active in the casting of cannons. After the war, financial fortunes waned until the closing of the operation.

The Shields family were pro-Revolutionary activists from the mounting of anti-Crown sentiment in the 1760s through the end of the war itself. During the war, various family members became military officers or provisional government officials. The family held a high social position and frequently held social gatherings in their home. It is unknown whether or not the Harringtons ever were invited to those gatherings or whether the Shields and Harrington families interacted socially.

Remains of the Shields Furnace, including walls standing nearly 12 feet high, are still visible at the site today.

Background on the Provenience of the Document

The document that follows was found in the collections of the Benningboro Historical Society in 1971. It was stored in a packet with several other documents of various ages, ranging from 1745 to 1932; so far as is known, all the other documents are authentic. The packet of documents came to the Historical Society from a posthumous donation of Peleg Matthewson, but it is unknown how he came to possess the documents. Mr. Matthewson died in 1964, and no relatives or friends with information on the packet of documents are known. Mr. Matthewson is known to have been an amateur historian with an interest in local history and was a man of considerable financial means.

The document is written on two pages of high rag paper, still in very good condition. There are no obvious stains or worm holes. The pages are of the same size. The writing in the pages is the same throughout, and, although no extant examples of Nathan Harrington's handwriting are known, the style is consistent with middle to late eighteenth-century English handwriting in colonial America. The ink is pure black ("India ink"), and the writing appears to have been executed with a hand-cut crow quill pen.

Local historians interpret this document as an authentic espionage report, prepared by Nathan Harrington for delivery to the British military to assist them in an attack on the Shields Furnace, in order to stop its production for the American Revolutionary War effort. Some historians believe the attack on the furnace was to have been coordinated with an attack on nearby Benningboro. (No attack ever was made on the ironworks, and local historians differ in their opinions about whether the document was never delivered or ignored or mistrusted by the British.) Some local historians believe that there originally was a third page to the document showing a map of the ironworks and grounds, but there is no evidence to support or refute this notion.

The Document to be Analyzed

A DESCRIPTION OF THE IRONWORKS OF A. SHIELDS

Along the cart track from Benningboro to Dummerville, fully one English league east of Benningboro and less than one mile from the center of Woodbridge settlement restes the works. The buildings form an orderly lot, in the grounds of the Shields house, though at one side as toward the track. The whole is surrounded by a low wall of dry stones layed one upon another to the heighth of three feet. At the western most edge of the property is the storage shed where ore and flux are held before consumption in the furnace. This building is some 50 feet by 40 feet at its base and nearly 20 ft. high with piles of ore sometimes behind it and to the east. To the w. of this shed is the furnace, where the ore and flux are throne into a great opening in the top of the furnace, led to by a ramp which extends outward from the side of the hill to allow the rolling of barrows to the opening, at which point the ore and flux may be poured in. The charcoal for the furnace is stored in many sheds and open piles to the e of the house and to the n and w of the fournace. The charcoal seems to be brought to the works by ox cart from charbonniers who make it in small heaps in the woods in the surrounding area, for there is no charcoal making at the works. The furnace faces to the s and the track, for the smell and heat of the fournace other wise would be carried to the house and be most offencive. The furnace itself consists of a high stack with an iron ring about the upper opening, to protect it from the batterring of the ore that is poured down it. The stack is of mortarred stone to a heighth of perhaps 45 ft, though it seems higher because [illegible]. At the base of the stack is the casting room, where the moulten iron is formed to make cannon and other devices, and here work the skilled labourers, of which there are four. The iron master supervises all, while his assistant produces the sand moulds which must be broken after each casting. The monkie tends the fire to see that enough flux is added to flote off the impurities in the ore and the rasper attends to the cleaning and smoothing of the objects as they cool. There are also all manner of other men and boys who work at sundrie tasks that require no skill, but they come and go as the fit strikes them. To the left of the furnace is the tuyere and the bellows that fill it and the channel of Cold Spring Creek where it has been diverted to run an undershot wheel of the sort usually used in this country for all manner of mills. The greatest danger to the furnace is that the Creek has weakenned the support for its w wall over the years and it may collapse into the Creek and wheel pit if given sufficient force, as by a goodley charge of powder. The finished cannons are carried to a shed on the w end of the property on a line even with the houses and out of sight of the track to be stored befor they are carted away. The iron that is produced at this fournace is of the highest quality and is sought after by all those of this country. It is said to have greater ability to stand abuse than other irons of this district, so that an empty cast kettle may be dropped and it will not break as it strikes a wooden floor. It is this quality of the metal that makes it so desirable for the making of cannon, so that the owners, with no love or respect for their sovreign King, produce fully one hundred cannon in a week, all provided to the rebellious forces that oppose the rightful Government. The complexion of this iron is that of a deep blue black like to that of a peacock and the iron from this fournace can be known by its colour. The works located as it is along the road but not near on to the other houses is a nest of loiterers and travellers who have chosen to stop for sustenance, though it is less than a mile to the inn at Woodbridge. The family encourages this, as they live an isolated existence and are by nature friendly and eagre to share gossip with any traveller. There are many dogs at the works, though most spend there time at the fields and woods behind the houses. The family keeps a few cows, pigs, &c. for there own sustenance, as well as a goodly stocked larder and barrelhouse for there guests.

[on a separate sheet:]
N. Harrington   October 8th 1778

BIBLIOGRAPHY ON SOURCE ANALYSIS

Clark, G. Kitson. 1967. *The Critical Historian*. Basic Books, Inc., New York. A book-length treatment of historical criticism of all sorts.

Garraghan, Gilbert J., and Jean Delanglez. 1946. *A Guide to the Historical Method*. Fordham University Press, New York. (Reprinted by Greenwood Press, Westport, Connecticut, 1973.) Part Three presents seven chapters treating criticism; the treatment of internal criticism is largely current, though some of the treatment of external criticism is dated.

Langlois, Charles V., and Charles Seignobos. 1898. *Introduction to the Science of History*. Duckworth and Company, London. Translated from the French by G. G. Berry. (Facsimile reprint by Barnes and Noble, Inc., New York, 1966.) The classic that first established the concepts of internal and external criticism. Largely dated.

Shafer, Robert Jones (ed.). 1980. *A Guide to Historical Method*, third edition. The Dorsey Press, Homewood, Illinois. Chapters VI and VII treat source analysis in a basic, down-to-earth manner. Probably the best brief treatment.

BIBLIOGRAPHY ON WORD USAGE SOURCES

Bartlett, James. 1989. *The Dictionary of Americanisms.* Crescent Books, New York. Originally published in 1848, this is a compendium of uniquely American words and word usage, including both conventional and colloquial usages.

Partridge, Eric. 1961. *A Dictionary of Slang and Unconventional English,* fifth edition. Macmillan Co., New York. A major compilation of slang words in English, including dates of usage.

The Dictionary of American Regional English. This multi-volume work is being published piecemeal and probably will be completed by the late 1990s. Until that time, only volumes dealing with the earlier letters of the alphabet will be available. The DARE provides detailed regional coverage, although dates of usage are not always provided.

The Oxford English Dictionary. There are two editions of this massive work by different editors and at different dates, but either is quite satisfactory for this exercise. The OED is available as a multi-volume book, as a reduced-print compact edition, and as a computer-accessible disk.

There also are many other excellent unabridged dictionaries, foreign dictionaries, and other sources that might be useful in this exercise.

— EXERCISE 2 —
TOPONYMY

OVERVIEW

The names given places can give strong hints to their past. This exercise asks you to examine the names given to a series of places in California's gold country and to develop possible interpretations.

BACKGROUND

Toponymy—the study of the names of settlements and other geographical features—sometimes can provide the historian or historical archaeologist with valuable insights, leads, and hypotheses. In particular, toponymy can be valuable in:

- dating settlements, especially old settlements where founding dates are unrecorded;
- assessing the ethnicity or origins of the occupants or founders of a settlement; and
- recognizing past geographical features that may no longer be extant.

A major assumption behind toponymy is that people name things in ways that have significance to the namers. A community might be given a particular name because its founders came from a community of the same name or because the new community had characteristics that reminded them of a community in their place of origin. On the other hand, a place might be named for a prominent physical or cultural feature that dominated it. There are many other possibilities, and many of these can provide insights into a place in the past or into the people who inhabited it.

TYPES OF PLACE NAMES

For convenience, toponymists categorize place names into eight major types, each of which is distinguished by the genesis of the name. These types are defined below.

1. Descriptive names. These names simply describe the landscape of an area, literally or metaphorically. *E.g.*, "Twin Peaks," "Green River," "Thousand Oaks," or "Furnace Creek" (in the heat of Death Valley).

2. Associative names. Associative names are ones that relate an area to its cultural features. *E.g.*, "Frenchman's Creek," "Mill Creek," or "Furnace Creek" (where associated with an iron furnace).

3. Incident names. An incident name is based on a particular event, either real or fictional, associated with the area. *E.g.*, "Big Bear" (any of several places where a large bear was seen) or "Show Low" (the Arizona town where a card game reportedly decided which of two rival families would leave town).

4. Possessive names. A possessive name indicates a person who is intimately associated with a place, often as a major landowner. Sometimes the name is merely a commemorative of a person of national or local importance, especially former rulers. *E.g.*, "Sutter's Mill," "Smithville," or "Jefferson."

5. Commendatory names. These names praise the places they describe. A commendatory name frequently is a public relations ploy to convince potential immigrants of the virtues of a place; sometimes, however, it is merely an extolling of the purported virtues of a place by its contented inhabitants. A special category of commendatory names includes mining camp names, where the founders often gave grandiose names in hopes of stimulating their good luck. *E.g.*, "Pleasant Valley," "Happy Camp," "Clearwater" (especially in an area with limited drinking water), "Running Springs" (especially in arid lands), or "Big Glitter" (for a gold mining camp).

6. Transfer names. These names have been transferred from their original (or at least earlier) homes along with immigrants. Consequently, they are often an excellent clue to the place of origin of the immigrant founders. *E.g.*, "Paris" (the Missouri town was named for a French prototype), "New Boston" (the Texas and Illinois towns were named for the Massachusetts city, which in turn was named for an English town), or "New York" (clearly named for "old" York in England).

7. Mistake names. A rare category, mistake names fossilize errors made by mappers or transcribers. Some are corruptions of the original names based on the dialect or accent of a region. For example, in Australia, "Coldegar" is a corruption of "collector," "Camboura" is a corruption of "gunblower," and "Dilliget" is a corruption of "delegate." A few mistake names are simple errors, such as "Nome, Alaska," whose name originally appeared on a map as "no name" and was miscopied to its present form.

8. Manufactured names. These are made-up words, often whimsical, *e.g.*, "Zzyzx" (a California desert settlement whose founder and namer swore that it would always be the last listing in a gazetteer). One category of manufactured names is those that combine parts from names of adjacent areas, such as "Arrowbear" (a California community located between Big Bear and Arrowhead), "Kenora" (the area between Keewatin, Norman, and Rat Portage in Canada's Northwest Territories), and "the Delmarva Peninsula" (which includes land from the states of Delaware, Maryland, and Virginia).

This typology of place names is neither exhaustive nor perfect. Some names fit no category well, and others may fit more than one category. Nonetheless, the terminology and concepts should be of use to you in completing this exercise.

USING TOPONYMY

To analyze place names sensibly, the analyst must ask why a place may have been named as it was and what that may imply about the place, its namer, or its occupants. Much of toponymy is based on common sense informed by a knowledge of words, their meanings, and their chronologies.

The dating of town founding on the basis of place names, for example, is based on the slow and more or less regular change in language over time. Over the centuries, typical word endings denoting towns have changed, and a local chronology of these endings can be used to date the founding of towns. (This method is predicated on the assumption that names of the towns have not changed in recent times, and that assumption usually can be reasonably assessed on the basis of documentary evidence. It also is based on the assumption that transfer names are not important in the area under study.) This type of analysis is most useful in a place with considerable time depth to its dominant cultural tradition, a place like Japan, England, or Italy; areas where the dominant cultural tradition is a modern overlay (*e.g.*, the United States or Australia) are less amenable to this type of analysis, partly because the time depth is so shallow and partly because transfer and manufactured names are so common.

An example of dating on the basis of town names comes from England. There, place-name endings are associated quite strongly with distinct periods, as Table 2-1 shows. These dates are applicable only to England, of course, and there might be significant regional variations in the dates within that country. By examining maps and dating the towns on them by the endings of their names, one can arrive at a preliminary picture of the history of the settlement of England.

On a different issue, the ethnicity or point of origin of the founders of a settlement often is indicated by the name they choose for their community. Naming a settlement with a French word, using the name of a French saint for a settlement name, or using a transfer name from a French community elsewhere can indicate that the initial settlers were French. Alternatively,

TABLE 2-1   Typical place-name endings in England and their dates of greatest usage.

ENDING	PERIOD	DATES
-enc	Celtic	pre-200 B.C.
-ain	Celtic	pre-200 B.C.
-ium	Roman	ca. 1 A.D.
-ham	Angle	ca. 500 A.D.
-burg	Saxon	ca. 800 A.D.
-ton	later Anglo-Saxon	ca. 1000 A.D.
-thun	Norman	post-1066 A.D.
-ville	Norman	post-1066 A.D.

transfer names from Connecticut appearing in Indiana may give a clue to where the settlers of a particular community originated.

Finally, features of the past landscape sometimes can be recognized in the names given an area. An area presently swathed in California tract homes may have descriptive or associative names like "Badger Hill," "Bear Canyon," or "Big Cat Spring," suggesting that its pre-domestication past may have featured a somewhat wilder environment than the present land use would suggest. The neighborhood of Boston called "Back Bay" is a reminder of the era before wetlands were so extensively filled in, when that area was salt marshes, mudflats, and tidal water. "Lime Kiln Creek" gives a clear suggestion of a prominent past industrial use, and "Wild Horse Potrero" suggests a grassland. (*Potrero* is Spanish for "pasture.") In areas where native languages have been replaced by other languages, place names may fossilize a descriptive or associative name, such as "Squamcut" in Rhode Island, a place name from the Algonquian Indian language meaning "salmon fishing place." (Since Squamcut is entirely subsumed by urban Providence, the name is one of the few ways to recognize the former relationship to salmon.)

Some Cautions

The use of place names for historical reconstruction, of course, has its dangers. Names can be misleading, especially when it is unclear into which of several types a name should be classified. For example, "Potter Creek" could be named for the pottery-makers who lived along it (descriptive or associative name), for the Potter family who formerly owned the land (possessive name), or for a Potter Creek that was prominent in the area from which the original settlers of the region emigrated (transfer name); further, the name might originally have been "Potrero Creek" and Anglicized (a mistake name derived from a descriptive name), or it might even be related to the folklore that Jesse Potter, the famous outlaw, passed there once (incident name). Some names, like this one, will be ambiguous if there is no additional documentary or oral evidence to aid analysis.

Commendatory names are especially susceptible to lies, as when an unscrupulous developer labels a desert tract "Lakeview," in hopes of attracting unwary speculators who might purchase land unseen. Wily developers have been especially active in California, peppering it with unlikely names in unlikelier places: "Apple Valley" in the Mojave Desert (where no apples could grow), several settlements named "Oro Grande" (Spanish for "Big Gold") where no significant amounts of gold were ever found, and various "Clearwaters," "Sweetwaters," "Running Springs," and "Cold Wells" in the middle of inhospitable and blazing deserts. Sometimes a namer wants to promote an old-fashioned or historical feeling and uses a purposefully old-fashioned-sounding name. Again, this has been particularly common in California, where most Spanish (or Spanish-sounding) place names date to periods considerably after the political dominance of Spain and Mexico in that state; using Spanish in a name evokes a feeling of history that most California communities have not developed by virtue of their age.

Another danger in the interpretation of place names is related to ethnic references incorporated into them. While "Chinese Bar" or "Hungarian Flat" probably reflect early settlements by those ethnic groups, not all names are so straightforward. For example, "Germantown Flats" might have been settled by Germans, but it might have been settled by Dutch instead, since Anglo-Americans frequently confused those groups, and since most names preserved in records are those used by Anglo-Americans. Other groups often have been confused in naming, such as Serbs with Russians and Norwegians with Swedes.

Further, place names may be nicknames for ethnic groups, often derogatory ones imposed on the community from outside. For example, "Greasertown" in the Southwest and California usually indicated a Mexican settlement, though there normally was another, often unrecorded name used by the inhabitants of that settlement. The power of racist thinking sometimes has been strong enough to lead to the naming of a community because of the presence of only a single member of an especially despised ethnic group, as with some of the many "Niggertowns" across the southern part of the United States from Georgia to California.

Some names are whimsical and of limited value in reconstructing the past. For example, the sidings along the Atchison, Topeka, and Santa Fe Railroad between Needles and Barstow, California, are in alphabetical order from A to H with names coming from Greek mythology. These names were assigned by an anonymous administrator who had never seen the terrain and certainly had no idea what sorts of towns might develop along the railroad. The variety of far-fetched interpretations that an overly zealous toponymist might develop from this case is sobering.

Finally, it is important to remember that the name of a community (providing the name has not been changed over the years) reflects only the conditions at the time of founding. The founders of a community may move on or quickly be submerged in a deluge of immigrants from different backgrounds, but the name lives on. "Chinese Camp" in California's gold country has no Chinese residents among its current 150 residents.

YOUR ASSIGNMENT

Prof. Theresa Highpockets, a well-known historical archaeologist and former student of Leslie Squarkmuffin, is planning a large-scale project in Plumador County, part of California's gold rush country. As part of her planning, she is conducting preliminary studies in a number of districts, enlisting the aid of selected graduate students, including you. Your task is to examine the data available and to draw what conclusions you can on the basis of toponymy. This research is exploratory, so you should feel free to explore any avenue that seems productive relative to toponymy, but you probably will have greatest success trying to learn something of the ethnicity of settlers in the area on the basis of transfer names. (To do this, you will have to consult gazetteers and other sources to trace where names occur elsewhere, at earlier dates.) You may also be able to find some sort of pattern that relates ethnicity to the locations and dates of settlements.

The information necessary to complete your task is given in this exercise. Figures 2-1 through 2-4 provide information on the topography, settlement, and land use of your section of Plumador County, and Table 2-2 presents what is known about founding dates for the settlements, based on documentary research. A thumbnail sketch of the history and geography of Plumador County is contained in this section.

Plumador County lies in the mountains and western foothills of central California. It has moderate rainfall and good agricultural land in its valleys, as well as mineral wealth (principally gold) in its hills and mountains. At the moderate elevations of the area under consideration, there will be only a little snow in winter.

Euro-American settlement began in the 1840s and exploded with the gold rush of 1849. Most of these settlements have been abandoned and now are ghost towns (archaeological sites); a few are still inhabited, especially in the valleys. Documentary sources are very good for a few communities and virtually non-existent for others, especially the more ephemeral mining settlements. Early roads were passable only in drier seasons, but improved roads that were passable most of the year were built around 1860. The railroad came through this area in 1878 and established a station at Germantown Flats.

TABLE 2-2   Settlements and founding dates, selected section of Plumador County, California.

SETTLEMENT	FOUNDING DATE
Cork	1849
Germantown Junction	1878
Greasertown	1850
Montenegro	1853 or 1854
New Chillicothe	1848
Oro Grande	1849
Peiping	1851?
Penzance	1849
St. Ide	1850

FIGURE 2-1

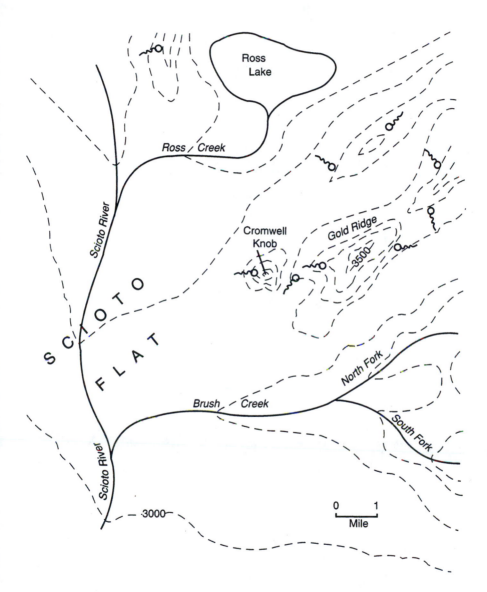

FIGURE 2-2

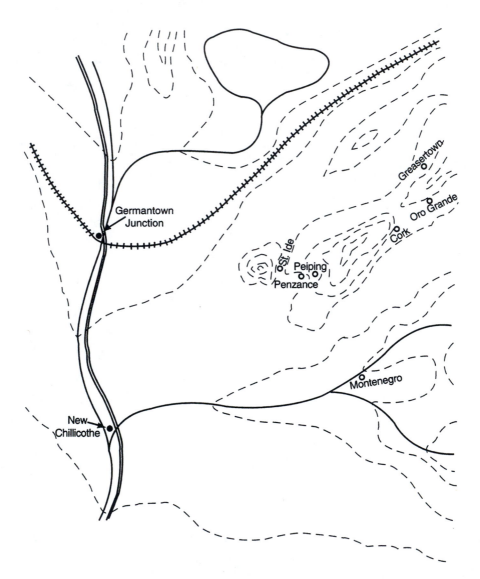

FIGURE 2-3

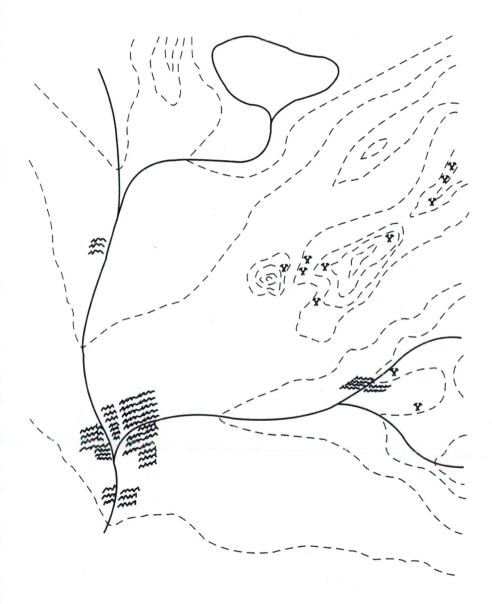

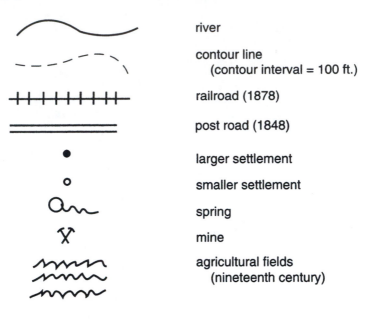

river

contour line
(contour interval = 100 ft.)

railroad (1878)

post road (1848)

larger settlement

smaller settlement

spring

mine

agricultural fields
(nineteenth century)

FIGURE 2-4

BIBLIOGRAPHY ON TOPONYMY

Andriot, John L. (compiler). 1987. *Township Atlas of the United States.* Documents Index, Inc., McLean, Virginia. Includes detailed U.S. gazetteer.

Gudde, Erwin G. 1969. *California Place Names: The Origin and Etymology of Current Geographical Names,* third edition. University of California Press, Berkeley, California. The basic reference on California place names. Neither this nor other sources on California place names are necessary for this exercise, but they provide abundant examples of the sorts of place names found in California and the reasons behind their naming.

———. 1975. *California Gold Camps: A Geographical and Historical Dictionary of Camps, Towns, and Localities Where Gold Was Mined: Wayside Stations and Trading Centers.* (Edited posthumously by Elisabeth K. Gudde.) University of California Press, Berkeley, California. The title tells it all: the basic reference on mining camp names in California.

Lambert, Eloise, and Mario Pei. 1959. *The Book of Place-names.* Lothrop, Lee, and Shepard Co., New York. A basic primer on toponymy.

Marinacci, Barbara, and Rudy Marinacci. 1980. *California's Spanish Place-names: What They Mean and How They Got There.* Tioga Publishing Co., Palo Alto, California. Detailed treatment on Spanish place names in California. More geared toward principles than encyclopedic treatment.

Paxton, John. 1986. *The Statesmen's Yearbook and Gazetteer,* third edition. St. Martin's Press, New York. World gazetteer.

Smith, Benjamin (ed.). 1894. *The Century Cyclopedia of Names.* The Century Co., New York. Large compendium of geographical and other names. Since more recent works often drop obscure references from earlier volumes, it often is necessary to consult older works.

Stewart, George R. 1975. *Names on the Globe.* Oxford University Press, Oxford, England. The best single text on toponymy.

Webster's New Geographical Dictionary. 1977. G & C. Merriam Co., Springfield, Massachusetts. World gazetteer.

— EXERCISE 3 —
ORAL HISTORY

OVERVIEW

Much knowledge about any period is never written down, and historical archaeologists working in relatively recent periods have the opportunity to collect information orally from informants. This exercise asks you to collect oral information to address one of five tasks presented.

BACKGROUND

Many academic disciplines tap the extensive body of knowledge that normally passes from individual to individual orally, never being written down. When anthropologists collect information orally, it is part of *ethnography;* when historians collect similar information, it is part of *oral history.* In either case, the people passing on the information are called *informants.*

This exercise uses the term "oral history" to refer to any collection and analysis of oral evidence to gain information and insights about the past. This can be a valuable adjunct to historical archaeology, and it has been used extensively around the world. Particularly in the twentieth century, the methodology for oral history has been developed and refined, sometimes drawing on the methodology of ethnography, where more scholarly attention has been directed. In the United States, oral history has increased in popularity among historians since around 1970, coinciding more or less with the increased popularity of social history.

The distinction often is made between *oral history* (where the informant actually witnessed the events, processes, conditions, or items under consideration) and *oral tradition* (where the period under study is too remote from the present for informants to have witnessed these things and where the information has been passed down through generations as folk knowledge). While many researchers consider oral historic evidence more reliable than oral traditional evidence, the methods of collecting and evaluating data are similar for both.

Despite any drawbacks, oral history can provide information of value to historical archaeology, including the following and other topics:

- the physical structure of buildings or other facilities;

- the use of artifacts, equipment, etc.;
- the social makeup of the groups using a facility or area (*e.g.*, young Greek immigrants, French-Canadian nuns, or convicts);
- the relations between the group under study and other social groups;
- the ideology of a group under study, a class of information particularly difficult to reconstruct archaeologically; and
- diverse information on activities practiced by a group under study.

For many projects, oral history is the only way to flesh out the archaeological record, especially in the study of recent groups poorly represented in the documentary record.

As with any other source of information, the historian or historical archaeologist must assess the likely validity of the information gained through oral history. This amounts essentially to internal analysis of the sort to which documents are subjected.

YOUR ASSIGNMENT

Your assignment is to carry out an oral historic project of limited scope that could have value to historical archaeological research. In particular, you are asked to complete one of the five tasks discussed below. Although an oral historic project usually profits from interviews with several informants, you probably will have to restrict your project to a single informant.

Task 1. Assemble the structural history of a building. Many buildings are described only sketchily in written records, but individuals may remember a great deal more detail; this is particularly true for outbuildings, such as garages, sheds, outhouses, and the like. For this task, you will need to select a building (preferably an outbuilding) and find an informant who can fill in details on it. Your informant may be able to fill in details for the entire period of the building's existence or only for some portion of that period. You will want to collect information that includes approximate dates of different construction events, the nature of those events, the appearance of the building after each event, and the use of the building during different periods. You also may collect information on the furnishing or decor of the building. If appropriate, you will wish to collect information on the destruction of the building.

Task 2. Collect information on the traditional methods used by a particular ethnic group for the cutting up of one type of food animal. This task will involve locating a butcher or meatcutter who caters to a particular ethnic group and gathering information on how that group traditionally cuts up chickens, ducks, or some other animal. This kind of information can assist in the interpretation of archaeological faunal remains, yet it can be very difficult to find in documents. (Exercise 10 treats faunal remains and butchering patterns a bit further.) You probably will want to include illustrations, perhaps skeleton diagrams with lines showing cut positions; you may or may not want to compare to typical Anglo-American butchering patterns for the same animal.

Task 3.   Collect information on the differing functions for a set of tools. Many of the tools used in any specialized occupation can look very similar to the outsider, yet they may have quite different uses. A slight curve in the blade of a chisel, for example, converts it into a gouge; a woodworker uses the chisel primarily for making joints, while the gouge is used primarily for fancy carving, a very different function. Knowledge of such uses can be valuable in archaeological interpretation. (Exercise 17 treats this issue further.) This task asks you to select a set of tools used in a particular occupation, to locate an informant knowledgeable regarding their use, and to collect information on their different uses.

Task 4.   Collect information on traditional gender roles. While most societies have marked differences between expected male and female behaviors, archaeology is weak at being able to identify these critical distinctions. Information on traditional gender patterning in activities can aid in the interpretation of archaeological remains, such as recognizing typically female or male work areas or toolkits. For this task, you will need to select a set of activities that will leave archaeological traces, find appropriate informants, and collect information on who traditionally performed those activities.

Task 5.   Collect information on a topic assigned by your instructor.

No matter which of these tasks you attack, you will need to follow similar steps:

- deciding on the appropriate set of information you want to collect;
- finding an appropriate informant who probably can provide that information;
- meeting with the instructor *early* in the term to work on the goal of the project and its design;
- conducting the interview(s);
- organizing and analyzing the information from the interview(s); and
- writing a report of the results.

Your report must include the following information, and you may find it convenient to make these labeled sections of your report:

- your goal: what did you want to find out, and what is its potential relationship to archaeology?

- your methods: what were the strategy and circumstances of the interview(s)? Who was your informant, and what was his or her claim to expertise? Why did you select that informant?
- a transcript of relevant portions of your interview(s);
- an analysis of the results of the interview relative to the goal, including a source analysis; and
- a conclusion or set of conclusions: what have you learned?

A Few Hints

This is not an easy assignment, but the following hints can help you be successful.

1. Allow more time for this project than you think you should need. Any fieldwork can develop problems; fieldwork that involves living people can develop more snags than most. Trying to complete this type of research under a pressing time schedule is not only nerve-racking but also likely to produce poor results.

2. Meet with your instructor *early* in the term to discuss your proposed topic and how to approach the project. You may have to meet several times, but begin early. An early meeting can help you avoid the many pitfalls of oral historic research, such as selecting an overly ambitious project or failing to take advantage of local opportunities. Also, your instructor may be able to assist you in locating an appropriate informant.

3. Select a narrow topic. By keeping your topic narrow, you help yourself in many ways. First, you aid your self-preservation, since a broad topic clearly requires a great deal more work. Second, the narrower topic allows you to focus the interview more, leading to an easier time at the analysis and writing phases.

4. Select an appropriate set of information you want to collect. First, it must be of potential use to archaeology. This means that you should keep in mind how an archaeologist conceivably could use your information to help interpret archaeological remains. Second, it must be feasible. Studying Chinese methods of duck butchering is not feasible if you have no access to a Chinese community or butcher. Try to take advantage of the opportunities peculiar to your area, letting its resources shape your choice of topic.

5. Be sure to do some reading prior to the beginning of the project if you feel you need it. There is a considerable literature on the methodology of oral history, and you may wish to sample it before you begin your project in earnest. The bibliography to this exercise notes major methodological works in oral history.

6. Prepare for the interview. Always bring appropriate questions with you to the interview; you may decide to ask somewhat different questions when the time comes, but at least you will be prepared. Be sure that you have your objective clearly in mind going into the interview, and let your informant

know early what your area of interest is. Your informant may not stick to that topic, and you may want to redirect the discussion tactfully if it strays.

7. Make your informant comfortable during the interview. Don't jump immediately into information collection; instead, begin by chatting informally with your informant, getting acquainted with one another. Making your informant more at ease will make the experience more pleasant for everyone and will increase the likelihood of gathering the information you seek.

8. During the interview, most oral historians will use an unobtrusive tape recorder, providing the informant approves its use. They will rely on the tape to catch all the details but still will take notes on main points, points that cannot be captured in sound (such as hand motions or actions), and ideas that occur to them during the interview. You may wish to modify this approach, however. Some informants will be made nervous by a tape recorder, in which case it might prove counterproductive. If you take notes, be sure that you don't stifle the flow of conversation from your informant by forcing him or her to slow down to let you complete your notes.

9. Depending on your objective, you may want to take photographs. This is particularly true for topics revolving around artifacts or activities, such as Task 3 or perhaps Task 2. Always get permission from your informant before taking photographs.

10. After the interview is over, you will need to go over your records as soon as possible. This involves clarifying your notes and transcribing your tapes. The longer you wait to do this, the more likely it is that you will be unable to decipher unclear passages.

11. Remember that your informant is doing you a favor. Accordingly, arrangements, such as the scheduling of any interview, should be at the informant's convenience.

12. This exercise is complicated by the ethics of oral history. The informant is providing you with information, but you must be mindful of the effects on the informant. Sometimes an event being recalled might be very painful, perhaps a mass or personal disaster; you must be sensitive to such a situation. Alternatively, informants might unthinkingly reveal information that would be harmful to themselves or others, sometimes even having legal ramifications. There are times when an oral historian, in good conscience, must refrain from utilizing information that has been provided by an informant. The literature cited in the bibliography to this exercise has many discussions of the ethics of oral history.

13. Universities and colleges have rules and guidelines regarding "the use of human subjects." These usually are most applicable to psychological experiments, but this research could fall under their control. If that is the case, you and your instructor will have to submit a proposal for approval before conducting this exercise.

BIBLIOGRAPHY ON ORAL HISTORY

Allen, Barbara, and William Lynwood Montell. 1981. *From Memory to History: Using Oral History Sources in Local Historical Research.* American Association for State and Local History, Nashville, Tennessee. Theory and methods.

Baum, Willa K. 1977. *Transcribing and Editing Oral History.* American Association for State and Local History, Nashville, Tennessee. Methods, particularly relating to transcribing and editing.

————. 1987. *Oral History for the Local Historical Society.* American Association for State and Local History, Nashville, Tennessee. Basic methods.

Cullom, Davis, Kathryn Black, and Kay McLean. 1977. *Oral History: From Tape to Type.* American Library Association, Chicago. Methods.

Evans, George Ewart. 1987. *Spoken History.* Faber and Faber, London. Theory and examples.

Grele, Ronald J. 1975. *Envelopes of Sound.* Precedent Publishing, Chicago. Theory and examples.

Harris, Ramon I., Joseph H. Cash, Herbert T. Hoover, and Stephen R. Ward. 1975. *The Practice of Oral History: A Handbook.* Microfilming Corporation of America, Glen Rock, New Jersey.

Havlice, Patricia Pate. 1985. *Oral History: A Reference Guide and Annotated Bibliography.* McFarland & Co., Jefferson, North Carolina. Bibliography.

Hoopes, James. 1979. *Oral History: An Introduction for Students.* University of North Carolina Press, Chapel Hill, North Carolina. General overview.

Lummis, Trevor. 1987. *Listening to History: The Authenticity of Oral Evidence.* Barnes & Noble, Totowa, New Jersey. Methods and theory, especially as relates to source analysis.

McMahan, Eva M. 1989. *Elite Oral History Discourse: A Study of Cooperation and Coherence.* University of Alabama Press, Tuscaloosa, Alabama. Advanced theory.

Olch, Peter D., and Forrest C. Pogue (eds.). 1972. *Selections from the Fifth and Sixth National Colloquia on Oral History.* The Oral History Association, New York. Various aspects.

Sitton, Thad, George L. Mehaffy, and O. L. Davis, Jr. 1983. *Oral History: A Guide for Teachers (and Others).* University of Texas Press, Austin, Texas. Methods, including teaching oral history and shaping student topics.

Stephenson, Shirley E. 1978. *Editing and Indexing Guidelines for Oral History.* Oral History Program, California State University, Fullerton, California. Methods, restricted to editing and indexing.

The Oral History Review. Periodical; covers all phases of study.

Vansina, Jan. 1965. *Oral Tradition: A Study in Historical Methodology.* Translated by H. M. Wright. Aldine Press, Chicago. Methods and theory.

————. 1975. *Oral Tradition as History.* University of Wisconsin Press, Madison, Wisconsin. Theory, especially relating to oral tradition carried over several generations.

Waserman, Manfred. 1975. *Bibliography of Oral History.* The Oral History Association, New York. Bibliography.

— EXERCISE 4 —
PROBATE INVENTORIES
AND ACCULTURATION

OVERVIEW

Probate inventories are a special class of documents that list individuals' possessions at the time of death. This exercise asks you to use a series of probate inventories from seventeenth-century American Indian communities in Massachusetts to study the degree to which these communities had adopted English technology.

BACKGROUND ON PROBATE INVENTORIES

In places where English Common Law has been the basis for inheritance, especially colonial New England and the Middle Atlantic colonies, *probate inventories* are valuable documents for archaeologists. A probate inventory is a list of an individual's property at the time of his or her death. This document was prepared by a public official and usually was mandatory; it generally is accepted by historians as a reasonable reflection of the material possessions of the deceased. Consequently, a probate inventory, in large measure, is functionally equivalent to the archaeological assemblage produced by a particular individual; each reflects the possessions of an individual.

There are very real differences, however, between archaeological assemblages and probate inventories. First, an archaeological assemblage accumulates over a long time, while a probate inventory is taken at a particular moment in time. Consequently, the assemblage will be dominated by remains from items with short use life expectancies, things that break or wear out frequently, swelling the archaeological assemblage and requiring replacement; broken bottles, sherds, and pipestems, though coming from items that never dominated a person's possessions numerically, are prominent in archaeological assemblages because those items break easily and require frequent replacement. In contrast, probate inventories often include expensive items that would be curated carefully, rarely making their way into the archaeological record at all, items such as pewter candlesticks and gold watches. Second, certain items that are prominent archaeologically are considered components of other items in probate inventories. Furniture, for example, might be reduced to metal nails and hinges in the archaeological transformation (as the wood rots away), yet it would not be analyzed into its component parts for an inventory. Third, some items apparently were not significant enough for inclusion in inventories, such as empty bottles, yet these clearly were reused and show up archaeologically. These factors suggest that probate inventories and archaeological assemblages are distinct sources of information on past material culture and that, while they reflect aspects of the same thing, they are not interchangeable.

Needless to say, probate inventories are a prime source of information for historical archaeologists. They can be analyzed in many of the ways that artifact assemblages can, and they are not subject to the same sources of distortion that archaeological remains are. Of course, they are a form of document, and they must be evaluated in the same way as any other document; such source analysis is discussed in Exercise 1.

There are issues relating particularly to probate inventories that must be considered in evaluating their appropriate use. It is clear that not everyone had a probate inventory, even in places and periods where it was mandated by law. It is estimated, for example, that 50% to 80% of the English in colonial Massachusetts had probate inventories made. (This number contrasts with an estimate of only 25% among Indians living in Christianized communities.) Of course, it would be best for historical archaeologists if everyone's goods had been inventoried upon a person's death, but the fact that this didn't happen would not be an extreme problem if those who were inventoried formed a representative sample of their communities. Unfortunately, this may not be the case. While there is disagreement currently, there is evidence suggesting that, at least in some places, those with probate inventories tended to be the more wealthy. As a result, these inventories may present a picture of colonial life that overemphasizes the well-to-do.

There are further complications regarding the use of probate inventories as they relate to Indians. Probate inventories, for example, were recorded more regularly for Indians living near English settlements than for those living further away. More troublesome, all probate inventories of Indians' goods, so far as is known, were produced by English officials. This means that the inventories incorporate the English value system and are likely to reflect limited knowledge of traditional Indian technology.

BACKGROUND ON ACCULTURATION

When one society abandons its traditional way of life to adopt that of another society, the process is called *acculturation*. In most usages, the term refers to the process as it applies to a subdominant segment of a society, such as an immigrant group or a conquered people.

In reality, of course, the process of acculturation is never so complete as implied by the simple definition given above. Any real society is likely to accept certain usages and reject others; these decisions to adopt or reject typically are patterned according to the values of the society in question and the circumstances of contact. How far a society is along the continuum between "pristine" and totally reoriented culture is described by the degree of acculturation.

In addition, the sociocultural process involved in the contact of peoples is more complex than that implied by this simple characterization. A society may adopt an item of technology from another but use it in a completely different manner, as when copper pots were first adopted by New England Indians from the English, not as cooking vessels, but as raw material for making copper arrowheads. Alternatively, an item might be accepted and used as originally intended, although its value might be seen as more symbolic than technical, as with steel axes adopted as status symbols among Australian Aborigines. While these and other complexities are clearly part of the process of cultural contact and change, acculturation retains a value as a simple concept providing an overall summary of the unfolding of complex sociocultural changes.

There is no fixed measure for degree of acculturation, but there are various indexes that can be used. (An index is an approximate measure, whose value is only a rough indication of the characteristic that it gauges.) One way to construct such an index is to assemble a list of cultural traits that characterize the traditional lifeway of the society in question and a list of the traits characterizing the society toward which it is believed to be acculturating. Looking at the acculturating society, one can calculate the number of its traits that can be traced to its traditional form and the number that can be traced to the dominant society. The proportion of borrowed traits is an index of the degree of acculturation of the society in question. Clearly, the value of the index will vary, depending on the particular data that are examined.

For example, we could examine the degree of acculturation of early twentieth-century Serbian immigrants to America as of 1950. If we were using personal possessions as our data set, we would compile one list of typically Serbian possessions (as of the early twentieth century) and another list of typically American possessions. Then, we would look at the lists of personal possessions for a series of Serbian-Americans from 1950. For each individual in our sample, we would count up the number of items that could be considered Serbian and the number that could be considered American. (Some items, of course, might fall under both categories, and these should be counted in both places.) Finally, we would divide the number of American items by the total number of items under consideration (both Serbian and American). The resulting figure will range from 0 (totally unacculturated, traditional Serbian) to 1 (totally acculturated to American ways). Of course, a study of Serbian-American foodways or religious practices would come up with a somewhat different figure for the index, but each figure would contribute to our understanding of acculturation among Serbian-Americans.

YOUR ASSIGNMENT

You and several other of Prof. Leslie Squarkmuffin's graduate students at Miskatonic University have decided to present papers at the Society for Historical Archaeology's annual meetings, and you have successfully proposed a symposium on acculturation. Each of you is preparing a brief paper to present at the meeting.

Your task is to use probate inventories to assess acculturation at two historic American Indian towns in eighteenth-century Massachusetts: Ponkatick and Natog. This exercise provides you with probate inventories and trait lists of expectable items for the English and for unacculturated Indians of seventeenth-century Massachusetts. You will have to compare the probate inventories from the Indian towns to the trait lists. Your report should include a table showing how the items from the Indian town probate inventories fit into one or both of these trait lists, your calculations of the acculturation index, a discussion of the results, and your conclusions. Remember that an index is only an approximate measure. You may find further information in the probate inventories that supports or argues against the findings of your index; be sure to include any such discussion in your report.

The Data Set

Tables 4-1 and 4-2 present partial lists of items that characterized pre-contact Indian cultures of eastern Massachusetts and early eighteenth-century English culture as it was transplanted to eastern Massachusetts. Many of the English tools were similar in function to Indian tools but were made of iron (knives, harpoons, etc.). New England Indians had no skills in the working of brass, pewter, or iron before the arrival of Europeans, so pre-English items were made primarily of wood, stone, shell, and bone.

The probate inventories from the Indian towns of Ponkatick and Natog are presented in Tables 4-3 and 4-4. These towns are both in eastern Massachusetts, about 30 miles respectively west and southwest of Boston. The individuals whose goods are inventoried in all cases were Indians. For your ease, the spellings (and in some cases, wordings) of the inventories have been made consistent with modern usage; some words, of course, have no modern equivalents. Certain portions of the inventories have been omitted, particularly assessments of value and the names of the inventoriers. These comprise all the inventories filed in these communities for the year 1722.

TABLE 4-1   A partial list of material culture items known to have been in use by the Indians of eastern Massachusetts on the eve of the entry of Europeans. Synonyms or types are given in parentheses.

Housing:	wigwam (hut)
Furnishings:	woven mats (rush mats)
	wicker baskets (reed baskets, rush baskets, osier baskets)
	barks (bark baskets)
	pottery
Foods:	maize (corn)
	squash
	beans
	tobacco
	wild animal meat
Food procurement items:	bow and arrow
	spear
	nets (pigeon nets, bird nets, fish nets)
	fish traps (eel pots, lobster pots)
	bone harpoon
	traps (wood and sinew)
Food preparation items:	samp mortar (corn mortar, corn grinding stone)
	pottery (earthenware)
Food consumption items:	bone or shell spoons
Clothing:	skin clothing
	skin leggings (Indian stockings)
Other:	stone tools of various sorts
	shell beads (wampum, wompanpeaque, suckonhock)
	tumpline (mattump)
	snowshoes
	stone and buffware smoking pipes
	woven bags (fiber bags)
	bark canoes

TABLE 4-2   A partial list of material culture items in use by the English in eastern Massachusetts by the late seventeenth and early eighteenth centuries.

Housing:	frame house (house)
	clapboards
	iron nails
Furnishings:	wooden furniture
	blankets
	iron hardware (hinges, nails, latches, locks)
	pottery
	splint baskets
Foods:	wheat
	livestock (cows, pigs, sheep, goats)
Food procurement items:	firearms
	iron plows
	iron hoes
	fish traps (eel pots, lobster pots)
	fishing nets
	iron traps
	iron harpoon
Food preparation items:	pottery
	iron pots
Food consumption items:	pottery
	trenchers (wooden plates)
	knives, forks, spoons (iron or pewter)
Clothing:	clothing made of textiles, with buttons
	leather boots
Other:	books
	iron tools in general
	whiteware and redware smoking pipes
	brass items
	glass beads
	horses
	barrels
	rope
	wooden boats

TABLE 4-3. Summary of items in probate inventories, Ponkatick.

Ben Quady:
- 1 frame house
- 1 table
- 1 samp mortar
- 1 barrel of Indian corn for seed
- miscellaneous cooking gear
- 1 bed
- 1 blanket
- 1 skin jacket
- 1 shed
- 2 cows
- 1 milking pan

Peter Netowa:
- 1 frame house
- 1 table
- 2 chairs
- 1 samp mortar
- 1 basket of corn
- 1 bag of beans
- 1 pewter spoon
- 1 pewter tankard
- 1 chest
- 1 waistcoat
- 1 pair English leather boots
- 1 bed
- 2 blankets
- 1 barn
- 2 oxen with yoke
- 1 pitchfork
- 1 shovel

Joseph Micah:
- 1 frame house
- 1 boat
- 1 iron pot
- 1 rifle
- 1 samp mortar
- 1 basket of corn

Ben Micah:
- 1 frame house with shutters
- 1 table
- 2 chairs
- 1 sideboard
- 1 wash basin
- 1 iron pot
- 1 samp mortar
- 1 basket of corn
- 1 bag flour
- 1 Bible
- 1 pewter candlestick
- 1 bed
- 2 blankets
- 1 shed
- 1 keg of nails
- 1 anvil
- 1 hammer
- 1 tongs
- 1 hand bellows, leather
- 1 horse

TABLE 4-4. Summary of items in probate inventories, Natog.

Mattacachame Duch:	Phillip Tashime:
1 frame house	1 frame house
1 samp mortar	1 samp mortar
1 iron pot	1 bag corn
1 bag of beans	1 bag beans
3 barks, one with Indian corn	3 wicker baskets
miscellaneous cooking gear	1 splint basket
1 fowling piece	1 brass kettle
1 horn of powder	nets
1 leather bag of shot	1 leather waistcoat
nets	4 traps
1 mattump	1 rifle
1 string suckonhock	1 pair snowshoes
1 bed	Peter Abel:
3 buckskins	1 wigwam
1 eel pot	4 woven mats
James Peleg:	2 pigeon nets
1 Indian cottage	1 fowling piece
1 large wicker basket with corn	5 traps, one of iron
1 samp mortar	1 iron pot
1 bag of beans	1 bark canoe, large
several rush mats	1 samp mortar
1 flintlock	1 box of corn
1 powder horn	Joshua Duch:
2 pots	1 frame house
1 Indian harpoon	1 samp mortar
2 buckskins	1 bag of corn
1 sinew snare	1 bag of beans
1 canoe	2 ceramic cooking pots
	1 chest
	2 buckskins
	1 flintlock
	4 wooden traps
	1 fish harpoon
	1 pigpen
	2 pigs
	1 large iron knife

A Note on Indian-English Relations in Early Eighteenth-Century New England

The first permanent English settlement in New England was at Plymouth in 1620, but the English (and other Europeans) had been in contact with the Indians of New England for decades before that, trading from fishing ships off the coast. Initially, relations between the two groups were friendly, and trading was regular. By 1650, the English had set up "praying towns"—the English counterpart of Spanish missions—where Indians could learn English ways and Christianity. These praying towns were successful at attracting Indians, since they provided access to trading and acquisition of technical skills (such as gun repair); in addition, they permitted individuals and communities on the wrong end of political hierarchies to escape intertribal tributary obligations or to aspire to leadership under the protection of the English. On the negative side, the praying towns established a dependent relationship on the English and served as a reservoir for European diseases, against which Indians had little immunity.

Praying towns ended with the bloody King Philip's War of 1675-1676, during which some Indian tribes battled the English and their Indian allies. This war resulted in the essential destruction of independent Indian polities in New England. From this point onward, Indians would have to fit into a larger, English-dominated society. It is against this backdrop that these probate inventories must be considered.

BIBLIOGRAPHY ON PROBATE INVENTORIES AND ACCULTURATION

Bragdon, Kathleen J. 1988. The material culture of the Christian Indians of New England, 1650-1775. In Mary C. Beaudry (ed.), Documentary Archaeology in the Old World (New Directions in Archaeology series), Cambridge University Press, Cambridge, England, pp. 126-131. Uses probate inventories to assess degree of acculturation at Indian towns.

Little, Elizabeth A. 1980. Probate records of Nantucket Indians. Nantucket Algonquian Studies 2. Archaeology Department, Nantucket Historical Association, Nantucket, Massachusetts. A review of the probate records and their usefulness for acculturation studies.

Vaughan, Alden T. 1965. New England Frontier: Puritans and Indians, 1620-1675. Little, Brown and Co., Boston. A classic historical treatment of acculturation and interaction.

— EXERCISE 5 —
INTEGRATING DOCUMENTS
AND ARCHAEOLOGICAL DATA

OVERVIEW

Documents and archaeological remains—the two most important types of data for the historical archaeologist—can be tricky to use together. This exercise asks you to use both sets of information in examining an urban area in Maryland.

BACKGROUND ON THE GENERAL ISSUE

Curiously, while virtually all historical archaeologists would agree that the integration of documentary and archaeological evidence is at the heart of historical archaeology, there are virtually no rules or conventions on how it should be done. In fact, there are few published treatments of the subject.

Probably this is a result of a feeling that such integration is either pretty straightforward or so variable from case to case that there can be no general rules. The disagreements that historical archaeologists get into over proper interpretation suggest that perhaps it isn't so straightforward as some might guess. Some suggestions and hints that might make your task in this exercise easier are given below.

1. Be critical of both your documents and your archaeological data. Neither set of data is the yardstick by which the other is validated or rejected. Each presents its own unique inputs, each has its gaps, and each can be distorted by a variety of factors. Documents have to be criticized internally, as discussed in Exercise 1. Archaeological data can be altered in confusing ways by site formation processes of the sort discussed in Exercise 9 and the introduction to Part V. In particular, when examining archaeological evidence, remember that a site can be reused after the period that may be most obvious or interesting to a researcher, and some remains may postdate the occupation under study. For example, a fort might be used as a dump by local trappers after it has been abandoned by the military; the presence of huge numbers of bones from fur-bearing animals does not mean that the soldiers were eating muskrats or moonlighting as fur trappers.

2. Try to be creative in envisioning possible ways that an archaeological deposit could have come about. You will have to come up with a variety of possible interpretations, many of which you will reject as soon as you examine

them. Others, however, may be a bit more enduring. For these, you will have to assess the competing interpretations and reject the less likely ones.

3. Use your critical thinking skills. Much of your success in this kind of activity rests on your ability to think clearly, to conceive of possible explanations, and to critically assess them. Remember to:

- assess everything, even the obvious;
- beware of false leads;
- watch out for logical fallacies; and
- avoid confusing similar concepts.

YOUR ASSIGNMENT

Various laws and regulations demand that public agencies usually assess archaeological and historic sites ("cultural resources") that potentially will be destroyed by public development and building. Consequently, archaeological surveys and other fieldwork must be completed by archaeological consultants under contract to the developing agency. You are working as a summer intern at such an agency, and you are asked to independently evaluate the conclusions of Prof. Leslie Squarkmuffin, the archaeological consultant who conducted the field studies for the project under consideration. You are provided Squarkmuffin's data, but his conclusions are kept from you until you complete your evaluation.

Your task is simple in concept, though perhaps a bit more complicated in practice. You are given a document that describes a series of adjacent buildings along Wulfing Street in Baltimore, Maryland, in 1824. You also are given a set of archaeological data from a small excavation conducted at Wulfing Street in 1988. The excavation was located such that it must have cut into the remains of at least one of the buildings described in the document. Your job is to decide which building or buildings were sampled by the excavation.

Background on the Document

The document comes from the archives of the Maryland State Museum, where it has been since shortly after its writing; there is no doubt about its authenticity. The document was written by Edwin Dodd, an insurance officer for the Republic Surety Company, based in Philadelphia. As was common practice, this company drew up a document covering an entire neighborhood, even though not all the businesses there were insured with their company. The purpose of the document was primarily to substantiate claims if a fire or other natural disaster were to wipe out the area. Insurance companies often shared one another's documents in the case of such a disaster. Normally, such insurance documents were produced on the basis of personal inspection by the officer, usually quite shortly before the date given on the document; occasionally insurance companies would share such information, so that some of the information in a particular document might not be firsthand.

This document is clearly written, and there are no possibilities of misreading because of illegibility.

Edwin Dodd was born in Baltimore in 1781 and began working in 1797 as a shipping clerk for E. Solomon Company, a Baltimore firm that specialized in international shipping. He left Solomon for Republic Surety in 1811, where he worked as a clerk until 1814, at which time he became an officer and began doing the sort of assessments considered here. Republic Surety had a Baltimore office, and apparently Dodd worked out of that office until 1844, when he died from injuries sustained when he was struck by a runaway milk truck.

Background on the Archaeological Excavation

The archaeological research was conducted by Dr. Leslie Squarkmuffin of Miskatonic University. Squarkmuffin was hired by the Maryland Department of Public Works to do preliminary testing of a small area where the state wants to build an underground water pumping facility, the construction of which would destroy completely any archaeological site on the property. This archaeological work was mandated by the Federal Environmental Protection Act and by state legislation and regulation. Squarkmuffin is a competent archaeologist who has experience in the historical archaeology of the nineteenth-century Mid-Atlantic Seaboard.

Because the work was designed merely to locate and identify whatever building(s) or other sites might be on the property in question, it was relatively small in scale, consisting of five test pits, each two-meters square. These test pits were distributed as shown in Figure 5-1. The contents of these pits are given in Tables 5-1 through 5-5. The section following these tables gives some background on the categories of remains recovered. The only intact evidence recognizable as being part of a building is the segment of masonry wall shown in Test Pit 1.

The Document

[An excerpt from an insurance area description prepared by Edwin Dodd and dated August 14, 1824.]

On the north side of Wulfing Street, between Calvert and Bothrop Streets, are a series of small shops and businesses. Passing along the street from west to east, these are the harness shop of Dennis Velorme, the pottery of Henry Harris, the butchery of Chas. Cutler, the cabinetry shop of Richard Whittlesey, and the chandlery of Vittorio Vincenzi.

The harness shop of D. Velorme is a small wood frame building with a stone foundation and half-cellar, dimensions about 30 by 45 feet. In the front is a workshop and storage area for completed work, while in the rear is a storage area for raw materials. He keeps on hand about $40 of raw materials, $85 of finished materials, and $35 of tools. The street frontage is 68 feet.

The pottery of H. Harris is a somewhat larger establishment, consisting of a woodframe building, an outdoor kiln, and two outbuildings in the rear of the property. The woodframe building is on a mortared stone foundation, while the outbuildings are without foundations. The woodframe building contains his workshop and showroom of completed pottery; in this workshop the vessels are formed and decorated. Clay is purchased and stored in a wood shed in the rear of the property. Charcoal for the kiln is stored in the other wood shed. The kiln is a brick and mortar affair, measuring about 12 ft wide, 12 ft deep, and 4 ft high, with three doors in front and one in the rear. The workshop has water piped in to a sink and has a drain to remove the water. Stock ready for sale: $160. Raw materials: $20. Tools, exclusive of kiln: $45. Frontage: 142 ft.

The butchery of Charles Cutler is a small shop where the proprietor cuts meat but does no slaughtering. The rear half is devoted to a cold storage with blocks of ice brought in every two days. There usually about 12 sides of beef, 4 sides of pork, and 2 sides of mutton are kept in various stages of aging. The value of the meat is about $140. The value of his knives and other tools of the trade is $35. The front portion of the shop is for customers to enter and for the sale of meat, as well as sweetmeats made by Mr. Cutler's wife. The building is of wood frame with a mortared stone foundation and no cellar. There is a water barrel that is refilled weekly by the merchant who delivers ice. Frontage is 71 feet.

The cabinetry shop of Richard Whittlesey is a building more spacious than required by his trade, with a frontage of 135 feet. The building is of wood frame on a mortared stone foundation with a fine, large cellar. The building is one large room, with a small room as an office behind. Wood is stored to the east end of the building, while the workshop is in the center and the finished stock is stored at the west end. The proprietor works in very fine woods, whose value at any time is around $200. Because he mostly works by orders, he usually has little finished stock on hand, value $45. The value of his tools is $200. There is no water in his shop.

The chandlery of Vittorio Vincenzi is a small shop, with a frontage of 68 feet and a wood frame building of 55 feet by 45 feet. It has no cellar or outbuildings, but it is divided into three rooms. The front room is where the candles are sold and the rear room which makes up most of the building is for storage of materials and the workshop. In addition, there is a small room to the rear and west where the proprietor resides alone. He stores wood which is required in large quantities for his work under a roof extending into the area behind the building. Value of raw materials: $45. Value of tools: $35. Value of completed merchandise: $75.

The Archaeological Results

[Excerpts from the report of Leslie Squarkmuffin, "Preliminary Excavations along Wulfing Street, Baltimore, Maryland, July 1992."]

Test Pit 1, located in the southwest corner of the property, was the only unit to encounter structural remains in place. Passing through the square from north to south was a mortared stone foundation wall, 27.5 inches (0.7 m) in thickness. This wall began at 44 inches (1.1 m) below surface and was overlain by rubble fill.

Soils to both the east and west of the wall were dense and solidly packed, indicating an original land surface and not a cellarhole. Materials on the east and west of the wall were tabulated separately in Table 5-1.

Test Pit 2 was located in the central portion of the property and encountered an upper layer of fill to 40 inches (1.0 m) below surface. The underlying soil was littered with artifacts and lenses of tan-gray clay; the soil was moderately dense and appears to represent a former soil surface.

Test Pit 3, located at the northwest corner of the property, was nearly sterile in terms of archaeological remains.

Test Pit 4 was located in the southeast corner of the property. The uppermost fill was some rubble to a depth of about 40 inches (1.0 m) below surface. Underlying this was a layer of apparently original land surface.

Test Pit 5 was located in the northeast corner of the property and showed the same pattern as elsewhere: an original land surface overlain by about 40 inches (1.0 m) of rubble-laden fill.

The archaeological remains from the test pits are summarized in Tables 5-1 through 5-5.

Notes on the Remains Described in Tables 5-1 through 5-5

The following notes give some information on the general archaeological occurrence of the classes of remains that were found in the Wulfing Street testing, and they may assist you in interpreting the archaeological evidence. For convenience, the remains are grouped into categories.

Structural Remains:

BRICK FRAGMENTS: common near brick structures, near brickyards, and in fill

CONCRETE FRAGMENTS: common near concrete structures and roads and in fill

MORTAR FRAGMENTS: common near mortared stone or brick walls; mortar tends to break down in fill but may occur

WINDOW GLASS: common near walls where the glass formed a window; typically more common on the outside of the wall than on the inside

Ceramics:

SHERDS: broken fragments of pottery; among the more common archaeological remains, sometimes occurring far from habitations

TABLE 5-1 Archaeological remains from Test Pit 1, Wulfing Street testing. Numbers in parentheses indicate numbers of fragments recovered.

LEVEL	ARCHAEOLOGICAL REMAINS
0-40 inches	brick fragments (37) concrete fragments (22) redware sherds (5)
40-45 inches	mortar fragments (43) leather fragments (34) small iron rivets (4) nail (1)
45-70 inches, west of wall	mortar fragments (23) nails (8) redware sherds (5) buffware sherds (3)
45-70 inches, east of wall	mortar fragments (31) nails (14) window glass (21) redware sherds (44) buffware sherds (15) ceramic wasters (3) ceramic trivet fragments (3) iron hinge (1) brass button (1) fragment of iron knife blade (1) iron wire (3) miscellaneous iron fragments (5)
70-80 inches, both sides of wall	[culturally sterile]

REDWARE: the most common kind of pottery in most American archaeological sites before the late nineteenth century; a soft, porous earthenware pottery (like a flowerpot); cheap and easy to make; used without glaze for a wide variety of purposes

BUFFWARE: a less common kind of pottery, made from the similar clay to redware but fired differently; somewhat more expensive than redware, but still inexpensive; often glazed to enable the holding of liquids

CERAMIC WASTERS: attempts at pottery that failed during the firing process, usually collapsing or otherwise deforming; wasters cannot be used for their intended purposes and normally are discarded by the potter

CERAMIC TRIVET: a small (about 3 inches across) redware piece shaped something like a three-bladed propeller with its tips raised at right angles to one

TABLE 5-2 Archaeological remains from Test Pit 2, Wulfing Street testing. Numbers in parentheses indicate numbers of fragments recovered.

LEVEL	ARCHAEOLOGICAL REMAINS
0-40 inches	brick fragments (22) concrete fragments (7) nails (3) redware sherds (2)
40-45 inches	leather fragments (4) redware sherds (11) nails (4) wood fragments (4)
45-70 inches	redware sherds (23) clay nodules (11) ceramic trivet fragments (2) nails (11) wood fragments (8) fragment of iron shovel blade (1)
70-80 inches	[culturally sterile]

side; these trivets are used as stands in the firing of pottery to keep the pots from fusing onto one another and the kiln interior

PIPESTEM FRAGMENTS: white ("kaolin") one-piece pipes were the predominant smoking apparatus in America before the late nineteenth century, and the stems were rather fragile and broke off easily; they can be found anywhere people smoked pipes

TABLE 5-3 Archaeological remains from Test Pit 3, Wulfing Street testing. Numbers in parentheses indicate numbers of fragments recovered.

LEVEL	ARCHAEOLOGICAL REMAINS
0-40 inches	brick fragments (38) concrete fragments (8) redware sherds (2) nail (1)
40-45 inches	nail (1) redware sherds (2)
45-70 inches	nail (1)
70-80 inches	[culturally sterile]

TABLE 5-4   Archaeological remains from Test Pit 4, Wulfing Street testing. Numbers in parentheses indicate numbers of fragments recovered.

LEVEL	ARCHAEOLOGICAL REMAINS
0-40 inches	brick fragments (4)
	concrete fragments (21)
	nails (9)
	redware sherd (1)
	coin (1)
40-45 inches	leather fragments (6)
	small iron rivets (2)
	nails (12)
	wood fragments (5)
	cow bones (3)
	pig bones (2)
45-70 inches	wood fragments (13)
	nails (9)
	iron hooks (4)
	iron wire (3)
	fragment of an iron knife blade (1)
	pewter button (1)
	pipestem fragments (7)
	cow bones (11)
	pig bone (1)
	sheep bones (3)

Iron:

NAILS: very common anywhere there are structural remains and in fill; they also occur in areas where they were used for industrial purposes (the making of furniture, carriages, etc.)

SMALL IRON TIVETS: iron rivets about 1/4 inch across at the head; they probably were used in the attachment of some flexible, sheet-like material

FRAGMENTS OF IRON KNIFE BLADES: iron was less sturdy in the early nineteenth century than today, and knife blades snapped with considerable regularity when they got heavy use; a snapped-off fragment could occur anywhere knives were used

FRAGMENT OF IRON SHOVEL BLADE: the same considerations hold true for shovel blades as for knife blades (see above)

IRON HINGE: a strap hinge from a swinging door, of a size to have been used either on a building or on a large piece of furniture

IRON HOOK: a fairly heavy bent piece of iron with a pointed end and a looped end (for nailing to a wall or similar area), about the size of a modern coat hook;

TABLE 5-5 Archaeological remains from Test Pit 5, Wulfing Street testing. Numbers in parentheses indicate numbers of fragments recovered.

LEVEL	ARCHAEOLOGICAL REMAINS
0-40 inches	brick fragments (21)
	concrete fragments (7)
	nails (2)
	redware sherds (3)
40-45 inches	leather fragments (13)
	small iron rivets (4)
	nails (8)
	iron hook (1)
	cow bones (7)
	pig bones (7)
	sheep bones (3)
	pipestem fragments (4)
45-70 inches	nails (2)
	iron hooks (4)
	iron wire (5)
	iron knife blade fragment (1)
	redware sherds (4)
	wooden comb (1)
	pipestem fragments (11)
70-80 inches	[culturally sterile]

such hooks could have served any purpose where something heavy would be hung and could be perforated with no damage

IRON WIRE: iron wire was used for many purposes in the early nineteenth century, including baling, holding things together, and the making of other items (*e.g.*, coarse wire was used to make nails)

MISCELLANEOUS IRON FRAGMENTS: iron decomposes in the ground, and it is common to have bits that cannot be identified in terms of the object they once composed

Other metal items:

BRASS BUTTON: brass was not an altogether common button material, since it was a bit expensive

PEWTER BUTTON: pewter was a more common button material

COIN: coins occur rarely yet regularly throughout archaeological deposits, especially in areas frequented by people

Bones:

BONES: bones preserve in all sorts of environments, although the smaller ones often decompose; bones may be moved from their original point of disposal by rats, dogs, and other scavenging animals

COW BONES: heavy and easily preserved

PIG BONES: heavy and easily preserved

SHEEP BONES: less heavy and less frequently preserved

Other items:

WOOD FRAGMENTS: bits of wood will preserve for a couple of hundred years in many preservation environments, so their presence here is not amazing; they can occur any place where people are using wood or discarding the waste from using wood; they sometimes occur in fill

LEATHER FRAGMENTS: leather preserves much less well than wood, and the presence of leather in this assemblage is slightly unusual, though by no means

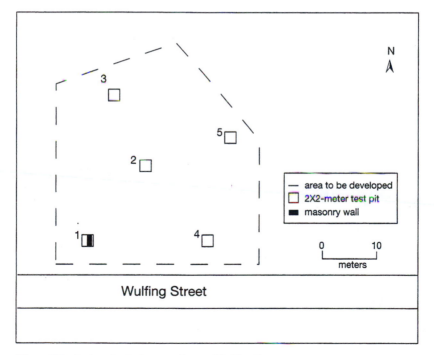

Figure 5-1. Archaeological excavations at Wulfing Street, Baltimore, Maryland, 1988.

unheard of; leather usually occurs in quantities only near some area where it was worked; leather fragments often are transported by scavenging animals, especially rats; untanned skin would not have preserved under the conditions at Wulfing Street

WOODEN COMB: in this period, combs typically were made of wood or bone; they were used as a grooming tool, just as today

CLAY NODULES: clay can occur naturally in soil or can be brought there as part of human activity, usually associated with filling in areas for construction or with ceramic production

Culturally sterile: bearing no artifacts or other humanly accumulated remains

PART TWO

Spatial Analysis
and Stratigraphy

MOST OF THE INTERPRETATIONS of archaeological remains that archaeologists can make are based on the answers to only two important, basic questions about those remains. What are they? And where did they come from? Parts III and IV of this exercise manual discuss the first question, and this part discusses the second.

It's no secret that archaeological remains, if they are removed from their original positions without recording them, have lost much of their information value. In the same way that Sherlock Holmes needed to know where the tobacco ash came from, so do archaeologists need to know the origin of the remains they study. Hence, archaeologists are awfully concerned with recording the *context* of their finds: where these materials were found, both in absolute terms and in relation to one another.

This concern with spatial patterning of archaeological remains is based largely on a recognition that human behavior tends to be organized spatially, and that the spatial patterning of remains can be used to reconstruct the behavioral or cultural patterns that produced it. Archaeologists who study these patterns are concerned with *settlement patterns*, recognizable and significant patterns of spatial organization. A great deal of archaeological effort has been expended in studying settlement patterns, but geographers have had the greatest success in understanding spatial patterning, and archaeologists often borrow theory from them to interpret their remains.

Geography, of course, concerns itself primarily with the spatial aspects of human behavior. There are many geographical models, some of which are discussed in exercises in this part, that aim at explaining and interpreting patterns of human use of the land. Most of these work from the recognition that human beings will place their activities on the land in response to the distribution of resources over space, the ease of transportation between places, and the distribution of other people.

Two terms will be useful in considering the first three exercises in this section. A *region* is a contiguous area in which there is considerable interaction between people and settlements and there is some similarity of environment. A *settlement* is a unitary location of human activity with some sort of boundary where the activities fall off dramatically, as at the edge of a town or city.

Using spatial patterns to make inferences and interpretations about the ways people have organized their behavior in the past is important. But there also is a second major reason that archaeologists pay so much attention to context: stratigraphy. Stratigraphy, the interpretation of soil layers and deposits in the ground, can provide information about the activities—both human and natural—that shaped an archaeological site. It also can tell a great deal about the sequence in which the deposits that form that site were accumulated. This latter use of stratigraphy is an important means of dating in most archaeological excavations.

The first three exercises in this part of the manual treat the three basic levels of spatial analysis. Exercise 6 examines the way an entire region is organized, looking at resource endowment, transportation routes, population distribution, and the relationships between settlements. Exercise 7 explores a single settlement, primarily looking at how internal forces shape its growth. Exercise 8 examines the architecture of single houses to investigate the mutual effects that housing and human activities have on one another. Finally, Exercise 9 provides an example of stratigraphy and presents guidelines for interpreting it.

— EXERCISE 6 —
REGIONAL SETTLEMENT
PATTERN ANALYSIS

OVERVIEW

Settlement within a region is shaped by the human reaction to the natural environment and to other settlements. This exercise asks you to examine settlement in a Kansas county and to discuss its probable origins and effects in terms of the central place model.

BACKGROUND

Social scientists define a *settlement* as any place where regular human activity takes place, including domestic sites (where people live), extractive sites (where they remove resources from the land), industrial sites (where those resources are turned into products), commercial sites (where goods and services are exchanged), ritual sites (where religious and other ritual activities take place), and other types of sites.

These settlements are spread across nearly every part of the world, but their distribution is anything but even or haphazard. In any part of the world, settlement is more likely to occur in certain zones than others, and there is a geometry that typically characterizes the distribution of settlements in relation to one another. In a word, settlement is spatially patterned.

This patterning that underlies human settlement is the focus of a variety of analytic approaches, most of which have been pioneered by geographers, and a few of which have originated with other social scientists, mostly archaeologists.

Reduced to basics, human settlement is patterned in response to two factors: natural environment and social environment. The *natural environment* includes terrain, soil, climate, plant and animal distributions, mineral distributions, and anything else in the natural world that can affect human survival and happiness (as defined culturally). The *social environment*, on the other hand, consists of other settlements, developed transportation routes, and the mutual effects that settlements have on one another. These concepts warrant a bit more examination.

The natural environment affects human activities at their base: without resources there can be no life and no culture. Some zones are better endowed with resources for agriculture—or at least for agriculture based on certain crops—than others; other zones have mineral wealth; still others have timber, fish, or whatever. In addition to these resources, there are other natural environmental factors that also affect the desirability of a zone, including climate and the ease with which humanly acceptable or desirable conditions can be obtained, incidence of diseases, ease of travel, and so forth. If there were no social factors to consider, the world's population would all be crammed into a relatively few zones with rich resources and desirable characteristics.

But the presence of other human beings and their settlements affects the desirability of an area. To a degree, there is a natural repulsion of human settlements, at least in terms of resource use. Too many settlements in an area, for example, can overtax the food or water supplies or lead to deforestation and erosion. At the same time, however, there is a natural attraction of settlements because of the importance of exchanging goods and services. In the extreme case, a mining camp with few other resources can survive very well if it can establish relationships with other communities that can trade the necessities of life for minerals produced at the mines; this can happen only if the camp is located in an area convenient enough to those other settlements to permit the economical transportation of the various goods between them. At a less extreme level, an industry will not locate in a place so far from other settlements that its workers will have no access to the goods and services that they expect, at least not unless resource distribution allows no other alternative. In the social arena, the spatial relationship between settlements can be seen as a tension between these attracting and repelling forces. These forces, of course, act as an overlay on the natural zones discussed above, forming a complex interplay.

The analysis of the natural environment's effects on settlement, in many ways, is simpler than the analysis of the effects of the social environment. Basically, the former consists of ascertaining what natural resources are needed for the activities that take place in a region, then finding what settlements fall in the appropriate zones to provide those resources. Presumably, there will be relatively few settlements in zones that are poorly endowed with critical resources or in zones that are well endowed with some resource for which there is little demand.

A few terms will be useful as we enter a further discussion of the social environment. A *settlement system* is the set of closely interacting settlements that occupy a contiguous area or a region. It is not necessary that all the settlements be nearly identical; indeed, there will almost always be diversity, as settlements of different sorts make their differing contributions to the system as a whole. One characteristic of most settlement systems is a *settlement hierarchy*, where different settlements are related to one another in an ordering from *higher-order settlements* (with greater size and greater numbers of functions that are carried out in them) to *lower-order settlements* (with smaller size, fewer functions, and simpler organization); the higher-order settlements also are known as *central places*. The *settlement pattern* is the set of characteristics shared by the elements of a settlement system, a description of how the various settlements are arrayed in relationship to the land and to one another.

One of the major models of geography deals with settlement hierarchies and is known as the *central place model*. This model originally was formulated over a century ago for application to places like the Central European Plain, where transportation is more or less equally easy in all directions and where resource endowment is similar everywhere. This sort of an area demands few choices of settlers in terms of natural environment, since few spots have particular advantages over others, and this model is based entirely on the effects of the social environment on settlement. (Its proponents argue that the model also is appropriate to areas where these conditions do not prevail, merely that the patterns will be "stretched" or "compressed" by the effects of the natural environment in places with greater natural diversity.)

According to the central place model, one should expect a more or less regular spatial distribution of settlements in patterns approximating hexagons. (Hexagons are the geometric figure that can be most closely packed in an array, apportioning the landscape into "territories.") The largest settlements in a region ("first-order settlements") will be surrounded by slightly smaller settlements ("second-order settlements"); second-order settlements, in turn, are surrounded by smaller, third-order settlements, and so forth to the smallest settlements. (Perversely, larger settlements are known as "higher-order centers," despite the fact that the number associated with their ranking is smaller.) In all cases, the lower-order settlements surrounding a higher-order center will approximate a hexagon. Higher-order settlements will be larger and provide more goods and services than the settlements below it in the hierarchy. This means, of course, that there will be progressively more settlements in a system as one passes from the larger, higher-order settlements to the smaller, lower-order settlements. It also means that, in general, larger settlements will serve a greater number of functions than smaller settlements, allowing settlement size to be used as an index of number of functions served.

According to the central place model, individuals living in a settlement will serve most of their everyday needs there. When they have a less usual need, they will go to the nearest settlement that can satisfy it. Normally this will be the next higher order settlement and will be fairly close, but a particularly exotic need will be served only by an even higher order center at a greater distance. The hierarchic settlement and hexagonal geometry, then, is the result of individuals trying to satisfy their needs with a minimum of effort expended in travel.

If you consider your local area, you will recognize first-order and lower-order settlements. There is some central place (often known as "the big city") where all or most goods and services are available, while there are smaller settlements around it that provide a smaller number of goods and services, and perhaps smaller settlements around them. Finally, there are very small, lower-order settlements that service only their local area, providing gasoline stations and convenience stores and little else. These local settlements illustrate the settlement hierarchy of the central place model, and the placement of these settlements over the land may approximate the hexagons predicted by the model.

(The nature of a model in social science requires a bit of explaining at this point. A model is simply a picture of what would happen if certain conditions were met. In the case of the central place model, the conditions are that individuals try to minimize travel time and effort, that resources are distributed equally over the landscape, that travel is equally easy in all directions, and that human beings are completely rational decision makers. Clearly, these conditions are not fully met in any real case, so there is no reason to expect that the predictions of the model will be fully realized. Consequently, the model is a device to predict what a simplified version of reality would be like; one of its greatest strengths lies in the examination of real-world deviations from its predictions and the search for the reasons why those deviations occurred.)

YOUR ASSIGNMENT

You are a student in Prof. Leslie Squarkmuffin's graduate course in historical settlement patterns at Miskatonic University. He has assigned you the project of examining historic settlement in McSaline County, Kansas, in 1881. The assignment requires that you:

1. apply the central place model;
2. look for deviations from it that may result from violations of its assumptions; and
3. be sure that your analysis takes both the natural environment and the social environment into consideration.

Figure 6-1 summarizes the settlements in McSaline County in 1881, providing size information, as well. Figures 6-2 and 6-3 provide information on the landscape. The following section provides a thumbnail sketch of the relevant history of McSaline County. Your report should present your analysis of the settlement of McSaline County in 1881 and any conclusions you can draw from it.

A Brief Sketch of the Relevant History of McSaline County

Euro-American settlement of McSaline County began in earnest around 1858. The settlers were mostly corn farmers who favored the bluestem prairie along rivers, where their preferred crop grew so well. Following the Civil War, irrigation expanded the areas where corn could be grown into areas away from flood plains, although the bluestem prairie continued to be the focus of agricultural settlement. Around 1873, farmers began growing wheat in quantities in McSaline County, particularly in irrigated areas of the sand prairie. The irrigation networks in the sand prairie, however, could be established only with great expenditure of labor, and the lack of investment capital made the expansion of wheat agriculture relatively slow. By 1895, however, wheat had become an important crop in McSaline County. Throughout the history of McSaline County, crop growing has supported the vast majority of its occupants.

McSaline County was not endowed with great mineral wealth. The south-central hills had small deposits of salt and potash, both of which were mined from the early 1860s through the mid-1870s. By 1881, however, only a single mining community (Dusty) remained active and occupied.

The Bathsheba River and West River, both of which were permanent and ran from west to east, provided water for drinking and irrigation; Salt Creek, despite its name, carried fresh water and was used for drinking water. Wells also supplemented supplies for irrigation.

The rivers served as local transportation corridors, with roads along their sides, but they never were major transportation routes to areas outside the county, since portions of them were too shallow to support boats in all seasons. Bridges spanned the Bathsheba River at Aroma (1864), Bouquet (1871), and Brut (1872). There were no bridges over the West River or Salt Creek until the twentieth century. The railroad came to McSaline County quite late, in 1891.

With the establishment of the county in 1866, Aroma became the county seat.

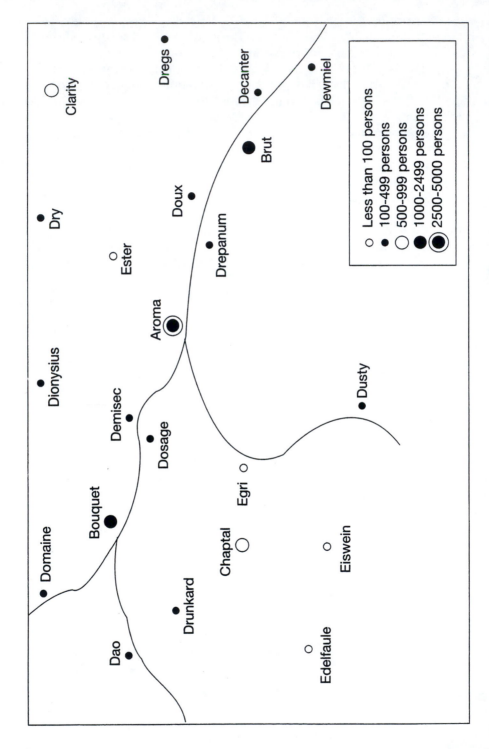

Less than 100 persons ○
100-499 persons •
500-999 persons ◯
1000-2499 persons ●
2500-5000 persons ◉

Dregs
Decanter
Dewmiel
Clarity
Brut
Doux
Dry
Ester
Drepanum
Aroma
Dionysius
Demisec
Dusty
Dosage
Bouquet
Egri
Domaine
Chaptal
Drunkard
Eiswein
Dao
Edelfaule

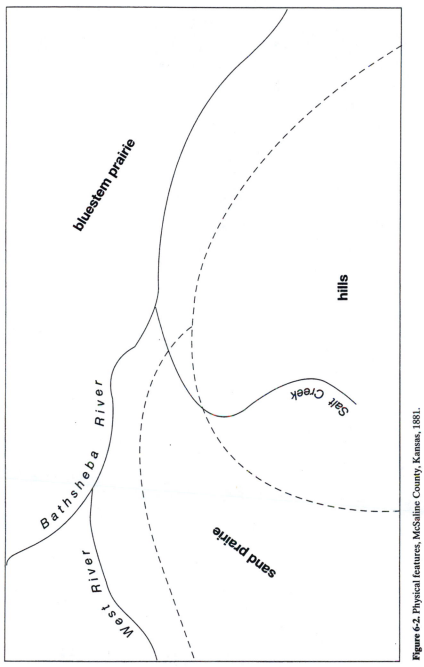

Figure 6-2. Physical features, McSaline County, Kansas, 1881.

bluestem prairie

hills

Bathsheba River

West River

Salt Creek

sand prairie

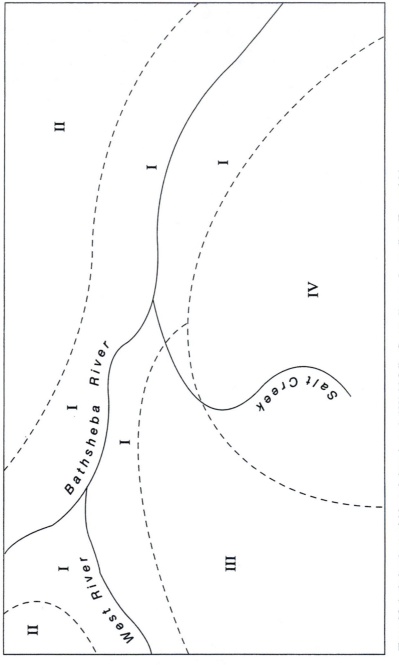

Figure 6-3. Agricultural potential for techniques in use in 1881, McSaline County, Kansas . I = excellent; II = good-fair; III = limited; IV = poor.

BIBLIOGRAPHY ON SETTLEMENT PATTERN ANALYSIS

Chorley, Richard J., and Peter Haggett (eds.). 1967. *Models in Geography*. Methuen Press, London. A highly technical but classic treatment of theoretical models in geography, including those discussed in this exercise.

Haggett, Peter. 1972. *Geography: A Modern Synthesis*. Harper and Row, New York. A classic introductory text in theoretical geography, treating central-place and other theories. Sometimes a bit difficult to understand.

Hartshorn, Truman A., and John W. Alexander. 1988. *Economic Geography*, third edition. Prentice-Hall, Englewood Cliffs, New Jersey. A widely used and easily understandable treatment of economic geography for beginners. Includes treatments of the models discussed in this exercise.

Hodder, Ian, and Clive Orton. 1976. *Spatial Analysis in Archaeology*. Cambridge University Press, Cambridge, England. An excellent—though technical—treatment of settlement pattern and other spatial analyses in archaeology.

Makower, Joel (ed.). 1986. *The Map Catalogue*. Vintage Books, New York. Not really a catalogue, but a description of the variety of maps available, their uses, and how to obtain them.

— EXERCISE 7 —
ANALYSIS OF
COMMUNITY PATTERNING

OVERVIEW

A human settlement typically shows spatial patterning of neighborhoods, zones, and districts. This exercise asks you to examine the historic changes in Armadillo, Texas in terms of the general patterns and processes discussed.

BACKGROUND

A human settlement is not a random collection of buildings, activity areas, and transportation links. Rather, it develops according to the needs of the inhabitants and the constraints of existing conditions. Many of the most sophisticated ways of analyzing the evolution of settlements, of course, come from geographers.

The twin concepts that underlie much geographical theory as it relates to community patterning are function and rents. *Function* refers to the way that a piece of land is used, such as a cotton field, a habitation, a factory, or a store. Function can be drawn as narrowly or broadly as the analyst believes will be useful. In practice, a historical archaeologist infers the function of a district on the basis of either documentary or archaeological information. Sometimes a directory or insurance map will provide the needed information; other times, one might need to do archaeological testing and infer the function of a district on the basis of the structures and artifacts found there.

The concept of *rent* refers to the costs associated with using a piece of land. Those costs may be "rent" in the normal sense (money paid to an owner to secure the rights to the use of the land), or they might be costs associated with purchasing, homesteading, or developing land. In most cases, rents will include taxes or other continuing costs.

Function and rent are intimately related. Certain plots of land are intrinsically preferable to others, because they are located more centrally to a community and access to them is easier. Those properties will have higher rents, assuming an economy that permits competition and a free market. Because these properties are so expensive, they will be used only for functions that can support those costs, such as luxury housing (where price is irrelevant) or certain types of retail stores (where ease of access directly affects the success of the business). Given this intimate relationship, it is possible to construct various models of how functions will be distributed over space within a settlement.

All of these models share the concept of the *central business district* (CBD). The CBD, as the name implies, is a zone near the center of a settlement where the major businesses are focused. This zone usually has the highest rents in the community, so the CBD is dominated by retail businesses, governmental buildings, and other high-end uses. Large cities, of course, have the most highly developed CBDs, and some have several foci around which the settlement develops. Smaller communities also have CBDs, though they are more modest; in the smallest communities, there may be no CBD, if there are no businesses or rent differentials.

As a settlement grows, rents in various areas change. In part, this is related to the changing face of the settlement, as areas that once were on the periphery are submerged by urban sprawl. Also, some areas will be degraded by the nature of the activities that take place there, as with industrial and low-cost housing zones. The pattern of changing spatial distribution of functions in a settlement as it grows is known as *urban succession*. There are various models of urban succession that are based on differing expectations of acceptable rents for different functions.

On the surface, it might appear that a community would grow equally rapidly in all directions, retaining a more or less circular shape. In reality, however, growth will be much more rapid along transportation routes. After all, the main reason that anyone wants to use high-rent land in the first place is that it is more convenient in terms of transportation. Consequently, land along a major highway will be more desirable than other land. This leads to a pattern of growth known as *stellate growth* ("star-shaped growth"). Looking down at a community from an airplane at night almost always reveals that its edges are "drawn out" along the major highways that cut through it, starkly revealing stellate growth.

Another form of asymmetrical growth is *sectorial growth*, where one zone expands faster than other parts of the settlement as changes in a community require that extraordinary amounts of land be devoted to a particular function. The zone or zones already devoted to that function expand outward rapidly, since that is the only direction in which appropriate unused land is available. For example, external changes may make a settlement into a bedroom community that provides housing to nearby (probably more expensive) communities. As residential areas grow faster than other zones, they will require large areas of land. People don't want to live next to a tire incinerator or coat hanger factory, so low-rent areas closer to the center of town but adjacent to these functions will not be used for housing; instead, existing housing areas will be extended outward, probably into previously unused land. In this sense, sectorial growth often is based on the earlier distribution of functions within the community.

The foregoing ideas relate basically to the class of settlements termed *nucleated*. Nucleated settlements have moderately high population densities, more or less distinct boundaries, and usually some diversity of business functions. They usually develop where populations are high enough to warrant the development of a CBD, where there is special access to a transportation network, or where some special resource is focused. These settlements can be contrasted to *dispersed* settlements, where there is no CBD and where houses and other land use features are spread out over the landscape. Dispersed settlement usually characterizes areas with lower populations, where the benefits of nucleated living are offset by the travel time to work areas, particularly agricultural fields.

These factors fit together to reveal certain things about an evolving community. The presence or absence of a CBD and where a settlement rests along the continuum between nucleation and dispersal are indications of the basic character of the community. The size and nature of the CBD can tell whether it serves primarily the single settlement or whether it may serve a broader region. Stellate growth can point out the important transportation routes, and sectorial growth can tell which functions are growing at an exceptional rate. Through the examination of urban succession, the analyst can see the changing face of the community. And the examination of these factors and others in the perspective of rents and functions can lead the analyst to insights unique to the community under study.

YOUR ASSIGNMENT

Dr. Cecilia Bump, well-known historical archaeologist and cousin of Leslie Squarkmuffin, is conducting a cultural resource management project examining the construction corridor for proposed Interstate Route 007 in Dasypus County, Texas. Federal law requires that public projects must locate and assess the importance of archaeological and historical sites that they may destroy, and Bump's project is the first phase of location and assessment.

At present, 11 different corridors are being considered, and Bump's study must deal with all of them. Consequently, it is not practical to examine all the areas intensively until the number of corridors has been reduced. As a first step, Bump plans on examining the overall development of each town through which the interstate may pass, in order to see which areas were developed at which dates and for which land uses. To truly understand this development, Bump argues, you have to understand the forces that shaped the growth of the town. Then you will be able to predict which zones are likely to contain significant archaeological and historical sites. Further, since some historic sites will not be noted in documents, this approach will reduce the likelihood that a zone with archaeological potential will be overlooked simply because no documents have been found that describe a specific site in it.

As part of this study, Bump needs a picture of the overall development of several towns along the corridors. She has hired an archaeologist to study each town, and you have been selected to study the town of Armadillo. Your job is to trace the development of Armadillo, paying special attention to the development of zones and districts. Your interpretation should relate the historical events and processes known at Armadillo to their spatial expression in settlement, using the concepts of nucleation-dispersal, urban succession, sectorial growth, and stellate growth as appropriate.

Fortunately for you, much of the information you will need already has been collected in a Master's thesis at Glyptodont University. The author, William Curmudgeon, has reproduced all the known historic maps of Armadillo and has done some digesting of the material to infer zones of land use. The thesis, however, is a bit short on interpretation, and your task essentially is to use Curmudgeon's data to support the sort of analysis discussed above. The most important of Curmudgeon's maps are reproduced in Figures 7-1 through 7-5; Table 7-1 presents data on relative acceptable rents to support various functions.

Your report for this exercise doesn't need to be so detailed as would your report to Bump. It should include sections treating your objective, the interpretation of the maps, and your conclusions. For this report, you needn't try to draw conclusions regarding which zones will have more significant sites or which corridors might destroy fewer sites.

Sketch of the Economic History of Armadillo, Texas

The first Euro-American settlement of Dasypus County began around 1834, but that settlement was sporadic and light. The first settlement at Armadillo itself was probably around 1860, although frontier hostilities with Indians kept substantial settlement from occurring until after the "pacification" of the local Indians in 1876. The area's fertile soils and permanent water sources supported several farms, and a small business district was located at the junction of the Dasypus River and Gurteltier Creek.

TABLE 7-1 Ordering of acceptable relative rents for different land uses, Armadillo, Texas. The land uses with the highest rents are at the top of the list.

1. retail business and services
2. residential, high rent
3. governmental
4. residential, middle rent
5. residential, low rent
6. manufacturing
7. transportation facilities
8. warehouses
9. farming

In 1884, a disastrous fire at Glyptodont, the only other settlement of any size in the county, destroyed its capacity to serve as the county seat, and Armadillo was made the county seat. The community responded with a great show of civic pride and built a complex of courthouse and county buildings in the center of town. Its status as county seat stimulated the economy, leading to a variety of new businesses developing there.

In 1889, the Southern Edentata Railroad completed the section of track that would connect Armadillo to the outside world. It set up its station and river crossing to the west of town, where the engineering task of crossing the river was easiest.

In 1892, Meyer Lemon and Charles Albacore, local entrepreneurs, set up a factory to produce corset stays by a new and improved process. The great success of this enterprise led to major expansion of the operations around 1900, which in turn led to an influx of unskilled laborers to work in the plants and associated facilities. The demise of corsets in the 1930s led to a scaling down of the Armadillo operations. Most of the factories were able to remain open—but less profitably and with a smaller work force and output—by converting to the manufacture of other products. Most of the industrial operations closed shortly after World War II.

Automobiles came to Armadillo in the early 1900s, but they first made a considerable impact around 1930. By the end of World War II, the railroad was a losing business, and the line closed in 1947.

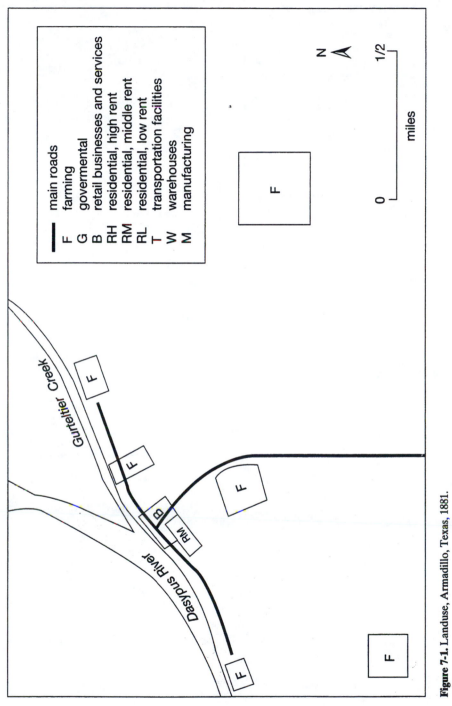

Figure 7-1. Landuse, Armadillo, Texas, 1881.

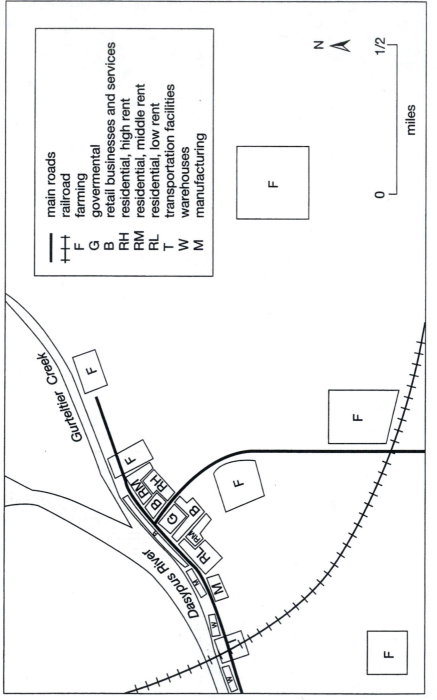

Figure 7-2. Land use, Armadillo, Texas, 1864;

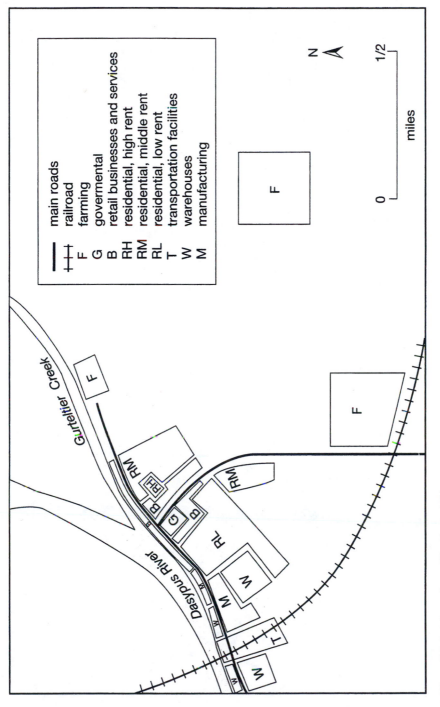

Figure 7-3. Land use, Armadillo, Texas, 1911

Legend:
- main roads
- railroad
- F farming
- G govermental
- B retail businesses and services
- RH residential, high rent
- RM residential, middle rent
- RL residential, low rent
- T transportation facilities
- W warehouses
- M manufacturing

N

0   1/2

miles

Gurteltier Creek

Dasypus River

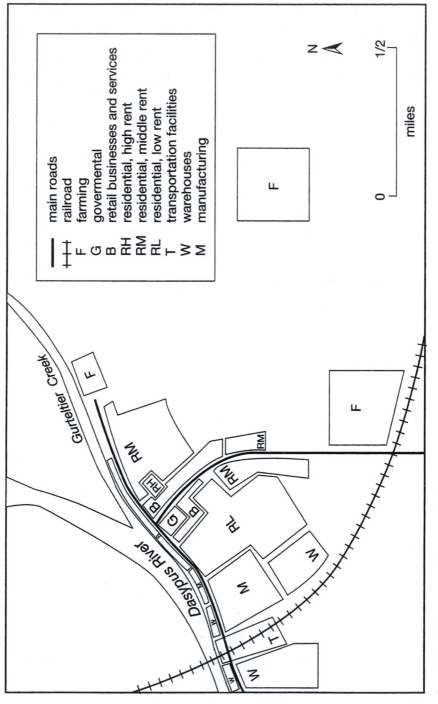

Figure 7-4. Land use, Armadillo, Texas, 1923.

Legend:

——	main roads
+++	railroad
F	farming
G	govermental
B	retail businesses and services
RH	residential, high rent
RM	residential, middle rent
RL	residential, low rent
T	transportation facilities
W	warehouses
M	manufacturing

N

0   1/2
miles

Gurteltier Creek

Dasypus River

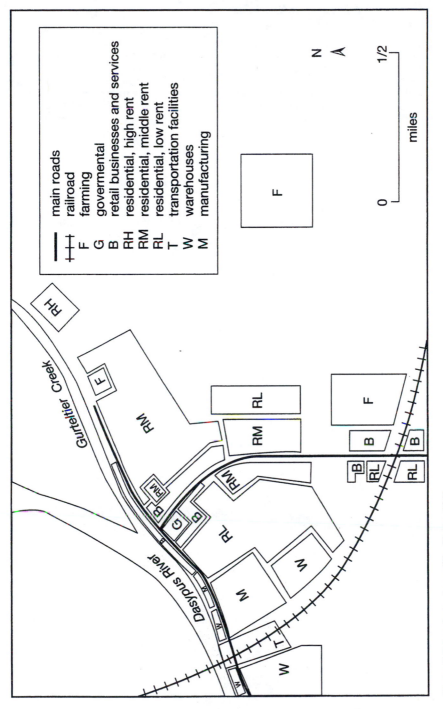

Figure 7-5. Land use, Armadillo, Texas, 1941

Legend:

	main roads
	railroad
F	farming
G	govermental
B	retail businesses and services
RH	residential, high rent
RM	residential, middle rent
RL	residential, low rent
T	transportation facilities
W	warehouses
M	manufacturing

N

0   miles   1/2

BIBLIOGRAPHY ON THE ANALYSIS
OF COMMUNITY PATTERNING

Chorley, Richard J., and Peter Haggett (eds.). 1967. *Models in Geography*. Methuen Press, London. A highly technical but classic treatment of theoretical models in geography, including those discussed in this exercise.

Hartshorn, Truman A., and John W. Alexander. 1988. *Economic Geography*, third edition. Prentice Hall, Englewood Cliffs, New Jersey. A widely used and easily understandable treatment of economic geography for beginners. Includes treatments of the models discussed in this exercise.

— EXERCISE 8 —
SOCIAL ANALYSIS
OF ARCHITECTURE

OVERVIEW

Architecture provides evidence about past attitudes regarding the activities that properly should take place in buildings and how those activities should be organized. This exercise asks you to examine the structures of two buildings of different periods in the Pacific Northwest and interpret what attitudes and behavior patterns they reflect.

BACKGROUND

There can be no doubt that the architecture of our dwellings reflects, at least in part, our attitudes about how our activities should be organized. A huge, elegant ballroom was *de rigueur* for any Victorian aristocrat, but most families today have little trouble getting along without one, although they might be lost without a small television room for the kids. Sensible architects try to design new homes with the needs of the occupants in mind; as times change, so do the activities of those occupants, the sizes and sorts of social groups that take part in those activities, and the types of spatial organization that will be most appropriate. Of course, other factors enter into the equation, such as coping with the physical challenges of the climate and the economic challenges of the times. Snow requires good insulation, sloping roofs, and materials that resist breaking up with freezing; and, no matter how desirable a design or material, you can't use it if you can't afford it.

But once a building has been completed, few of us have the option to simply reject it when times change further and it no longer reflects the life style that we would like to maintain. Instead, most occupants must stay on, and the structure of the house becomes a conservative factor, encouraging its inhabitants to continue the types and organizations of activities in a way similar to those current when the house was built. What was once molded to the owner's will now itself becomes the mold.

Archaeologically, houses usually are examined and interpreted largely on the basis of two sets of information: floor plans and artifact distributions within the house. The floor plan provides a spatial framework, and the artifacts provide evidence about how the different rooms and areas were used. For modern houses, we can obtain similar information in a considerably more direct way. The floor plan can be drawn by observing the extant house, and the functions of the rooms can be determined by observing activities or questioning the occupants.

Regardless of how the information is obtained, a floor plan and list of room/area functions can be the basis for a social analysis of architecture. Many scholars from different disciplines have produced excellent analyses of this sort, and one of the best known is James Deetz's analysis of seventeenth- and eighteenth-century folk houses in New England, presented in his *In Small Things Forgotten* (1977). In that work, Deetz focuses on the development of attitudes favoring increased privacy. The front door that opens into the main communal room in the earlier portion of this period is replaced by a front hall that "protects" the household (symbolically) from the intrusions of outsiders; the communal room itself is replaced by more specialized and private rooms, set off from one another by walls and doors. The primary thrust of such an analysis is asking the question: What are the social consequences that follow naturally from this architectural arrangement? In effect, what does an elegant ballroom or a small television room for the kids *mean* in terms of everyday activities?

A social analysis of architecture of this sort usually will focus on the following questions and issues:

- What amounts of space are allocated to different functions? Functions allocated large amounts of space probably are deemed quite important, just as those given little or no space are considered less critical.
- How do barriers (especially walls) break up or unite functional areas? Uniting functional areas usually means that the functions are seen as somehow related, or at least compatible and able to share an area. Segregating areas devoted to different functions usually means the functions are deemed distinct or incompatible.
- What transition zones buffer the progression from one area to another, and what are their functions? Hallways, passages, and other architectural areas may serve to make the barriers between areas more impenetrable, or they may serve to soften the abruptness between areas and their different functions. Some buildings have many such transition zones; some have few or none.
- How are public and private areas set off? Some portions of a house are accessible to all who enter, while others are available only to the occupants and possibly their intimate friends and relatives. Walls, doors, transition zones, stairways, and other architectural devices can divide the public from the private areas. It tells much about a society to know what it considers to be private and public functions.
- How and to what degree does the house serve as a symbol of the occupants' prestige? Various architectural devices have taken on symbolic meaning as indicators of wealth, taste, high status, or at least aspiration to some of these qualities. These include fountains, walls separating the yard from the street, sculpture, sheer size, and many others.

A good social analysis of a house (or other building) will address these questions and others that may be relevant to a specific case. By using reason and knowledge about the period in question, the analyst can better understand the tangible expression of attitudes and behavioral norms in architecture, sometimes revealing new insights into society at that place and time.

YOUR ASSIGNMENT

Figures 8-1 and 8-2 provide floor plans of two houses from Amocat, Washington. The first is for a mid-Victorian house, built in 1871, and the second is for a modern house, built in 1987; both are still standing and in use as family housing. The functions of the various rooms are given on the figures.

Your assignment is to compare the two houses in terms of their social implications. Your comparison should focus on the differences between the activity patterns of the 1870s and those of the 1980s and the ways that those are reflected in housing. Some of the differences you come up with will be ones that you know to be true from your store of information on modern life and that in the 1870s, but your analysis might also lead you to inferences that you cannot verify from your knowledge; that is fine, and you should include your inferences, labeled as such.

Your report should consist of a brief introduction and a comparison of the social implications of the two houses.

A Note on the Houses

The 1871 house was built for Reynold S. Rapp, a district manager for the J. J. Castor Company, a successful fur-trading company. Rapp spent most of his time in town, and this was his regular residence. By the standards of the time, he was of the upper-middle class, and his house was moderately expensive. It was set on a 1/4-acre plot in a neighborhood with houses of similar value on the hill at the end of what was then the south side of Amocat. Rapp's property also had a carriage barn and a work shed. At the time the house was built, the Rapp family consisted of Reynold Rapp, his wife Sharon, and three children. The family subsequently expanded with the birth of another child. While the Rapp family had no live-in servants, they did have a maid and handyman who worked for them during the day. Rapp selected the design of the house from John Riddell's *Architectural Designs for Model Country Residences,* a well-known collection of house designs published in Philadelphia in 1864. At the time when the house was built, the adult Rapps were 28 and 30 years of age.

The 1987 house was built by Slash and Burn Development Company, a local firm. It was part of a housing development of 260 units, each of the same basic plan with a few variants. The development was designed for the upper-middle class and was priced accordingly. The house was purchased by the Prufer family in 1988. Rusty Prufer is the manager of an auto body shop; his wife, Molly Page-Prufer, is an editor with a publishing house in Amocat. Their combined income places them in the upper-middle income bracket. They have two children and no intentions of having others. The house is on a 1/16-acre plot and has an attached garage and storage shed; there are no other outbuildings. At the time of purchase, the adult Prufers were 37 and 38 years old.

BIBLIOGRAPHY ON SOCIAL ANALYSIS OF ARCHITECTURE

Blumenson, John J. G. 1977. *Identifying American Architecture: A Pictorial Guide to Styles and Terms, 1600-1945*. American Association for State and Local History, Nashville, Tennessee. Handy both for finding meanings of architectural terms and for finding proper terms to describe architectural features, elements, and styles.

Bourdier, Jean-Paul, and Nezar AlSayyad (eds.). 1989. *Dwellings, Settlements, and Tradition: Cross-cultural Perspectives*. University Press of America, Lanham, Maryland. A wide-ranging collection of essays on the social interpretation of architecture in many cultures.

Ching, Frank. 1975. *Architectural Graphics*. Van Nostrand Reinhold Co., New York. Detailed treatment of conventions in architectural drawings, including floor plans.

Deetz, James. 1977. *In Small Things Forgotten: The Archaeology of Early American Life*. Anchor Books, Garden City, New York. Chapter 5 analyzes colonial New England housing using the approach of this exercise.

Glassie, Henry. 1968. *Pattern in the Material Folk Culture of the Eastern United States*. University of Pennsylvania Press, Philadelphia, Pennsylvania. Examples of architectural analysis are spread throughout.

———. 1975. *Folk Housing in Middle Virginia: A Structural Analysis of Historic Artifacts*. University of Tennessee Press, Knoxville, Tennessee. An excellent though difficult treatment.

Gowans, Alan. 1992. *Styles and Types of North American Architecture: Social Function and Cultural Expression*. HarperCollins Publishers, New York. A series of essays treating the major styles of North American architecture, emphasizing domestic housing. Each essay includes a treatment of the style's sociocultural underpinnings, treated in the tradition of architectural history.

Upton, Dell, and John Michael Vlach (eds.). 1986. *Common Places: Readings in American Vernacular Architecture*. University of Georgia Press, Athens, Georgia. Almost any of the 23 previously published essays in this collection can serve as a model of how social analysis of architecture can proceed. Essays by Cummings and Cohen are especially appropriate for this exercise. There also is a good topical bibliography included.

Tables and figures for this chapter follow.

roof

nursery

bath
room

chamber

chamber

passage

dressing
room

chamber

chamber

roof

roof

second story

wash room

kitchen

closet

store room

dinning
room

library

porch

parlor

hall

veranda

first story

0   6   12

feet

Figure 8-1.

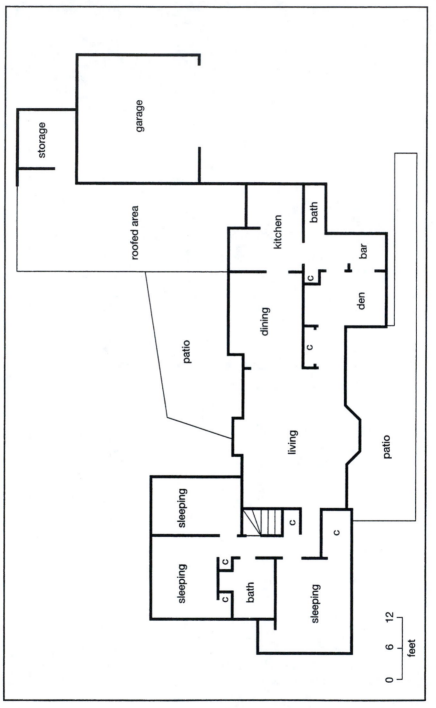

Figure 8-2.

— EXERCISE 9 —
STRATIGRAPHY

OVERVIEW

Stratigraphy—the layering of soils—provides archaeologists with critical information on the formation and relative ages of the different parts of an archaeological site. This exercise asks you to use stratigraphy to interpret the sequence of deposits that formed an urban site in Minnesota.

BACKGROUND ON STRATIGRAPHY

An archaeological site potentially contains artifacts and other remains from the earliest date of occupation for that patch of land to the present day. A variety of *site formation processes* (such as the purposeful dumping or removal of soil, the gradual accumulation of soil that blows or washes in, the erosion of existing deposits, and the slumping of soils into hollows and depressions) have formed or reshaped the site, often producing a complex series of intertwining deposits. Archaeologists try to sort out this complicated picture, coming up with periods into which the remains fall, and one of their primary tools is stratigraphy.

Stratigraphy is the structure of soils that are divided into layers or other deposits that can be distinguished from one another. These deposits usually are differentiated visually by color and texture, but compactness, ability to hold moisture, presence of other materials (such as artifacts or shell), and other factors also can aid the archaeologist in recognizing different deposits in the field. Archaeologists usually describe deposits in terms of *soil types,* defined principally by the grain size of the mineral components of the soil and the amount of organic material in the soil. Some of the more common soil types are *gravel* or *pebbles* (coarse pieces of rock), *sand* (finer grains of rock, sometimes admixed with decomposed organic material), *silt* (very fine grains of rock, usually admixed with organic material), *clay* (extremely fine grains of rock, forming a sticky or slippery mass), and *loam* (sand, silt, or mixed sand and silt, admixed with considerable amounts of organic material). It can be a difficult task to translate field stratigraphy, sometimes with indistinct or ambiguous boundaries between deposits, into an accurate *profile,* the stratigrapher's name for a scale drawing of stratigraphy. Fortunately, however, this skill can be learned, and experienced field archaeologists will produce nearly identical profiles from the sidewall of an excavation.

A few more definitions are necessary before carrying the discussion further. A *stratum* (plural *strata*) is a layer within a stratigraphy; a stratum of limited extent that lies between two other strata and thins to nothingness at its edges is a *lens*. An *intrusion* is any deposit that cuts into pre-existing deposits, including such diverse phenomena as a woodchuck burrow, an erosion channel, and a foundation trench. An intrusion or other deposit that is produced purposefully by human beings is called a *feature*. Features can range from the small and discrete (such as a post hole into which a fence post was driven) to the large and diffuse (such as a broad area of dumping). They include trash pits, privy pits, wells, and foundations, to name but a few. The boundary between two deposits most commonly is called a *soil interface*, and a soil interface where there has been erosion of the lower stratum before the deposition of the upper stratum is called an *unconformity*. (Figure 9-1 illustrates many of these kinds of deposits.)

The importance of stratigraphy in archaeology is twofold. First, the correct identification and interpretation of deposits, particularly features, can tell the archaeologist much about the events that took place at a site and helped form it. A *destruction level*—the deposit formed by the razing of a building—

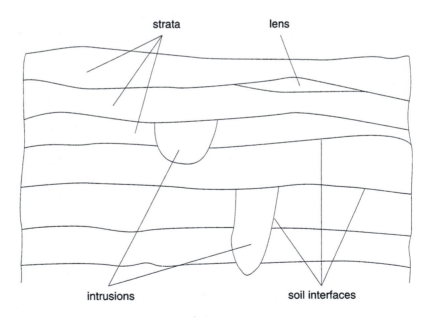

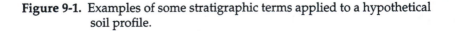

Figure 9-1. Examples of some stratigraphic terms applied to a hypothetical soil profile.

says much about the history of a place, as do *trample levels* (caused by traffic breaking up artifacts and other materials on the surface), *middens* (sizable deposits formed by purposeful dumping of refuse), *sheet refuse* (refuse thinly scattered over the former surface of the ground), and many other kinds of features and other deposits. Second, the spatial relationships of deposits to one another indicate the sequence in which they were formed, providing a preliminary framework for the history of a site. The stratigraphy of a site allows the archaeologist to place events that took place there into a chronological order, and it is this use of stratigraphy on which this exercise focuses.

Archaeological dating falls into two broad categories: relative and absolute. *Relative dating* involves putting things into order from earliest to latest, but not assigning specific dates to any of the things. *Absolute dating*, in contrast, assigns a specific date to something. Relative dating, for example, may place deposit A before deposit B, but it provides nothing more specific; deposit A might be ten minutes older than deposit B or ten millennia older. Absolute dating, on the other hand, assigns a numerical date to something: 1492 A.D., 230 years before present, the thirteenth year of the reign of Pepin the Short, or the like. Obviously, accurate absolute dating is preferable to accurate relative dating, since it provides a greater level of specificity. In archaeology, however, both are important, providing one reason why stratigraphic dating—a relative dating technique—remains so important.

While there are many ways of determining absolute dates for deposits, some deposits do not contain the materials necessary for such dating. Deposits with no artifacts, for example, may defy absolute dating. Even if they contain artifacts or other datable materials, deposits formed with only a short interval between them may pose a problem for absolute dating, since the accuracy of the dating may be low enough to obscure the true relationship of the deposits. Deposit A may actually be eight years older than deposit B, but the date derived for deposit A might be 1760-1790, while the date for deposit B might be 1770-1810; the true relationship of the two deposits is compatible with the absolute dating, but the absolute dates taken alone would suggest a different (and incorrect) interpretation. A relative dating technique, such as stratigraphic dating, can provide a valuable check on the results of absolute dating. The wise archaeologist takes advantage of as many dating techniques as possible, both relative and absolute, using their combined results to arrive at the most plausible sequence and dates.

The chronological interpretation of a complex soil profile may appear difficult and obscure because of the seemingly chaotic intersection of deposits, but it is based on four simple principles: the Principle of Association, the Principle of Superposition, the Principle of Reversal, and the Principle of Intrusion.

The *Principle of Association* was first formalized by the Danish archaeologist J. J. A. Worsaae in 1843. He recognized that items in graves had to have been deposited together at the same date. Since Worsaae's time, the principle has been expanded to apply to other depositional units and now states that items in the same deposit are of essentially the same age. This is a powerful recognition, permitting all the items in a deposit to be dated on the basis of the relatively few items that can be independently dated. A single coin in a deposit, therefore, can provide a date estimate for all the remains in the deposit, including bones, artifacts, and structural remains that might otherwise be undatable.

There are three important cautions, however, that must be remembered about the Principle of Association. First, some items may find their way into an archaeological deposit long after their dates of manufacture. This is especially true of rare or valuable items such as a fancy ceramic dish, which may be cared for meticulously, extending its use life before it finally breaks and has to be discarded. Consequently, a single heirloom in a trash deposit may be considerably older than the other materials associated with it. Similarly, old artifacts, such as a family wedding ring, may be included as purposeful grave offerings long after the date of the artifact's manufacture. (This lengthy lag between the manufacture of an object and its eventual incorporation into the archaeological record is known as the *curatorial effect*.) The only thing that an archaeologist can be absolutely sure of is that remains must have been produced at or before the date of the deposit in which they occur.

Second, some items may make their way into a deposit considerably after they were discarded by human beings. A rodent burrow, for example, may undermine a former ground surface where a pipe bowl was dropped. As a result, the pipe bowl may drop into a deposit that predates the true age of the pipe. Such site formation processes can jumble parts of a site, and the field archaeologist has to be vigilant to recognize the telltale signs of such movement of remains.

Third, Worsaae's original formulation referred to grave pits, features that were open only for a short period and whose contents all had to date to that brief period. Extending the principle to other kinds of deposits means that some of them will have taken substantially longer periods to form, and the stratigrapher must use good sense in terms of what "essentially the same age" might mean. A stratum that formed over a century could have remains deposited over that entire span.

A deposit often contains hints of how long it took to form. Internal divisions such as *laminations* (very fine layers, indicating discrete depositional episodes) or *subaerial surfaces* or *unconformities* (lines showing previous ground surfaces that have altered as a result of exposure to the elements) are indications that a deposit formed in stages, probably over a considerable period of time. Fill and other deposits that show no such characteristics, on the other hand, often can be considered *unitary*. That is, they can be considered to have formed during a single, brief episode, and the items within them can be considered to have been deposited at nearly the same time.

The *Principle of Superposition* states simply that more recent deposits overlie older ones. This principle is the same one that guides someone searching for something on a messy desk littered with papers. The letter that arrived today should be in the uppermost layer, since it would be placed atop the papers previously deposited; a letter arriving a month ago might be two inches beneath the surface, depending on the rate of accumulation and the exact spot on the desk where it was placed. The same thing is true of soil deposits; the most recent ones typically are at the top, the older ones further beneath the surface. Since accumulation rates of deposits can vary greatly, there is no guarantee that five centimeters of soil at the top of Stratum D took the same amount of time to form as did five centimeters in Stratum F or even at the bottom of Stratum D. While the Principle of Superposition also was formalized by Worsaae, it had been used by earlier archaeologists, including Thomas Jefferson.

The *Principle of Reversal* describes the result of digging through a normal stratigraphy (with the oldest stratum at the bottom) and depositing it in reversed order. The result, usually called a *reversed stratigraphy*, is moderately uncommon but can have disastrous effects on interpretation if it is not recognized. There are a number of well-known prehistoric cases that have led to incorrect cultural sequences that went unrecognized for decades. Reversed stratigraphies are most commonly produced when digging or construction projects move quantities of earth. Reversed stratigraphies also can occur on a paper-laden desk, when the search for a letter results in the examination of a stack of papers one at a time. The papers are placed in a new pile, with the most recent papers (formerly uppermost on the desk) now at the bottom of the new (reversed) pile. The Principle of Reversal was first presented formally by F. M. Hawley in 1937, although it and its effects had been known before.

The *Principle of Intrusion* states that an intrusion must be more recent than the deposits through which it cuts. This is only sensible, since an intrusion clearly must have had some material to cut into. There are two steps to finding an intrusion's relative position in a sequence. First, find the deposit that immediately overlies the intrusion; the intrusion is earlier than this deposit. Second, find the uppermost deposit that underlies the intrusion and is cut by it; the intrusion is later than this deposit.

Intrusions cause another problem the stratigrapher must solve. Shown on a profile, the intrusion may divide pre-existing strata into separate units, no longer connected. With no further information, it is possible that these two units either are part of the same deposit or are separate and distinct deposits. There are two ways of inferring which is the more likely. First, if other stratigraphic information is available (perhaps a profile from a few feet away, beyond the extent of the intrusion), the problem can be resolved there. Second, if only the single profile is available, it usually is reasonable to infer that units on both sides of an intrusion are really the same deposit if they have similar characteristics in terms of soil type, compactness, color, artifact content, and so forth. This process of inference is called *stratigraphic correlation*.

These four principles are the basis for all interpretation of stratigraphic profiles. Of course, absolute dating, where available, can assist in determining the sequence in which deposits were formed. Beyond this, one must use logic and good sense. As with so many forms of archaeological interpretation, each case is unique and requires the analyst to examine the particulars and use reason in drawing conclusions. Alas, it is not always possible to determine the exact placement of every deposit in a stratigraphic sequence; there are limits to the information contained in any profile.

YOUR ASSIGNMENT

Nagasawa Street lies in the heart of the Japanese district of Minneapolis, Minnesota. The area has been intensively occupied since around 1870, and it has undergone a series of changing land uses and spasms of urban development.

Today, Nagasawa Street is undergoing further urban redevelopment. Since this project is partly funded by federal money, there is a requirement that an environmental impact statement be prepared, and one area of concern is archaeological and historical properties that will be destroyed. Dr. John Benjo, a professional archaeologist and an in-law of Squarkmuffin, has been hired by the Minneapolis Redevelopment Agency to assess the archaeological potential of Nagasawa Street. He has completed his documentary study of the area and has consulted with the appropriate agencies that keep records of known historic and archaeological sites. He now has begun his field testing of the area by excavating a test trench with a backhoe in a vacant lot. This test trench has yielded large numbers of artifacts and other remains, and Benjo needs to establish a relative chronology before he can start making sense of the information he has recovered.

You have been hired by Benjo to assist in the study. After assisting in the excavation, you are the lucky crew member who has been selected to stay on and work out the chronology as indicated by the stratigraphic profile (Figure 9-2) and a few bits and pieces of other information that are available currently. Using this information, produce a relative chronology for the Nagasawa Street excavation. Your report should include:

- the sequence of deposits at the site, including deposits that are of the same date;
- deposits that cannot be placed unambiguously in the sequence; and
- reasons for your decisions.

You don't have sufficient information to try to explain how every deposit formed, although you probably will want to suggest formation processes for some of them.

Further Information on the Nagasawa Street Site

The stratigraphic profile of Figure 9-2 shows the structure of the soils at this section of Nagasawa Street, identifying stratigraphic units by letters. A letter has been assigned each discrete unit, even though some of these are merely portions of deposits that have been cut by intrusions and can be stratigraphically correlated. Excerpts from Benjo's field notes, presented in Table 9-1, provide some information on the composition of the deposits and a bit on their contents.

At this point in the analysis, there are only a few dates available on materials found in the excavation. Those dates, the basis for their estimation, and the units from which the dated materials were recovered are given in Table 9-2.

BIBLIOGRAPHY ON STRATIGRAPHY

Buckman, Harry O., and Nyle C. Brady. 1969. *The Nature and Properties of Soils,* seventh edition. Macmillan, New York. The basic text on soil and soil types, focusing on naturally forming soils. Technical.

Harris, E. C. 1979. *Principles of Archaeological Stratigraphy.* Academic Press, New York. A technical treatment of stratigraphy, focusing on complex examples and describing the use of Harris matrixes, a technique of recording the interpretation of complex stratigraphies.

Hawley, F. M. 1937. Reverse stratigraphy. *American Antiquity* 2:297-299. Basic treatment of reversed stratigraphy.

Pyddocke, Edward. 1961. *Stratification for the Archaeologist.* Phoenix House, London, England. A classic treatment of the subject in general that never goes out of date.

Stein, J. K. 1987. Deposits for archaeologists. *In* Michael B. Schiffer (ed.), *Advances in Archaeological Method and Theory,* vol. 11, Academic Press, New York, pp. 337-395. A useful update of Pyddocke, cited above.

Tables and figures for this chapter follow.

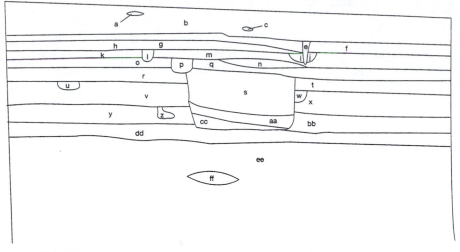

Figure 9-2. Nagasawa.

TABLE 9-1   Excerpts from Benjo's field notes, Nagasawa Street, Minneapolis.

a	dense lens of coal ash and cinders
b	unitary deposit of fill with no indications of exposed surface levels
c	dense lens of broken plaster, wood, and nails
d	yellow sand with sparse artifacts
e	loose, rocky soil with gas pipe at bottom
f	yellow sand with sparse artifacts
g	gray sand with pebbles, some artifacts
h	loose deposit of mixed yellow sand, gray sand, and gray clay with some artifacts, especially window glass
i	greasy black soil with high artifact density
j	greasy black soil with high artifact density
k	yellow sand with gray clay streaks
l	dense, black soil with butchered animal bones
m	yellow sand with gray clay streaks
n	rounded pebbles with almost no soil between them
o	gray sand with high artifact density, especially window glass
p	loose, brown sand with admixed rubble, including brick
q	gray sand with high artifact density
r	brown sandy loam with high artifact density
s	loose rubble with much construction debris
t	brown sandy loam with high artifact density
u	black soil with abundant artifacts
v	yellow sand with almost no artifacts
w	black soil with abundant artifacts
x	yellow sand, almost no artifacts
y	sterile orange clay, showing fine laminations
z	loose brown soil filling a rodent burrow
aa	fine gray sand and silt with some artifacts
bb	sterile, finely laminated, orange clay
cc	very fine brown silt with some artifacts
dd	sterile tan clay with fine laminations
ee	sterile, laminated, gray clay
ff	sterile lens of blue-black clay, no laminations visible

TABLE 9-2 Absolute dates, Nagasawa Street, Minneapolis.

STRATIGRAPHIC UNIT	DATE	DATING METHOD
d	1942	inscription on coin
r	ca. 1840	style of fancy pottery
	1890–1905	bottle technology
cc	ca. 1905	button style

PART THREE

Foodways

T HE TERM *FOODWAYS* REFERS to the distinctive cultural patterns that a group holds relative to food, including what is eaten, how it is procured, how it is prepared, how it is served, what artifacts are used in conjunction with food, and what place food holds in the social system, value system, and ideology of the eater. Foodways are one of the many ways that historical archaeologists can investigate the differing ways that social groups structure their everyday ways of life.

Foodways can be studied through three classes of archaeological data: faunal remains (animal bones, shell, etc.), floral remains (plant seeds, pollen, etc.), and food-related artifacts (preparation or serving vessels and tools). In addition, documentary and oral sources may provide valuable information on foodways.

Because of the nature of archaeological preservation, faunal remains tend to be better preserved than floral remains. The leaves, stalks, and other moist, soft parts of plants tend to rot readily and leave little for the archaeologist to recover. Consequently, most of the archaeological floral remains analyzed regularly by historical archaeologists tend to be the harder parts, especially seeds (including grain). While these remains can be readily identified, there are serious problems in estimating their relative importance in an archaeological site. Finding twice as many wheat grains as corn kernels may reflect the greater usage of wheat, but it also might reflect the greater preservability of wheat or a difference in the preparation techniques for wheat that led to greater spillage or better preservation.

In contrast, faunal remains generally provide the analyst with a richer data set to work with. Much of this is because food animals typically have bones or shells that preserve quite well archaeologically, providing a high likelihood that an animal's usage as food will be indicated in the remains. Equally important, however, is the fact that faunal remains provide an index of the relative usage of different animals. Finding twice as many deer bones as sheep bones in a trash deposit—so long as the means of calculating the relative frequencies is appropriate—*does* mean that deer were eaten twice as much as sheep. This ability to estimate quantitative relationships among different food animals permits the faunal analyst to investigate areas unavailable to the floral analyst.

Artifacts are particularly important in investigating the social dimension of foodways: food serving and its relationship to social organization, food preparation and its relationship to economics, and the like. But artifacts also can be used in some cases to help reconstruct the basic patterns of consumption themselves. Sardine cans, mustard pots, olive oil jars, and other distinctive packaging can allow the archaeologist to estimate the relative inputs of different purchased foodstuffs. Some items, such as beverages, may be able to be studied only in this manner.

Part III contains two exercises on foodways. Exercise 10 is a general treatment of two faunal assemblages, asking you to identify differences in two ethnic groups' eating behavior during California's gold rush. Exercise 11 focuses on alcohol consumption during local prohibition in Mississippi, asking you to examine the extent of alcohol usage as evidenced by artifacts.

— EXERCISE 10 —
FAUNAL ANALYSIS

OVERVIEW

Faunal remains—the remains of animals—are an important category at most archaeological sites. This exercise asks you to compare the faunal assemblages at two gold camps in California to find out about differing patterns of behavior among immigrants from China and New England.

BACKGROUND

While archaeologists realize that most people who have lived on earth have gotten most of their food from plants, the nature of archaeological preservation often leads them to focus on the analysis of faunal remains. The bones, shell, antlers, horn, and other hard parts of animals that are eaten will find their way into the archaeological record and often are preserved well enough to support sophisticated analysis and reconstruction of this aspect of foodways.

When archaeologists analyze the faunal remains from a site, they accumulate their data into a list usually called a *faunal list*. The faunal list gives the *taxon* (type of animal, identified to the species or variety level, if possible; the plural is *taxa*), the *element* (which bone and, if appropriate, which side of the body it came from), and the number of bones or fragments for that taxon and element; sometimes sex, age, or other information can be inferred and may also be included on the faunal list. There usually also will be a category of "unidentified" to include fragmented, immature, or deformed bones that cannot be assigned to a taxon. The faunal list is the basic set from which most calculations are made and most conclusions are drawn.

There are a number of simple calculations that faunal analysts make to help interpret their faunal assemblages, and a few of those are given here.

Minimum number of individuals (MNI): the smallest number of animals that could have produced the remains of a species (or other taxon). MNI is the most commonly used measure of the relative numbers of different species contained in an assemblage. MNI is calculated by examining the number of each element within a species; the greatest number is the MNI. *E.g.*, a faunal assemblage with 2 skulls, 4 right thigh bones, and 7 left thigh bones would have an MNI of 7. If several pieces of a left thigh bone could fit together to form a single bone, they are counted as one; if three left thigh bone fragments overlap, including the same portion of the bone, they must be from three individuals and are counted as three elements.

Number of individual specimens (NISP): the total number of bone pieces of a species, calculated by adding together the numbers of pieces of each element. NISP sometimes is used as a measure of the relative numbers of different species contained in an assemblage, but it has severe limitations in this role. If the bones of small animals are more fragmented than those of larger animals (and this often is the case), using NISP as a measure of relative frequency will make the smaller animals appear disproportionately important in the assemblage. Consequently, NISP is more appropriately used as a way to quantify the extent of breakage. (Breakage can be important in assessing remains, since some cultures break bones more thoroughly than others to extract a greater portion of the food on and in them [flesh and marrow]. Also, breakage patterns sometimes can point out areas of a site where disturbances, such as pathways, have led to increased fragmentation of bones.) NISP cannot be converted directly to MNI, since NISP is calculated by adding together numbers of *pieces*, while MNI is calculated from numbers of *elements*. *E.g.*, a species represented by 1 thigh bone in 37 pieces will have an MNI of 1 and NISP of 37. When a species ranks particularly high on MNI but low on NISP, check to see whether only particular parts of the carcass (*e.g.*, hind legs, torsos) are represented in the assemblage, indicating the consumption of selected cuts of meat; when a species ranks particularly low on MNI but high on NISP, check to see whether its remains might be especially fragmented.

Flesh weight: an estimate of how much meat would have been available from the animals represented by the remains of a species. The simplest way of calculating flesh weight (and the only way you will have available to you in this exercise) is to multiply the MNI times an estimated average amount of meat per individual of the species. There are more sophisticated ways to estimate flesh weights, many of which are based on calculated relationships between flesh weight and certain dimensions of bones of that species. There is a cultural element that enters into the calculation of flesh weights and makes them a bit tricky to use, since some social groups eat practically everything from horn to hoof, while others are more selective and throw away considerable quantities that really are edible. There is a more or less established convention that a rough estimate of flesh weight can be made by assuming that robust animals (like pigs and ducks) are 70% edible flesh, while more slender animals (like sheep, deer, and squirrels) are 50% edible flesh. While flesh weight calculation can be tricky, its value is obvious: Equal MNIs for bears and squirrels don't yield equal amounts of food.

Niche width index: a measure of how much variety was usual in the meat consumption of a group. It is possible to assess variety by simply counting up how many species were used, but there are certain limitations to this approach.

For example, this approach gives the same measure of diversity for Group A that eats equal amounts of four different animals and for Group B that eats almost exclusively one animal but occasionally eats an individual of one of the other three species. The primary alternative measure of this diversity is called *niche width*. To calculate niche width, follow these steps:

1. Using MNI, calculate the proportion that each species contributes to the whole (remember: proportions are decimals below 1.0).
2. Square each proportion (multiply it times itself).
3. Add these squared proportions together.
4. Divide 1 by the sum of the squared proportions that you just derived.

These steps are summarized by the following equation:

$$\text{niche width} = \frac{1}{\Sigma p^2}$$

where n = the number of taxa and p = the proportion of total MNI contributed by a taxon. Niche width always will be a positive number, ranging from 1 to infinity. The lower the value for niche width, the more specialized the diet (less diversity); the higher the value for niche width, the more generalized (more diversity). Normally any non-food species that are represented in the faunal assemblage will be omitted from the calculation of the niche width.

The faunal analyst also has to keep an eye out for confusing remains (red herring bones?). For example, a snake might have crawled into a hole on a site, perhaps during the period when a site was occupied and perhaps not, and died. The best field archaeology will not always be able to tell that these bones were not deposited by human agency. The faunal analyst, however, has to make some sort of decision about whether these bones represent a food animal or not. Sometimes butchering marks on bones will help; sometimes the circumstances of the find (*e.g.,* an articulated skeleton) will help; sometimes nothing helps.

The opposite effect also plagues the faunal analyst. Some animals may have been eaten—perhaps even in large quantities—but remain unrepresented or underrepresented in the archaeological record. Fish, for example, often are underrepresented for several reasons: Their bones are small and can decompose rapidly in some soils; those same small bones can be difficult to recover in the field; some modes of preparing fish involve mashing the bones up with the flesh for eating; and fish cleanings are very smelly and sometimes are disposed of at some distance from the usual dumping places for the settlement. Faunal analysts can't hope to reconstruct food sources that aren't evidenced in the record, but they can be alert to possible sources of bias in the archaeological record and note them.

YOUR ASSIGNMENT

Dr. Theresa Highpockets has been conducting research into Chinese Camp and New London, two gold mining camps from the 1850s in Plumador County, California. (You already have encountered some of her early studies in Exercise 2.) She has excavated at both of these sites and has a faunal collection from each. A faunal analyst has identified the remains, producing the species list included as Table 10-1 and the faunal lists included as Tables 10-2 and 10-3. But, for personal reasons, the faunal analyst is unable to continue with the project. Consequently, Highpockets has hired you as a consultant to complete the analysis. You have every reason to be confident in the accuracy of the original analyst's identifications. For your convenience, Figure 10-1 shows the basic skeleton and bone element names for generalized vertebrates, including mammals and birds.

The faunal lists are from comparable assemblages at Chinese Camp and New London. These camps were similar in many ways. Each was occupied for about five years, then abandoned; each was occupied by about 500 people, mostly young men; each procured its food from the countryside and from the provisioning town of Jackson (about 40 miles away by dirt road). But they differed in one essential respect: Chinese Camp was populated primarily by Chinese immigrants, while New London was populated primarily by Anglo-American immigrants from New England. With the same resources and

TABLE 10-1   Species list, Chinese Camp and New London sites. An asterisk marks domestic species; all others are either wild or feral.

	SPECIES	COMMON NAME
Birds:	*Cairina moschata**	Muscovy duck
	*Gallus gallus**	chicken
	*Meleagris gallopavo**	turkey
	Phasianus colchicus	ring-necked pheasant
	Laphortyx californicus	California quail
	Anas canadensis	Canada goose
	Ardea herodias	great blue heron
	Gavia immer	common loon
Mammals:	*Bos taurus**	cattle
	*Sus scrofa**	pig
	*Ovis aries**	sheep
	*Equus caballus**	horse
	*Canis domesticus**	dog
	Ursus americanus	black bear
	Cervus elephas	elk
	Odocoileus hemionus	mule deer
	Sciurus griseus	gray squirrel
	Lepus californicus	black-tailed jackrabbit

TABLE 10-2   Faunal list, Chinese Camp.

TAXA	ELEMENT	NUMBER OF ELEMENTS	NUMBER OF PIECES
BIRDS:			
Cairina moschata	ilium/ischium	14	37[a]
	femur, left	18	71[a]
	femur, right	22	68[a]
	tibia, left	11	44
	tibia, right	16	61[a]
	humerus, left	16	39[a]
	humerus, right	16	45[a]
	ulna, right	4	14
	ribs	—	73
	vertebrae	—	14
	skull	12	46[d]
	toe bones	—	11
Gallus gallus	ilium/ischium	1	4[a]
	femur, left	3	11[a]
	femur, right	2	7[a]
	tibia, left	2	7
	humerus, right	3	14[a]
	ulna, left	1	3
	radius, left	1	6
	ribs	—	14
	vertebrae	—	6
Meleagris gallopavo	ilium/ischium	2	9[a]
	femur, left	1	2[a]
	femur, right	1	3[a]
	tibia, left	1	1
	tibia, right	2	5[a]
	humerus, left	3	4[a]
	humerus, right	2	5[a]
	ribs	—	12
	vertebrae	—	5
	skull	2	17[d]
Phasianus colchicus	ilium/ischium	1	3[a]
	femur, left	2	2[a]
	tibia, left	1	2
	scapula, left	1	1
	humerus, left	1	1[a]
	ulna, left	1	1[a]
	ribs	—	3
	vertebrae	—	1
	skull	1	2

(continued)

TABLE 10-2   Faunal list, Chinese Camp, *continued.*

TAXA	ELEMENT	NUMBER OF ELEMENTS	NUMBER OF PIECES
	vertebrae	—	1
	skull	1	2
Laphortyx californicus	ilium/ischium	14	27
	femur, left	22	39
	femur, right	11	19
	tibia, left	9	12
	tibia, right	13	17
	humerus, left	24	31
	humerus, right	17	34
	ulna, left	6	8
	ulna, right	1	1
	radius, left	1	1
	ribs	—	63
	vertebrae	—	77
	skull	14	25
	toe bones	—	6
Anas canadensis	ilium/ischium	1	3[a]
	femur, left	1	2
	femur, right	1	1[a]
	tibia, left	1	2
	humerus, left	1	2[a]
	humerus, right	1	4[a]
	ulna, right	1	1
	ribs	—	7
	vertebrae	—	11
	skull	1	3
Ardea herodias	ilium/ischium	1	7[a]
	femur, left	1	3[a]
	femur, right	1	2
	tibia, left	1	1[a]
	tibia, right	1	2
	humerus, right	2	5[a]
	ulna, left	1	1
	scapula, right	1	1
	ribs	—	5
	vertebrae	—	2
	skull	1	1
Gavia immer	ilium/ischium	1	1
	femur, right	2	3
	humerus, left	1	2
	ribs	—	1

TABLE 10-2 Faunal list, Chinese Camp, *continued*.

TAXA	ELEMENT	NUMBER OF ELEMENTS	NUMBER OF PIECES
MAMMALS:			
Bos taurus	pelvis	1	12[a]
	femur, left	1	5[a]
	femur, right	2	8[a,g]
	tibia, left	1	2
	tibia, right	1	1[a]
	fibula, left	2	2[g]
	fibula, right	1	3
	humerus, left	1	3[a]
	humerus, right	1	5[a]
	ulna, left	1	2
	ulna, right	2	6[a,g]
	radius, left	1	2
	ribs	—	12[a,g]
	vertebrae	—	14[g]
	skull	1	89[a,d]
Sus scrofa	pelvis	3	41[a,f]
	femur, left	3	55[a,f]
	femur, right	6	56[a,f]
	tibia, left	1	3[a]
	tibia, right	4	22[f]
	fibula, left	2	17[f]
	fibula, right	4	26[f]
	humerus, left	4	11[a,f]
	humerus, right	7	14[a,f]
	ulna, left	1	4
	ulna, right	2	6[a,f]
	radius, left	1	3
	radius, right	1	1
	ribs	—	88[a,f]
	vertebrae	—	67[f]
	skull	4	122[a,d,f]
	toe bones	—	44
Equus caballus	femur, left	1	3[b]
Canis domesticus	pelvis	1	4[a]
	femur, left	3	11[a]
	femur, right	1	8
	tibia, left	1	1
	humerus, left	2	3
	humerus, right	1	2[a]
	ulna, left	1	3

(continued)

TABLE 10-2 Faunal list, Chinese Camp, *continued.*

TAXA	ELEMENT	NUMBER OF ELEMENTS	NUMBER OF PIECES
	radius, right	1	1
	ribs	—	9
	vertebrae	—	8
	skull	2	6
Sciurus griseus	pelvis	9	23[h]
	femur, left	11	19[h]
	femur, right	4	14[h]
	tibia, left	5	11[h]
	tibia, right	7	16[h]
	humerus, left	7	9[a,h]
	humerus, right	12	16[h]
	ulna, left	3	5[h]
	ulna, right	1	2
	radius, right	1	1
	ribs	—	112[h]
	vertebrae	—	44[a,h]
	skull	7	9[h]
Lepus californicus	pelvis	14	31[a,h]
	femur, left	22	30[a,h]
	femur, right	24	42[h]
	tibia, left	11	14[h]
	tibia, right	9	14[h]
	humerus, left	21	29[h]
	humerus, right	18	30[h]
	ulna, left	14	18[a,h]
	ulna, right	12	15[h]
	radius, left	8	9[h]
	radius, right	5	11[h]
	ribs	—	38[h]
	vertebrae	—	20[h]
	skull	17	23[h]
	toe bones	—	8
unidentified		—	152

Notes (for both tables)
[a] butchering marks present on at least some specimens
[b] no butchering marks present
[c] essentially intact and complete
[d] highly fragmented
[e] partially articulated
[f] all adults
[g] nearly all adults
[h] includes both adults and immature individuals
[i] mostly immature individuals

TABLE 10-3   Faunal list, New London.

TAXA	ELEMENT	NUMBER OF ELEMENTS	NUMBER OF PIECES
BIRDS:			
Cairina moschata	ilium/ischium	1	2
	femur, left	2	2
	femur, right	2	3
	tibia, right	1	1
	humerus, left	2	2
	humerus, right	1	2
	ribs	—	4
	vertebrae	—	5
Gallus gallus	ilium/ischium	14	20
	femur, left	11	17[a]
	femur, right	21	23[a]
	tibia, left	11	19
	tibia, right	9	13
	humerus, left	22	31
	humerus, right	16	22
	ulna, left	10	12
	ulna, right	7	7
	radius, left	3	3
	ribs	—	48
	vertebrae	—	66
	skull	9	10[c]
	toe bones	—	18
Meleagris gallopavo	ilium/ischium	1	2
	femur, left	1	1[a]
	femur, right	2	2[a]
	tibia, left	1	2
	tibia, right	1	1
	humerus, left	1	1
	humerus, right	2	3
	ulna, left	1	2
	ribs	—	8[a]
	vertebrae	—	12
	skull	1	4
Anas canadensis	ilium/ischium	1	1
	femur, left	1	1[a]
	femur, right	1	1[a]
	tibia, left	1	1
	humerus, right	1	2
	ribs	—	3

(continued)

TABLE 10-3   Faunal list, New London, *continued.*

TAXA	ELEMENT	NUMBER OF ELEMENTS	NUMBER OF PIECES
	vertebrae	—	6
	skull	1	2
MAMMALS:			
Bos taurus	pelvis	11	24[a,g]
	femur, left	17	36[g]
	femur, right	13	19[a,g]
	tibia, left	5	11[g]
	tibia, right	11	18[g]
	fibula, left	5	7[g]
	fibula, right	3	4[g]
	humerus, left	16	25[g]
	humerus, right	14	16[g]
	ulna, left	10	13[g]
	ulna, right	8	11[g]
	radius, left	4	4[g]
	radius, right	6	9[g]
	ribs	—	88[a,g]
	vertebrae	—	54[a,g]
	skull	14	14[a,g]
	toe bones	—	38
Sus scrofa	pelvis	2	5[a,g]
	femur, left	4	6[a,g]
	femur, right	4	7[g]
	tibia, left	1	2
	tibia, right	3	4[g]
	fibula, left	1	1
	humerus, left	4	5[g]
	humerus, right	3	7[g]
	ulna, left	1	1
	ulna, right	2	3[g]
	radius, right	1	2
	ribs	—	11[a,g]
	vertebrae	—	9[a,g]
	skull	2	2[b,c,g]
Ovis aries	pelvis	3	7[a,i]
	femur, left	6	9[i]
	femur, right	3	7[i]
	tibia, left	1	2
	tibia, right	5	7[i]
	fibula, right	1	1
	humerus, left	4	8[i]
	humerus, right	6	14[i]

TABLE 10-3   Faunal list, New London, *continued.*

TAXA	ELEMENT	NUMBER OF ELEMENTS	NUMBER OF PIECES
	ulna, right	1	1
	ribs	—	15[a,i]
	vertebrae	—	12[i]
	skull	5	8[b,c,i]
Canis domesticus	pelvis	1	1[b,e]
	femur, left	1	1[b,e]
	femur, right	1	1[b,e]
	tibia, left	1	1[b,e]
	tibia, right	1	1[b,e]
	toe bones	—	2[b]
Ursus americanus	pelvis	2	3[a,f]
	femur, left	2	5[e,f]
	femur, right	1	2[a,e]
	tibia, left	1	3
	tibia, right	2	2[e,f]
	fibula, left	1	1
	humerus, left	2	6[f]
	humerus, right	2	4[f]
	ulna, left	1	1
	ribs	—	14[a,f]
	vertebrae	—	8[a,f]
	skull	1	1[b,c]
	toe bones	—	4[e]
Cervus elephas	femur, left	7	7[a,f]
	femur, right	4	5[a,f]
	tibia, left	4	4[f]
	tibia, right	2	4[f]
	fibula, left	3	3[f]
	fibula, right	1	1
	toe bones	—	27[e]
Odocoileus hemionus	femur, left	12	14[a,f]
	femur, right	8	11[a,f]
	tibia, left	11	15[f]
	tibia, right	7	9[f]
	fibula, left	1	F1
	toe bones	—	27[e]
unidentified			111

similarity of general circumstances, differences in diet arguably were largely
the result of cultural differences in their behavior relating to food—differences
in their foodways.

Your job is to evaluate how different or similar the diets were at the two
communities, at least in terms of meat. What characteristics you consider and
how you make your comparisons are up to you, but be sure to use some
quantitative measures to support your conclusions. Topics that could be
supported by these data include the relative importance of wild versus domestic meat, preferences for particular species, patterns within hunted species,
selectivity of cuts consumed, food procurement practices, and others. Don't
feel obligated to cover all these issues, and don't feel limited by this list.

(You should assume that the samples on which the faunal lists are based
are comparable and accurately reflect the entirety of the faunal remains at the
sites. That is, you should assume that the quantity of food remains in each site
was of comparable size, that those food remains were a reasonable reflection
of the meat actually eaten there, that the sample excavated from each site
represents more or less the same percentage of the overall deposit, etc. It would
be poor research to compare a very well-preserved sample from one site with
a largely destroyed one from another site. In this case, the assumptions you
are asked to make are quite well warranted by the data. Keep in mind that the
sample of faunal remains is only a small percentage—probably less than
3%—of the entirety of animal refuse produced at the settlements during their
human occupation.)

A Note on Species Names

Species names, as presented in this exercise, follow the accepted rules. These
are very straightforward, and you should follow them in your write-up.

1. The usual way of identifying a species is by giving both its genus and species
   names, in that order. For example, *Homo sapiens,* where *Homo* is the genus and
   sapiens is the species.
2. The genus name always is capitalized; the species name never is capitalized.
3. Both genus and species names are underscored or italicized.
4. When it will be convenient and will not cause confusion, it is acceptable to
   abbreviate the genus name with a single letter followed by a period. This can be
   done *only* after the complete genus-species name has been used at least once. For
   example, *H. sapiens.*
5. To refer to a genus whose species name is unknown, follow the genus name with
   the abbreviation "sp." (not underscored or italicized). For example, *Homo* sp. It
   is not acceptable to abbreviate the genus when using this form.
6. Higher order taxa (family, order, etc.) are capitalized but not underscored or
   italicized; they usually are used alone (not with a higher or lower taxon name).
   For examples, Mollusca; Canidae.

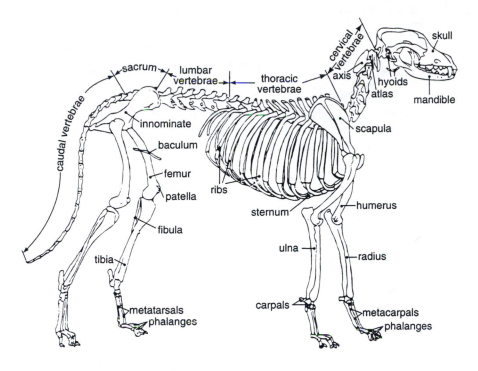

FIGURE 10-1

BIBLIOGRAPHY ON FAUNAL ANALYSIS

Anderson, E. N. 1988. *The Food of China.* Yale University Press, New Haven, Connecticut. Excellent treatment on the foodways of traditional China.

Chang, K. C. (ed.). 1977. *Food in Chinese Culture: Anthropological and Historical Perspectives.* Yale University Press, New Haven, Connecticut. Several articles that deal with Chinese foodways, divided by historical period; good bibliography.

Conlin, Joseph Robert. 1987. *Bacon, Beans, and Galantines: Food and Foodways on the Western Mining Frontier.* University of Nevada Press, Reno, Nevada. Thorough treatment of foodways in mining camps of western North America.

Jameson, E. W., Jr., and Hans J. Peeters. 1988. *California Mammals.* University of California Press, Berkeley, California. Basic guide to California wild mammals; includes weights for some species.

Klein, Richard G., and Kathryn Cruz-Uribe. 1984. *The Analysis of Animal Bones from Archaeological Sites.* University of Chicago Press, Chicago, Illinois. The best basic source of archaeological methods for analyzing vertebrate faunal remains.

Palmer, Ralph S. (ed.). 1974-1988. *Handbook of North American Birds.* 5 vols. Yale University Press, New Haven, Connecticut. Compendious; includes weight data on most species.

Small, Arnold. 1974. *The Birds of California.* Winchester Press, New York. Basic guide to the birds of California; few weight data.

Walker, Ernest P., and others. 1975. *Mammals of the World,* third edition. 3 vols. Johns Hopkins University Press, Baltimore, Maryland. Compendious; includes both wild and domestic species; includes weight data on many species.

White, Theodore E. 1953. A method for calculating the dietary percentage of various food animals utilized by aboriginal peoples. *American Antiquity* 18(4):396-398. Method and tables for calculating flesh weights of various animals; although considered crude by modern standards, this approach is still in use, and you will need to use it for this exercise.

Wing, Elizabeth S. 1980. *Paleonutrition: Prehistoric Foodways.* Academic Press, New York. Treatment of analysis of archaeological food remains; very different approach from Klein and Cruz-Uribe.

In addition, there are many nature guides and cookbooks that may provide further information of use. Also, for some domestic species, you may be able to draw on your own kitchen experience or make a visit to a supermarket for data.

— Exercise 11 —
Inferring Alcohol Usage
from Artifacts

OVERVIEW

Alcoholic beverages are sold in distinctive containers that can be used to infer the scale and nature of alcohol usage at a site. This exercise asks you to use bottle assemblages from Mississippi to test a hypothesis about whether alcohol usage decreases in times of local prohibition.

BACKGROUND

When products are packaged in distinctive containers, those containers can be used as evidence for the presence of those products, even if they have left no other archaeological traces. The bottles in which alcoholic beverages are sold constitute one such class of distinctive containers.

Alcoholic beverages traditionally are divided into five classes. *Beers* are produced by converting starch (especially from grains) to malt and fermenting it; their alcohol content typically ranges from 3% to 5%. Lager, ale, and stout are all types of beer. *Wines* are fermented from fruit juices, especially grape juice, and have alcohol contents ranging from 9% to 14%. *Liquors* include whiskey, brandy, gin, vodka, and the like; these are distilled from wines or beers and have much higher alcohol contents, typically around 40% to 50%. *Liqueurs* are liquors that have been sweetened with sugar, flavored with fruits, and (often) diluted with water; their alcohol contents, while highly variable, usually are around 25% to 30%. *Fortified wines* (*e.g.*, port and sherry) are a special category, consisting of a wine that has been strengthened by the addition of a liquor (usually brandy), resulting in an alcohol content around 18% to 20%.

In addition to these beverages, there are other commercial products that contain alcohol and have been drunk for their intoxicating effects. These include such unappealing substances as jellied alcohol fuel ("sterno"), hair tonic, and spot remover. Most of these products are poisonous or at least highly injurious to the health and often were the last refuge of severe alcoholics who had no access to more appealing inebriants; their consumption on a regular basis normally would lead to death.

There is, however, another class of alcoholic concoctions that were intended for human consumption. These include various patent medicines and flavor extracts. "Jamaica ginger" extract (or "essence"), for example, was a common product in the American South between the late nineteenth century and 1930. While it was sold as a curative agent and a flavoring agent in baking, its alcohol content ranged as high as 90%, and, often mixed with soft drinks, it was widely used as a cheap substitute for liquor, especially in periods of the prohibition of alcoholic beverages. (There is a sad postscript to the story of Jamaica ginger. Manufacturers were well aware that "jake" was being consumed as an intoxicant; the quantities purchased weekly would have kept all of America provisioned in gingerbread and free from gout for a year. Nonetheless, a major manufacturer changed the formula for the extract in 1930, utilizing a highly toxic—but cheaper—form of alcohol. The resulting wave of poisonings led to an epidemic in the South of "jake walk," a permanently palsied gait caused by "jake" poisoning.)

Another alcoholic concoction meriting comment is *bitters*. Bitters was the distillate of various roots and other substances, mixed with alcohol and sometimes sugar. Originally, bitters was used as a curative, and it has maintained this usage among some even today. But it took on an added status as a beverage in the nineteenth century; it still is used today as an additive in some mixed drinks. Alcohol content of bitters ranges from 20% to 40%.

The patent medicines were extremely varied in their contents. The Food and Drug Administration was not established until 1906, and it held no effective role in controlling patent medicines until after the passage of strengthened legislation in 1938. Consequently, patent medicines were odd mixtures of alcohol, narcotics, and ingredients that were argued to have magical healing properties. (One patent medicine of the 1890s was 60% alcohol, 1% laudanum [tincture of opium], and 3% to 5% extract of bull gonads; the remainder was inert ingredients.) Patent medicines were sold over the counter at general stores, pharmacies, and grocery stores, and they often were drunk for their intoxicating effects.

Both extracts and patent medicines were sold in distinctive bottles. These bottles, even after they have lost any label, typically remain identifiable, often to specific brand.

By the early to middle nineteenth century, the United States was a hard-drinking country. In many parts of the country, whiskey was considered a normal accompaniment to a meal, and alcohol consumption in general was quite high. Partly in response, there were various movements to outlaw the drinking of alcoholic beverages. The most famous of these prohibitions was the national prohibition mandated by the Volstead Act that lasted from 1920 to 1933. There were (and continue to be) various other prohibitions, often at the county level. The enactment of prohibition, of course, is no guarantee that the consumption of alcohol will be curtailed, merely that the consumption of certain forms of alcohol will be illegal.

YOUR ASSIGNMENT

Dr. Cecilia Bump has been studying the effects of local prohibitions in Yokna-patawpha County, Mississippi. This particular county had several periods of prohibition between 1880 and 1920, while neighboring counties remained "wet." Her minute study of newspapers and other documents of the period has produced mixed reports on the effects of these prohibitions. Some observers claimed that drinking and public drunkenness dropped off markedly during prohibitions, while others maintained that there was little if any difference. Recognizing the limitations of documents, Bump suspects that these differing reports relate more to the writers' attitudes toward drinking than to the realities of the effects of prohibitions. She has decided to turn to archaeology to help her sort out this problem.

There are several excavated archaeological sites from the county during the span from 1880 to 1920, some of which Bump has excavated herself. She has formulated a hypothesis to test with these data:

During periods of local prohibition, there is no significant decrease in alcohol consumption.

Tables 11-1 through 11-5 present summaries of the bottles found in a series of deposits around Yoknapatawpha County. Table 11-6 presents data on the various products whose bottles are contained in those deposits. Table 11-7 presents dates of the deposits.

Your job is to test the Bump hypothesis given above. You should present not only your conclusion but also the steps that led you to it. Your report should include the following information: an introduction stating the hypothesis and your plan to test it, your methods of calculating relative alcohol usage (with any relevant justification you feel necessary), your results, and your conclusion. Your results may be presented as a table or graph.

The Data Set

Your data set, summarized in Tables 11-1 through 11-5, consists of the bottle assemblages from five sites in Yoknapatawpha County. All of these sites were habitations or were associated with habitations. In Yoknapatawpha County during this period, trash usually was disposed of in pits behind a house; each pit would receive the accumulation from a few months, then would be closed. The features that appear in Tables 11-2 through 11-4 are these trash pits. The exception was when several households shared refuse disposal, in which case a dump (midden) was established; the levels of such dumps can be dated in the same way any other deposit can, provided they can be segregated.

The Faulkner Hotel was a "ladies' retirement hotel," an institution where elderly spinster or widowed women could live. While a private venture, rates were kept moderately low in light of the reduced circumstances of many of the occupants. Still, only moderately well-to-do women could afford to live

TABLE 11-1   Bottles from the Faulkner Hotel site.

DEPOSIT	BOTTLES	MININUM NUMBER OF VESSELS
dump, Level 1	gin	1
	Kennedy's East India Bitters	4
	S. T. Drake Plantation Bitters	7
	L. M. Hellman Bitters	5
	Dr. Kilmer's Swamp Root	1
	Jaynes Alterative	2
	Herbine	3
	ginger ale	14
	perfume	2
	hair dye	1
	milk	5
	cream	1
	pickles	2
dump, Level 2	gin	8
	brandy	4
	creme de menthe	3
	sherry	6
	wine	3
	L. M. Hellman Bitters	3
	Jaynes Alterative	4
	Herbine	2
	ginger ale	3
	perfume	2
	milk	7
	cream	2
dump, Level 3	sherry	1
	Kennedy's East India Bitters	11
	L. M. Hellman Bitters	7
	Jaynes Alterative	5
	Herbine	7
	ginger ale	13
	mineral water	8
	perfume	3
	cologne	1
	milk	9
	cream	2
	pickles	2
	ink	1
dump, Level 4	gin	4
	brandy	1

TABLE 11-1   Bottles from the Faulkner Hotel site, *continued.*

DEPOSIT	BOTTLES	MININUM NUMBER OF VESSELS
	creme de menthe	2
	sherry	2
	wine	3
	Kennedy's East India Bitters	1
	L. M. Hellman Bitters	1
	Herbine	4
	Jaynes Alterative	1
	ginger ale	4
	hair dye	2
	milk	5
	cream	2
	pickles	2

there. All or almost all of the residents were white. The number of residents remained essentially constant throughout the period under study.

The Joe Christmas site was the home of a low-income black family; the Lucius McCaslin site was the home of a low-income white family. The Thomas Sutpen Sharecropper's house was occupied by two sharecropping families during the period under consideration: the Richard Thomas family (1906-1912) and the Biff Williams family (1912-1926). Both of these families were white with low incomes.

The Beat Four District dump was an informal community dump for five or six families living in the district by that name. These families were mostly black, though there sometimes was a white family in the district. All had low incomes.

The Faulkner Hotel, Joe Christmas site, Lucius McCaslin site, and Thomas Sutpen Sharecropper's house all were excavated and analyzed by Dr. Bump; she dated the deposits on the basis of the bottles in them, calculating ranges on the basis of the probable dates of manufacture for the range of bottles. The Beat Four District dump, on the other hand, was excavated and analyzed by her cousin, Prof. Leslie Squarkmuffin, and he calculated summary dates of the deposits by a method analogous to mean ceramic dating (see Exercise 15).

A Note on the Quantification of Bottles

Tables 11-1 through 11-5 quantify the bottle remains from the deposits in terms of *minimum numbers of vessels* (MNV). Glass and ceramic vessels usually are found broken in archaeological contexts, and this measure is a common way of estimating the size of the assemblage and the relative frequency of its

TABLE 11-2   Bottles from the Joe Christmas site.

DEPOSIT	BOTTLES	MININUM NUMBER OF VESSELS
Feature 1	whiskey, 8 oz.	1
	N. K. Brown's Essence of Jamaica Ginger	5
	Brown's Highly Concentrated Essence of Jamaica Ginger	2
	Wait's Irish Moss	1
	Var-Ne-Sis	1
	milk	2
Feature 2	N. K. Brown's Essence of Jamaica Ginger	4
	Brown's Highly Concentrated Essence of Jamaica Ginger	3
	Wait's Irish Moss	2
	Var-Ne-Sis	1
	milk	1
	pickles	2
Feature 3	N. K. Brown's Essence of Jamaica Ginger	2
	Brown's Highly Concentrated Essence of Jamaica Ginger	4
	Var-Ne-Sis	1
	perfume	1
Feature 4	N. K. Brown's Essence of Jamaica Ginger	2
	Brown's Highly Concentrated Essence of Jamaica Ginger	2
	Wait's Irish Moss	1
	Var-Ne-Sis	2
	milk	1
	pickles	1
Feature 5	ale	1
	N. K. Brown's Essence of Jamaica Ginger	3
	Brown's Highly Concentrated Essence of Jamaica Ginger	3
	Var-Ne-Sis	1
	pickles	1
Feature 6	whiskey, 8 oz.	2
	whiskey, 26 oz.	1
	lager	6

TABLE 11-2 Bottles from the Joe Christmas site, *continued.*

DEPOSIT	BOTTLES	MININUM NUMBER OF VESSELS
	N. K. Brown's Essence of Jamaica Ginger	2
	Var-Ne-Sis	1
	cream	1
Feature 7	whiskey, 26 oz.	1
	whiskey, 8 oz.	3
	N. K. Brown's Essence of Jamaica Ginger	4
	Var-Ne-Sis	1
	milk	1
Feature 8	N. K. Brown's Essence of Jamaica Ginger	2
	Brown's Highly Concentrated Essence of Jamaica Ginger	1
	Wait's Irish Moss	1
	Var-Ne-Sis	2
	Kickapoo Indian Sagwa	1
	milk	1
Feature 9	whiskey, 26 oz.	1
	whiskey, 8 oz.	4
	Var-Ne-Sis	1
	pickles	1
Feature 10	whiskey, 26 oz.	2
	whiskey, 8 oz.	1
	lager	3
	Var-Ne-Sis	1
	milk	1
	pickles	1

component types. Its calculation consists of three steps. First, reconstruct (glue back together) as many parts of vessels as possible. Second, sort those parts (some of which will consist of a single fragment) into groups that could be parts of the same vessel, that is, pieces that are very similar in characteristics but do not overlap in their position on a vessel. Third, count the number of groups you have, and you have the minimum number of vessels. (This method of quantifying vessels is analogous to the calculation of minimum number of individuals in faunal analysis, discussed in Exercise 10.)

TABLE 11-3   Bottles from the Lucius McCaslin site.

DEPOSIT	BOTTLES	MININUM NUMBER OF VESSELS
Feature 1	Herbine	1
	ginger ale	3
	sarsaparilla	3
	hair dye	1
	milk	1
Feature 2	Dr. Kilmer's Swamp Root	1
	ginger ale	4
	sarsaparilla	3
	cologne	1
	hair oil	1
	milk	1
	pickles	2
Feature 3	Dr. Kilmer's Swamp Root	1
	ginger ale	3
	sarsaparilla	1
	milk	1
	cream	1
	pickles	1
Feature 4	sarsaparilla	4
	cologne	1
	hair oil	1
	milk	1
	ink	1
Feature 5	Dr. Kilmer's Swamp Root	1
	sarsaparilla	3
	cologne	1
	cream	1
	mustard	1
Feature 6	Herbine	1
	ginger ale	1
	sarsaparilla	1
	perfume	1
Feature 7	ginger ale	2
	hair oil	1
	milk	1
	mustard	1
Feature 8	ginger ale	4
	sarsaparilla	2
	milk	1
	pickles	1

TABLE 11-4   Bottles from theThomas Sutpen Sharecropper's house.

DEPOSIT	BOTTLES	MININUM NUMBER OF VESSELS
Feature 1	Kennedy's East India Bitters	2
	hair oil	1
	pickles	1
Feature 2	L. M. Hellman Bitters	1
	ginger ale	10
	hair oil	1
	pickles	1
Feature 3	L. M. Hellman Bitters	1
	ginger ale	8
	milk	1
Feature 4	Kennedy's East India Bitters	2
	Var-Ne-Sis	1
	milk	1
Feature 5	Kennedy's East India Bitters	3
	pickles	1
Feature 6	gin	3
	lager	3
	cream	1
Feature 7	whiskey, 26 oz.	1
	brandy	1
	ink	1
Feature 8	Kennedy's East India Bitters	3
	milk	1
Feature 9	whiskey, 26 oz.	2
	Jaynes Alterative	1
	milk	1
	pickles	1
Feature 10	gin	3
	lager	6

The minimum number of vessels is a useful measure, since it adjusts to help compensate for differential breakage. Thin vessels or fragile ones may break into far smaller pieces than heavier vessels, and a simple fragment count will overestimate the prominence of the more breakable types. Further, a large storage vessel will probably break into more pieces than a tiny perfume bottle, again leading to a faulty estimate of their relative frequencies if raw fragment counts were used.

TABLE 11-5   Bottles from the Beat Four District dump.

DEPOSIT	BOTTLES	MININUM NUMBER OF VESSELS
Level 1	whiskey, 26 oz.	7
	whiskey, 8 oz.	12
	gin	4
	lager	6
	L. M. Hellman Bitters	2
	N. K. Brown's Essence of Jamaica Ginger	3
	Brown's Highly Concentrated Essence of Jamaica Ginger	2
	Mellier's Essence of Jamaica Ginger	1
	Herbine	2
	Jaynes Alterative	4
	ginger ale	5
	milk	3
Level 2	whiskey, 26 oz.	5
	whiskey, 8 oz.	14
	gin	5
	lager	2
	ale	1
	L. M. Hellman Bitters	3
	N. K. Brown's Essence of Jamaica Ginger	1
	Brown's Highly Concentrated Essence of Jamaica Ginger	3
	Herbine	2
	Jaynes Alterative	4
	ginger ale	4
	milk	2
	pickles	1
Level 3	L. M. Hellman Bitters	6
	N. K. Brown's Essence of Jamaica Ginger	12
	Brown's Highly Concentrated Essence of Jamaica Ginger	14
	Mellier's Essence of Jamaica Ginger	8
	Herbine	5
	Jaynes Alterative	4
	ginger ale	2
	milk	3
	cream	1

TABLE 11-5   Bottles from the Beat Four District dump, *continued.*

DEPOSIT	BOTTLES	MININUM NUMBER OF VESSELS
Level 4	L. M. Hellman Bitters	5
	N. K. Brown's Essence of Jamaica Ginger	16
	Brown's Highly Concentrated Essence of Jamaica Ginger	8
	Mellier's Essence of Jamaica Ginger	11
	Herbine	3
	Jaynes Alterative	7
	ginger ale	4
	milk	2
Level 5	whiskey, 26 oz.	1
	gin	1
	L. M. Hellman Bitters	5
	N. K. Brown's Essence of Jamaica Ginger	11
	Brown's Highly Concentrated Essence of Jamaica Ginger	12
	Mellier's Essence of Jamaica Ginger	4
	Herbine	5
	Jaynes Alterative	4
	ginger ale	11
	milk	
Level 6	whiskey, 26 oz.	8
	whiskey, 8 oz.	8
	gin	4
	lager	11
	L. M. Hellman Bitters	1
	N. K. Brown's Essence of Jamaica Ginger	4
	Brown's Highly Concentrated Essence of Jamaica Ginger	1
	Mellier's Essence of Jamaica Ginger	1
	Herbine	2
	Jaynes Alterative	4
	ginger ale	7
	milk	2
	pickles	3
Level 7	whiskey, 26 oz.	6
	whiskey, 8 oz.	12

(continued)

TABLE 11-5   Bottles from the Beat Four District dump, *continued.*

DEPOSIT	BOTTLES	MININUM NUMBER OF VESSELS
	gin	4
	brandy	1
	lager	8
	L. M. Hellman Bitters	· 1
	N. K. Brown's Essence of Jamaica Ginger	3
	Brown's Highly Concentrated Essence of Jamaica Ginger	1
	Herbine	2
	Jaynes Alterative	3
	ginger ale	4
	cream	1
Level 8	whiskey, 26 oz.	11
	whiskey, 8 oz.	4
	gin	3
	lager	1
	L. M. Hellman Bitters	2
	N. K. Brown Essence of Jamaica Ginger	2
	Brown's Highly Concentrated Essence of Jamaica Ginger	1
	Mellier's Essence of Jamaica Ginger	1
	Herbine	3
	Jaynes Alterative	4
	ginger ale	5
	milk	1
	pickles	1

Sometimes students make the error of believing, however, that the minimum number of vessels is the exact number of vessels in the deposit or (even worse) the exact number used by the archaeological people under study. The minimum number of vessels is only an index, a rough approximation, of the relative numbers of vessels of different types in a deposit. Remember that archaeologists usually excavate only small percentages of archaeological sites, so the number of anything found in a site usually is far smaller than the total number actually there. Also, remember that many items either don't find their way into the archaeological record (*e.g.*, thrown away elsewhere or reused) or are destroyed before an archaeologist finds them (through rotting and such). Consequently, minimum numbers of vessels normally should be used to compare categories of vessels to one another but not to establish absolute frequencies.

TABLE 11-6   Information on alcoholic and other bottled products, Yoknapatawpha County sites.

PRODUCT	VOLUME (OUNCES)	PERCENTAGE ALCOHOL
Liquor:		
whiskey	26	40
whiskey	8	40
gin	26	40
brandy	26	42
Liqueur:		
creme de menthe	20	26
Fortified wine:		
sherry	26	18
Wine:	23	10
Beer:		
lager	24	4
ale	15	5
Bitters:		
S. T. Drake Plantation Bitters	30	28
L. M. Hellman Bitters	24	22
Kennedy's East India Bitters	30	40
Extracts:		
N. K. Brown's Essence of Jamaica Ginger	6	40
Brown's Highly Concentrated Essence of Jamaica Ginger	6	85
Mellier's Essence of Jamaica Ginger	6	50
Patent medicines:		
Dr. Kilmer's Swamp Root (laxative)	6	10.5
Wait's Irish Moss (tonic)	5	45
Herbine (tonic)	6	20
Kickapoo Indian Sagwa (tonic)	8	60
Jaynes Alterative	10	40
Var-Ne-Sis (rheumatism cure)	13	70
Toiletries:		
perfume	1	40
cologne	3.5	40
hair oil	5	10
hair dye	2	4

(continued)

TABLE 11-6   Information on alcoholic and other bottled products, Yoknapatawpha County sites, *continued.*

PRODUCT	VOLUME (OUNCES)	PERCENTAGE ALCOHOL
Soft drinks:		
ginger ale	11	<1
sarsaparilla	11	<1
mineral water	20	0
Dairy products:		
milk	32	0
cream	16	0
Miscellaneous:		
mustard	7	0
pickles	14	0
ink	3	0

The Prohibition History of Yoknapatawpha County

Yoknapatawpha County had a moderately small but influential prohibitionist element in the period between 1880 and 1920. The various referendums on prohibition or its repeal always were hotly contested, and usually the vote was close, regardless of the outcome. As a result, the county popped in and out of prohibition several times during the 40-year span under question. The county's prohibition history during this period is summarized in Table 11-8.

Of course, a period of prohibition was a period when alcoholic beverages (beer, wine, fortified wine, liquor, and liqueur) could not be sold in the county. Other fluids with alcohol (*e.g.,* bitters, patent medicines) continued to be sold throughout the period. Also, neighboring counties and the nearby state of Tennessee had no prohibitions during this period, and, while illegal, it was possible to buy alcoholic beverages outside and bring them across the border into Yoknapatawpha County.

Notes on Analysis

There is a critical subtlety in this problem. If Deposit A has 200 gin bottles and Deposit B has only 20, was alcohol usage ten times greater among those who formed Deposit A? Only if the number of people forming the deposits and the period of formation were the same. Five times as many people forming Deposit A over twice the period could mean that alcohol usage was exactly the same (calculated per person, per year). Or, the same number of people could produce five times as many bottles over a period five times as long.

TABLE 11-7 Site data, Yoknapatawpha County, Mississippi.

SITE	DEPOSIT	DATE
Faulkner Hotel	dump, Level 1	1892-1895
	dump, Level 2	1896-1901
	dump, Level 3	1902-1907
	dump, Level 4	1908-1910
Joe Christmas site	Feature 1	1904
	Feature 2	1918
	Feature 3	1906
	Feature 4	1916
	Feature 5	1907
	Feature 6	1914
	Feature 7	1911
	Feature 8	1908
	Feature 9	1912
	Feature 10	1914
Lucius McCaslin site	Feature 1	1911
	Feature 2	1882
	Feature 3	1893
	Feature 4	1884
	Feature 5	1887
	Feature 6	1901
	Feature 7	1892
	Feature 8	1890
Thomas Sutpen Sharecropper's house	Feature 1	1920
	Feature 2	1908
	Feature 3	1909
	Feature 4	1917
	Feature 5	1918
	Feature 6	1914
	Feature 7	1911
	Feature 8	1916
	Feature 9	1912
	Feature 10	1913
Beat Four District dump	Level 1	1891
	Level 2	1890
	Level 3	1889
	Level 4	1888
	Level 5	1887
	Level 6	1886
	Level 7	1885
	Level 8	1884

TABLE 11-8   The prohibition history of Yoknapatawpha County, Mississippi.

DATES	STATUS
1880-1886	no prohibition
1887-1889	prohibition
1890-1891	no prohibition
1892-1895	prohibition
1896-1901	no prohibition
1902-1910	prohibition
1911-1914	no prohibition
1915-1920	prohibition

Consequently, you will have to pay attention to the size of the groups that formed each deposit and to how long it took to form each deposit. If you are satisfied that these variables were more or less the same, then you can make direct comparisons. If not, however, then you will have to make some adjustment, such as using an index like "ounces of alcohol per year" or "ounces of alcohol per family." For this reason, you probably will want to restrict your comparisons to within each site.

You will have to decide how you wish to quantify alcohol usage. One approach would be simply to count the number of bottles you believe were consumed as alcoholic beverages, but bottles come in different sizes and with different contents. Another approach would be to convert the bottles into ounces of contents. Alternatively, you may wish to make some adjustment to account for the differing alcohol percentages in different substances. You must select which method of quantification best suits the objective of testing the Bump hypothesis.

Once you have made your calculations, you have to interpret your figures. One approach is to interpret them at face value. Alternatively, you can apply the methods of inferential statistics to them to assess how likely it is that the patterns you see are the result of chance. This manual provides no training in inferential statistics, so that option will be open to you only if you have other training in those methods.

A Note on Hypothesis Testing

The formulation and testing of hypotheses is a hallmark of the scientific method and has proven highly successful in the natural sciences. In the social sciences, however, there is more disagreement over whether this is the most productive way to frame research. Many archaeologists, particularly those who favor the processualist paradigm, would agree with Dr. Bump that hypotheses can be useful in archaeological research.

Generations of schoolchildren have learned that a hypothesis is an educated guess, but that definition is pretty inadequate. An hypothesis is a general statement that a researcher wants to test for accuracy. The Bump hypothesis fits the definition because it predicts what will happen (or retrodicts what has already happened) during periods of prohibition, at all times and all places. It also is reasonable as a hypothesis, since a researcher can formulate criteria against which it can be tested (*test implications*, in the jargon of the philosophy of science); in this case, the test implications will be that there is no significant change in the amount of alcohol consumed during periods of prohibition.

One of the problems of the "educated guess" definition of a hypothesis is that it makes the hypothesis appear random or arbitrary. In reality, a hypothesis reflects its formulator's theoretical or philosophical viewpoints and is based on previous thought. In this case, Bump is well aware that unloved laws can be ignored by the public and that the police are not always zealous in their enforcement, leaving open the possibility that the law will be little more than a political exercise. Sometimes, of course, a researcher will test a hypothesis that he or she feels probably is untrue, recognizing that the disproving of one hypothesis will leave a sole competitor as the only viable possibility. (Such a hypothesis is known as the *null hypothesis.*)

The testing of hypotheses always favors disproof. If the data from Yoknapatawpha County were to be exactly as predicted by the Bump hypothesis, would this prove the hypothesis true? No, because the hypothesis claims to have general validity, and it would have been tested in one county but not in all the other places where there have been local prohibitions. On the other hand, if the hypothesis were not to be borne out in Yoknapatawpha County, it certainly couldn't be entertained as generally true. This means that hypotheses cannot ever be proven true in the logical sense, although they usually are accepted as such when they have survived a series of tests. Because of the ease of disproving and difficulty of proving a hypothesis, it sometimes is sensible to use a null hypothesis, hoping that its disproof will mean that your actual expectation is proven true.

If the Yoknapatawpha County data fail to support the Bump hypothesis, does this mean that it is untrue and worthless? While it may not be true as a universal principle, it may be that the Yoknapatawpha County case is the oddball, and that the hypothesis holds true nearly everywhere else. Given the vagaries of archaeological evidence, it usually is wise not to reject a hypothesis too quickly, even if its initial test fails to support it.

BIBLIOGRAPHY ON ALCOHOL USAGE
AND ALCOHOL CONTAINERS

Asbury, Herbert. 1950. *The Great Illusion: An Informal History of Prohibition.* Doubleday and Co., Garden City, New York. A readable account of American prohibition, arguing for its ineffectiveness.

Fike, Richard E. 1987. *The Bottle Book: A Comprehensive Guide to Historic, Embossed Medicine Bottles.* Peregrine Smith Books, Salt Lake City, Utah. Largely an identification guide with some social commentary.

Kerr, K. Austin (ed.). 1973. *The Politics of Moral Behavior: Prohibition and Drug Abuse.* Addison-Wesley Publishing Co., Reading, Massachusetts. Includes original documents, some citing the success of prohibition and some citing its failure.

Kobler, John. 1973. *Ardent Spirits: The Rise and Fall of Prohibition.* G. P. Putnam's Sons, New York. Includes a chapter on bitters, jake, and other liquor alternatives.

Lender, Mark, Edward, and James Kirby Martin. 1987. *Drinking in America: A History,* revised and expanded edition. The Free Press, New York. General history of the subject in America.

Rorabaugh, W. J. 1979. *The Alcoholic Republic: An American Tradition.* Oxford University Press, Oxford, England. A classic history of alcohol use in America.

Wilson, Rex L. 1981. *Bottles on the Western Frontier.* University of Arizona Press, Tucson, Arizona. An excellent source on identifying bottles in the latter part of the nineteenth century; some discussion of the social context of the contents.

PART FOUR

The Analysis of Portable Artifacts

ARTIFACTS, OBJECTS FORMED BY HUMAN TECHNOLOGY, are one of the most important sources of information available to the archaeologist. As products of human design, they are subject to infinite variation, yet they are constrained by the technology that produced them and the ideas that conceived them. Consequently, they are storehouses of information about their manufacturers and users.

Archaeologists have developed many techniques and methods of analyzing artifacts in attempts to decode the information hidden in them. Many of these techniques are involved with the classification of artifacts into types, styles, and other categories, partially to simplify the task of coping with the many thousands of artifacts that are found on a typical historical site. Some of these categories carry the hidden benefit of assisting in establishing the date of a deposit, the ethnicity of its makers, or the function of the item. Other means of analyzing artifacts can provide further information on date, function, reuse, source of materials, place of manufacture, method of manufacture, cost, and many other characteristics of archaeological interest.

Some of these methods and techniques are very specialized, *e.g.*, identifying the place of manufacture of pewter vessels on the basis of maker's marks found on their bases. Others require complex equipment and procedures, *e.g.*, determining the original firing temperature of a ceramic on the basis of refiring. They are beyond the scope of this manual. Here, the exercises focus on more broadly applicable methods that require little or no equipment or specialized knowledge from the physical sciences.

Two of the exercises focus on classification. Exercise 12 leads you through the identification of artifacts into pre-established categories; Exercise 13 shows you how to establish categories to classify artifacts when none have been defined previously. The other exercises focus on methods of dating specific classes of artifacts or inferring their function. Some of the other exercises in this manual, particularly Exercise 11 and most of the cemetery exercises, also deal with artifacts.

Much of historical archaeology concerns the analysis of artifacts, and students pursuing careers or further training in the field will spend much of their time mastering a wide variety of those analytical methods. The more commonly encountered classes of artifacts, particularly ceramics, are critical to most historical archaeological research, and all historical archaeologists have to have moderately well-developed skills in their identification and analysis.

— EXERCISE 12 —
ARTIFACT IDENTIFICATION

OVERVIEW

Much of descriptive archaeology is based on the identification of artifacts or other remains—the placing of them in previously defined categories. This hands-on exercise asks you to identify the specimens in an assemblage of nails, a common class of historic artifacts.

BACKGROUND

One of the major tasks of archaeologists of all sorts is the placement of the artifacts they find into meaningful categories. Of course, some artifacts are unique and all have unique qualities, so there are times when they must be considered as individuals, but most of the time it is useful to place them in groups to simplify the data and see patterns. Analyzing an assemblage that may contain tens of thousands of bricks, sherds, or nails is made possible by the division of the mass of artifacts into categories that can be summarized, compared to one another, and compared to those in other sites. These categories often are a step toward determining the date of an archaeological deposit, the function of its artifacts, or the ethnicity or social status of its makers.

There is, however, an essential difference between most prehistoric archaeology and most historical archaeology in terms of these categories. Prehistorians normally must create the categories they use, since there are (by definition) no records left behind by the people under study. Consequently, they must use a variety of techniques to define categories and assign specimens to them, many of which are statistical. Categories of this sort that are defined by archaeologists are called *types*, and a system of types that divide up a class of artifacts is called a *typology*. For example, a typology of prehistoric stone axes from the American Midwest might consist of four types, each named and defined on the basis of a series of traits that consistently occur together.

Historical archaeologists, in contrast to prehistorians, have the advantage that they often have trade catalogues, encyclopedias, craft manuals, and other documentary sources that are contemporary with the archaeological remains they study. These sources often provide them with the categories that were in use by the makers or users of the artifacts under study. This tremendous advantage permits historical archaeologists, for the most part, to engage in *artifact identification* (the placing of artifacts into pre-existing categories) rather than *artifact taxonomy* (the definition and refinement of artifact categories). Of course, for some classes of artifacts there are no relevant documents, and historical archaeologists must turn to the methods of the prehistorian and define typologies; in other cases, archaeologists might want to produce typologies that differentiate between items in ways that their makers or users didn't find important. Typology will be discussed at length in Exercise 13.

Identification is a fairly straightforward process, but it requires a certain kind of mental discipline on the part of the analyst. Analysts first must become familiar with the characteristics of the categories that they are dealing with. To recognize an early seventeenth-century English wine bottle, for example, the analyst must know the typical overall shape (often well enough to recognize it in broken pieces), the size and placement of the handle (if any), the color and thickness of the glass, the amount of bubbles and other flaws in the glass, the height of kickup (indentation) in the bottom of the base, and the like. Each characteristic that is considered a basic element in technical terminology is called a *trait* or*attribute*. The traits distinctive to a category combine to characterize it.

When identifying an artifact as belonging to a particular category, you must ascertain that it truly possesses the traits that define that category. In many cases, this merely requires that you understand the traits and pay strict attention to their presence or absence. In other cases, however, things may be a bit more complicated. Especially when dealing with handmade items without the standardization of mass production, you may find that an artifact falls between the recognized categories. That is, it may have some of the traits for one category and some for another. How do you cope with this situation?

An example may help clarify the situation. Let's assume that you have two kinds of cast-iron cookware from early nineteenth-century Michigan. One category ("frying pan") is low and wide and has a handle projecting from one side; the other category ("stew pot") is somewhat narrower but much deeper and has a bail (wire) handle. Documents have defined these categories and have explained that the former was used for grilling and pan-frying and that the other was used for boiling and braising. You have found a variety of iron sherds from vessels and have so far been able to identify them as belonging to either the frying pan category or the stew pot category. But now you find sherds of a vessel that is as broad as the frying pan and as deep as the stew pot but has a projecting handle like the frying pan; in addition, there are iron sherds from a matching lid.

How you identify this vessel depends on how you judge the situation. For example, you may feel that the vessel essentially falls into the frying pan category, since most of its traits are in accord with that category, differing only in its depth and slightly narrower diameter. The anomalies would be viewed as simply quirks on the part of the maker; in a different example, the differences might be seen as the result of poor crafting or manufacturing error. On the other hand, perhaps you feel that the depth of the vessel makes it functionally a stew pot and consider the aberrant handle just an idiosyncrasy. A third alternative is to declare it a distinct and discrete category of its own, not represented in the documents available. (In this case, the aberrant form fits into the French-Canadian category of *casserole à frière* and would be found in Canadian documents.) The final alternative is to decide that you do not have enough information to identify the artifact, in which case you will place it into an "unidentified" category or deal with it uniquely. In any case, it is likely that you would want to note that the artifact was not a "classic" representative of one of the typical Michigan vessel categories.

YOUR ASSIGNMENT

The date is 2121, and your assignment is to identify the nails from the assemblage excavated by Prof. L. S. B. Capybara at the Wotacroc site in Wotacroc, Michigan. Capybara, a descendant of both Leslie Squarkmuffin and Cecilia Bump, is a well-known figure in twenty-second-century historical archaeology and has engaged you to conduct this aspect of the analysis of the Wotacroc site. Capybara has already dated the site by other means and knows that the assemblage you are dealing with was deposited around 1980. Capybara's interest in the identifications is twofold. First, the nails need to be described for the published site report. Second, your analysis may support further reconstruction of the activities that took place on this part of the site, including activities that led to the formation of the deposit. This exercise includes excerpts from a late twentieth-century document dealing with nails (*Reader's Digest Complete Do-it-Yourself Manual*, 1973), as well as a key to nails and related forms of the latter half of the twentieth century. You are expected to use these materials as your primary guides. The nail assemblage will be provided to you by your instructor.

Your report should list each specimen by its serial number and give its identification, including comments if you feel that a specimen is aberrant or unusual. Also, you should make any comments you feel would be helpful to Capybara in reconstructing activities and site formation processes at this portion of the site.

A Key to Nail Identification

A key is an aid to identification. It leads you through a program of questions, and the answer to each question leads you to the next; finally, you reach a single identification. Keys are systematic and have the advantage of leading you to a result, regardless of whether you know enough about the artifact category to ask appropriate questions on your own. They have the disadvantage, however, of being time-consuming, potentially wending their way through rare categories to arrive at a common one.

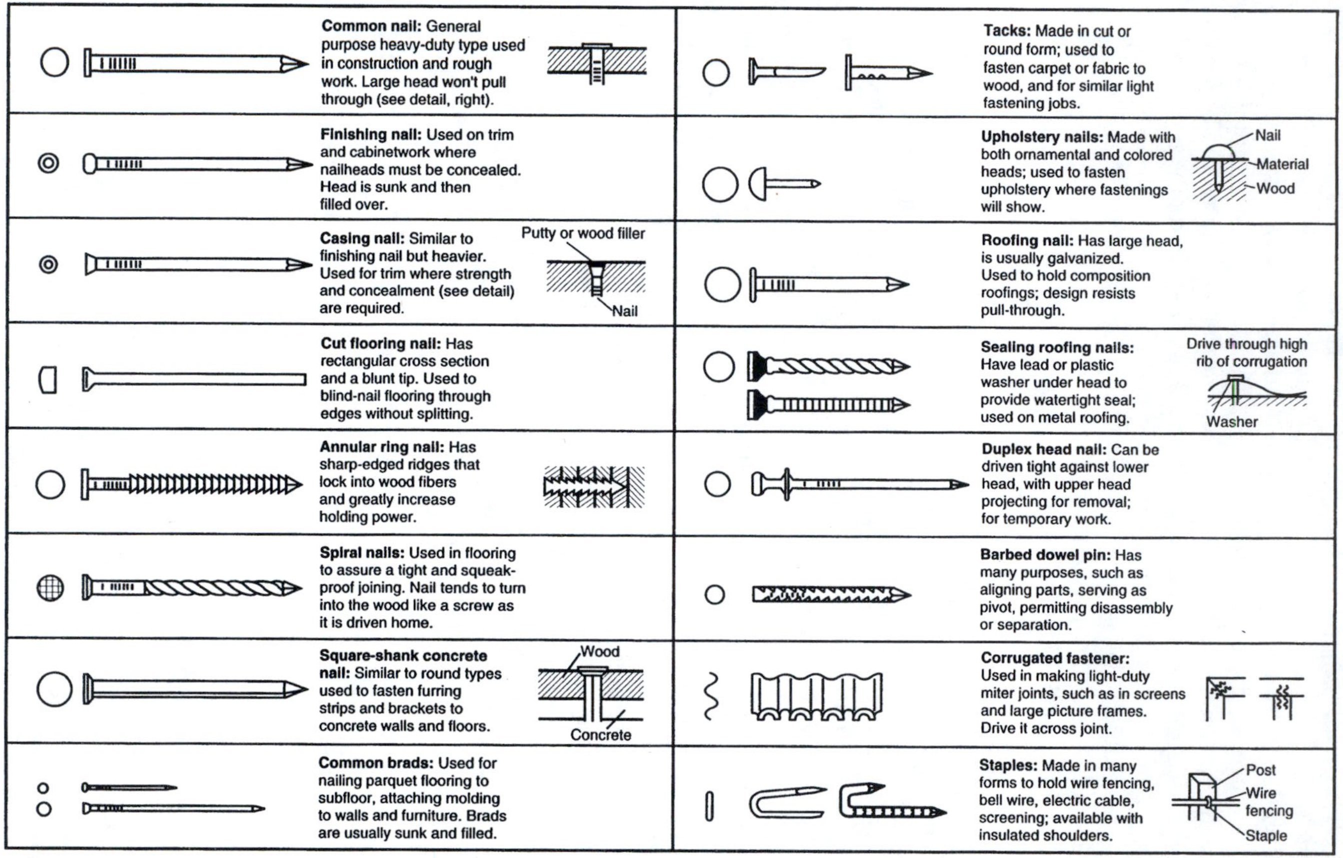

Common nail: General purpose heavy-duty type used in construction and rough work. Large head won't pull through (see detail, right).

Finishing nail: Used on trim and cabinetwork where nailheads must be concealed. Head is sunk and then filled over.

Casing nail: Similar to finishing nail but heavier. Used for trim where strength and concealment (see detail) are required.

Putty or wood filler — Nail

Cut flooring nail: Has rectangular cross section and a blunt tip. Used to blind-nail flooring through edges without splitting.

Annular ring nail: Has sharp-edged ridges that lock into wood fibers and greatly increase holding power.

Spiral nails: Used in flooring to assure a tight and squeak-proof joining. Nail tends to turn into the wood like a screw as it is driven home.

Square-shank concrete nail: Similar to round types used to fasten furring strips and brackets to concrete walls and floors.

Wood — Concrete

Common brads: Used for nailing parquet flooring to subfloor, attaching molding to walls and furniture. Brads are usually sunk and filled.

Tacks: Made in cut or round form; used to fasten carpet or fabric to wood, and for similar light fastening jobs.

Upholstery nails: Made with both ornamental and colored heads; used to fasten upholstery where fastenings will show.

Nail — Material — Wood

Roofing nail: Has large head, is usually galvanized. Used to hold composition roofings; design resists pull-through.

Sealing roofing nails: Have lead or plastic washer under head to provide watertight seal; used on metal roofing.

Drive through high rib of corrugation

Washer

Duplex head nail: Can be driven tight against lower head, with upper head projecting for removal; for temporary work.

Barbed dowel pin: Has many purposes, such as aligning parts, serving as pivot, permitting disassembly or separation.

Corrugated fastener: Used in making light-duty miter joints, such as in screens and large picture frames. Drive it across joint.

Post — Wire fencing — Staple

Staples: Made in many forms to hold wire fencing, bell wire, electric cable, screening; available with insulated shoulders.

FIGURE 12-1

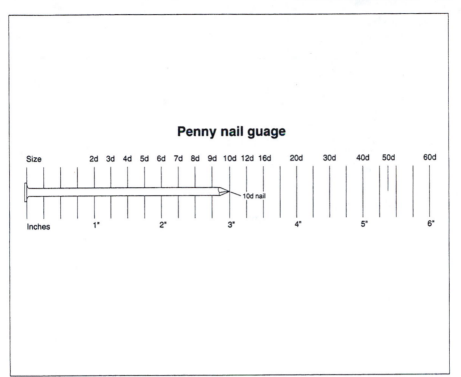

Figure 12-2. Nail sizes.

To use the key, start at #1. You must select either "a" or "b." If you select "a," you move on to #2, as the direction tells you; if you select "b," you have a staple, as the key tells you. You keep following the questions in order, following whatever directions the key gives you, until you find the category into which the artifact falls. You must not skip any step, however, since that could lead to gross misidentifications. For example, if you entered the key after #5, you would miss a critical division between headed and headless nails; trying to find a headless nail in #6-11 would be fruitless, since only headed nails are found there.

1. Number of shafts
    a. single shaft. . . . . (nails) see 2
    b. double shaft, usually bent . . . . staple
2. Shaft cross-section
    a. square. . . . . see 3
    b. round . . . . (wire nails) see 4

3. Head shape
   a. round . . . . square-shank concrete nail
   b. square, molded with shaft . . . . cut flooring nail
4. Multiple heads
   a. nail has one head at end of shaft,
      second a bit lower on shaft . . . . duplex head nail
   b. nail has single head . . . . see 5
5. Head type
   a. no head. . . . . barbed dowel pin
   b. prominent, broad head . . . . (headed nails) see 6
   c. distinct but small head . . . . (headless nails) see 12
6. Ribbing or twist
   a. shaft has twist or prominent ribbing over entire length . . . see 7
   b. shaft basically smooth (may have some ribbing
      near head only) . . . . see 9
7. Sealing
   a. sealing around base of head . . . . sealing roof nail
   b. no sealing. . . . . see 8
8. Twist versus ribbing
   a. shaft has twist . . . . spiral nail
   b. shaft has deep, barb-like ribbing . . . . annular ring nail
9. Flat versus round head
   a. flat head . . . . see 10
   b. rounded head . . . . upholstery nail
10. Length
    a. short, less than 1 inch. . . . . tack
    b. longer than 1 inch . . . . see 11
11. Head size
    a. larger head; nail often galvanized;
       often lightweight . . . . roofing nail
    b. smaller head; nail rarely galvanized;
       normal weight. . . . . common nail
12. Head shape
    a. torus-shaped (like a doughnut) . . . . finishing nail
    b. tapered, larger at top . . . . see 13
13. Size
    a. small (under 1 inch) and light . . . . common brad
    b. larger and heavier . . . . casing nail

— EXERCISE 13 —
TYPOLOGY

OVERVIEW

When appropriate or useful categories of artifacts do not already exist, archaeologists must define them. This exercise asks you to examine a class of historic Navajo Indian jewelry and formulate useful types.

THE IMPORTANCE OF TYPOLOGY

Exercise 12 introduced the distinction between *identification* and *typology*. Identification assumes that useful categories already exist and the analyst's job simply is to decide which item fits into which category. The typologist, on the other hand, is taking items for which there are no existing categories (or no appropriate ones) and creating categories; after this, items can be classified into these categories through identification. While typology is most prominent in prehistoric archaeology (where there are no documents to reveal the categories as conceived by the prehistoric people under study), there are several factors that also make it important in historical archaeology.

First, not all classes of historical artifacts are categorized in documents. Items produced by folk artisans or by local manufacturers with small distributions are particularly unlikely to appear in catalogues or other documents, yet the differences among them might be valuable indicators of date, place of manufacture, or some other piece of information of archaeological interest. And, of course, the further one retreats in time, the greater the likelihood that the appropriate document (if it ever existed) has failed to survive into the present. Consequently, many buttons, pipes, and other artifact classes can be classified only into categories devised by archaeologists.

Second, even if there are historical categories described in documents, they might not serve the same purpose in which the archaeologist is interested. Perhaps a document gives the different styles of sugar bowls in 1818 in England, or at least those made by a particular manufacturer. The archaeologist, on the other hand, might want some way to distinguish early nineteenth-century sugar bowls from late nineteenth-century ones; for this purpose, the historical categories might be of little use, forcing the archaeologist to construct new categories.

This last example leads to an important point about typologies: There is no such thing as *the* correct typology. Different typologies serve different purposes. Let's examine shovel blades for an example. One typology might differentiate the functions of shovels, perhaps focusing on shape and weight; types might be coal scoops, spades, snow shovels, and the like. Another typology might differentiate shovels of different periods, perhaps focusing on technology of manufacture, method of attachment to a handle, and so forth. A third typology might distinguish different countries of manufacture, ethnic styles, or other properties. No single typology can provide useful classification toward all ends, so it may be necessary or desirable to have several typologies for a single class of artifact. The most usual kinds of typologies are *descriptive* (all-purpose), *historical* (differentiating periods of manufacture), *functional* (differentiating uses), and *ethnic* (differentiating various cultural or national patterns). A special category of typologies is the *emic typology*, where the typology is argued to reflect the cultural values of the makers, embodying the characteristics that formed the "mental template" of the makers. Most archaeologists argue that constructing emic typologies is at best difficult, at worst impossible; certainly there is no conceivable way of testing whether a typology devised by an archaeologist indeed is emic.

CONCEPTS BEHIND TYPOLOGIES

The construction of typologies is based on the assumption that the items under consideration can be meaningfully divided into categories, each with its distinctive characteristics. Each of these categories is called a *type*, and the system of categories is called a *typology*. Ideally, any item in a class fits into one and only one type in a particular typology. In practice, of course, the situation can be less clear-cut, either because the typology has not been skillfully defined or because the items are not amenable to typological classification.

The primary assumption underlying typology is that items that are classified into a type are more like one another than they are like items in a different type. Stated differently, it is assumed that each type has a set of characteristics that consistently occur together and that typify it. There is a special terminology to refer to those characteristics. A *dimension* is a set of characteristics describing a certain quality, each of which is mutually exclusive with the others; a *trait* or *attribute* is one of those characteristics. For examples, color is a dimension, and red, green, and yellow are traits; size is a dimension, and small, medium, and large are traits; texture is a dimension, and smooth and rough are traits. A dimension may be coarsely divided, as when the dimension of material has traits like wood and metal; or it can be finely divided into traits like mahogany, pine, tin, and brass. In any case, any particular item should have only one trait for each dimension. This leads us to a formal definition of a type: a consistently co-occurring set of traits.

Depending on the dimensions you select and the way you set up traits for each dimension, you will derive different typologies. Are all of these equally good? No. In some kind of philosophical sense, all are equally valid, but they certainly are not equally useful. There are two major reasons for this.

First, not all typologies are equally good at discriminating types. There almost always will be a percentage of the items in any assemblage that cannot be assigned a type. Perhaps a specimen has a trait that appears nowhere in the typology or perhaps it has an uncommon cluster of traits that fits no defined type. If 23% of the items cannot be classified clearly with typology A and only 7% fail to be successfully classified with typology B, then typology B is superior, all else being equal. There are various statistical approaches that are aimed at minimizing the number of unclear, ambiguous, or overlapping classifications in a typology.

Second, you may have derived a typology that discriminates very well, but it may not be particularly useful for your purposes. For example, perhaps you want a typology that will help you identify the countries of origin for bricks. The typology that does the best job of discrimination (in statistical terms) may have no bearing whatsoever on country of manufacture. To be useful as anything beyond a descriptive typology, a typology must be tested against known data to see what the meaning of the types may be.

CONSTRUCTING TYPOLOGIES

There are many different techniques in constructing typologies, and this exercise will only scratch the surface in presenting approaches. One family of approaches is *statistical* and relies on mathematical approaches to maximize (or nearly maximize) the discrimination between types in a typology. Typically, the analyst loads data on a large number of dimensions and traits into a computer, and one of several commercially available programs performs the computations. Only dimensions that have major discriminating power will be incorporated into the final typology. These techniques probably are best for descriptive types, since the mathematical criteria involved are unrelated to any of the cultural issues involved in historical, ethnic, and functional typologies.

The other primary family of approaches is *impressionistic*, where the typologist becomes intimately familiar with the items to be classified and sorts them into groups that seem appropriate on the basis of experience; the traits that characterize these groups then become the definition of the types. Impressionistic typologies sometimes have been criticized because of the subjectivity involved in their construction. Their defense, however, lies in that they straightforwardly can be constructed for particular purposes. By starting with a set of dated wig curlers, one can devise a typology that will discriminate different periods. The typology then can be used to identify assemblages of undated wig curlers and to assign dates to them. So long as the data set from which the typology was derived is accurately dated and representative of wig curlers in general, the dates should be good estimates.

The paragraphs that follow describe one way to derive an impressionistic typology. For convenience, the process is divided into steps, even though those steps may not really be so discrete as they appear in this description.

1. Examine the items to be classified. It is critical to have familiarity with the overall data set before you start making decisions of dimensions to exclude or include in your typology. In some cases, the set of appropriate items available is so vast that you cannot possibly examine them all, in which case you should adopt a sampling strategy that attempts to ensure that you will see the entire range of diversity in the specimens you examine. What sample size is large enough? There is no simple answer, but you need a sample large enough so that you can recognize patterns of trait occurrence; the greater the diversity in the data set, the larger the sample size required to include that diversity. (See Appendix B for a further discussion of sampling.)

2. Sort the items in the data set into meaningful groups. If you are constructing a functional typology, your groups should represent uses; similarly, historical types will require date groupings, and ethnic types will require cultural or national groupings. At this stage, it probably is best to use as narrow groupings as your information will permit, since you can always merge groups later. If there appear, for instance, to be no significant differences in items from the 1810s and 1820s, you can merge them. Be sure that you always have at least a few examples in every group, if possible, since you are looking for recurrent patterns. If you are constructing a descriptive typology, your groups will be ones that you feel are quite distinct from one another in terms of traits and their clustering.

3. Decide on the dimensions you feel will be most useful. For example, if the colors of wig curlers appear to be the same in all periods, this is not a useful dimension for a historical typology of wig curlers. If the shape of terminals on early wig curlers seems different from the shape on later ones, then that dimension is probably useful. For certain kinds of typologies, certain dimensions are natural. The accumulation of technological expertise over time leads to greater technical complexity in later forms for some artifacts, so technological dimensions can be especially useful in historical typologies; functional typologies often utilize dimensions that are directly related to the use of the artifact. Are there any rules to ensure that you have selected the right dimensions? No, and this problem plagues both impressionistic and statistical typologies.

4. Make a trait list. For each dimension that you select to study, make a list of all the traits that occur along it. This list should define the traits as specifically as possible, so that you or someone else can be consistent in applying the typology. You may need "other" as a trait in some of your dimensions, since oddball traits show up from time to time. (Sometimes these "oddballs" occur with such frequency that they need to be added to your typology, but often they are just the result of mistakes, ideas that seemed good at the time, or other unique circumstances.) Be sure that your traits cover all the cases in your data set and that no specimen can possess two traits on the same dimension.

5. Make a specimen list. The specimen list includes the identification number of the particular specimen and its trait on each of the dimensions being considered. Specimens usually will have numbers on them from the institution

that curates them, but, if not, you will have to assign your own. The specimen list should be divided into the groups you decided to use in step 2. This is the drudgery part of typology construction, but it is critical that the data be properly recorded if the results are to be potentially useful.

6. Find trait clusters. At this step, you are actually defining the types. You are searching for patterns of traits that characterize the different groups. You may find that more than one group shares essentially the same cluster of traits, in which case you may decide to merge those groups, if that is sensible. (Merging 1810s and 1820s may make sense, but merging 1810s and 1920s—without the intervening years—probably doesn't.) You also may decide to omit certain dimensions from the definitions of certain types, because they are inconsistent. For example, terminal shape may be a useful dimension in early wig curlers but not in later ones. You also may find that some traits usually, though not always, occur in a certain group. It is perfectly acceptable to incorporate these "usually" attributes; such a typology is technically known as *polythetic*, and many theorists argue that polythetic typologies are the most useful sort.

7. Evaluate the typology. Use your typology to identify the specimens in your data set. Those that cannot be placed into any of your defined types should go into a residual category called "untyped." How accurately do you recreate the original groups based on function, date, or such? The perfect typology will exactly reproduce these groupings, but few typologies are that good. You can be assured that it is very likely that your typology will perform best with the data set on which it was based, so this evaluation is a wise step before actually using the typology on specimens of unknown characteristics. If you have constructed a descriptive typology, this step allows you to see whether it has any usefulness in dating, assigning function, and the like.

Once developed, typologies can be modified or expanded as new information accumulates. There can be a problem, however, if a widely used typology is modified, since it will be difficult to know whether a published reference to Dewdrop Painted redware is based on the original or the modified definition.

A Note on Lumpers and Splitters

Some types are very broad, encompassing many variants, while others are quite narrow. Those classifiers who favor broad types are colloquially known as "lumpers," while those who favor narrow types are known as "splitters." There are, of course, advantages to each of these polar philosophies. An extreme splitter would note with pride the great precision possible in dating with a historical typology based on very narrow types, while a lumper would note the greater percentage of misclassifications usual in such cases. Each approach has its advantages and disadvantages, and each typologist must decide where his or her typology should fall along the continuum from lumping to splitting.

ALTERNATIVES TO TYPOLOGY

While most archaeologists use typology for most of their basic description and much of their analysis, there are other systems of classification, as well. Most of these are really variants on typology, but attribute analysis stands out as a widely used adjunct to typology.

Attribute analysis is the study of traits of material culture individually, rather than as clusters. An attribute analysis, for example, might examine the distribution of brass versus iron jew's-harps in the eighteenth-century Mississippi Valley or the significance of the everted lip on Pennsylvania stoneware pitchers. Most historical archaeologists argue that complete reliance on typology can obscure simpler patterns (like these) and advocate that the two approaches be used together.

YOUR ASSIGNMENT

Prof. Kim Chee, professor of native studies at Four Corners University and a former student of Leslie Squarkmuffin, has been studying historical archaeological sites in and around Navajo country in the Four Corners region of New Mexico, Arizona, Colorado, and Utah. She has found a series of crescent-shaped silver ornaments ("najas") in some of the sites, but no good historical typology exists to assist her in their interpretation. You and Chee have been discussing her findings, and she has suggested that you construct such a typology. She has offered you access to the excellent collection of dated specimens of najas at the Four Corners University Museum, and you have decided that this study is a worthwhile one that you wish to undertake.

Your task, then, is to prepare an impressionistic historical typology for najas; your typology should be effective in discriminating different periods of najas. Information about dated najas in museum collections is provided in this exercise. Your report should include the dimensions and traits you will use, your specimen list, your type definitions, and a list of the specimens falling into each type. Also, be sure to discuss the typology in terms of difficulties you may have encountered. Since your typology probably will not be perfect in its discrimination of different periods, be sure to provide an evaluation of how useful it seems to be.

The Data Set: Najas

You are asked to make a typology of *najas,* a form of metal crescent used as part of Indian jewelry in the historic American Southwest. More background on this class of artifacts is given in the following section.

The najas in this data set all come from museum collections and have moderately good information about them. Historical archaeologists often use museum specimens for establishing typologies, since these specimens often were collected when the items were in use (rather than archaeologically) and typically have more detailed information associated with them.

Figure 13-1 shows a typical naja and labels its parts. Figure 13-2 presents drawings of specimens, and Figure 13-3 shows cross-sections of the specimens. Table 13-1 presents further information on the najas.

Background on Najas

The *naja* (pronounced na'-ha) is a kind of historic American Indian jewelry from the Four Corners area of the American Southwest. The word comes from the Navajo *najane*, meaning "crescent," and najas are crescentic ornaments that often were part of a necklace but could also be used alone as a pin or as part of other ornaments (including horse gear). Some najas have passed through various types of use over the decades.

The naja first appeared in the Southwest among the Navajo around 1868. Similar forms had been used by various Plains Indian tribes since the 1820s or 1830s, and they apparently diffused to the Navajo from the Spanish, ultimately deriving from Moorish ornament. The year 1868 marks the end of the five-year internment of the Navajo at Bosque Redondo by the United States government. During that detention, several Navajo learned metalworking skills (not part of earlier Navajo technology), and these skills formed the basis for the

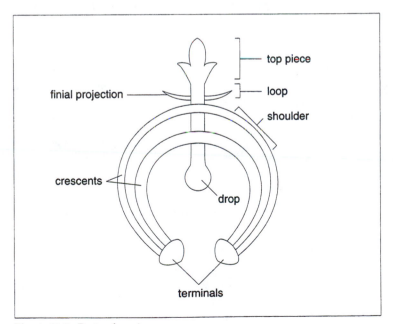

Figure 13-1. Parts of a naja.

Navajo silverworking tradition. The tools, skills, and even designs appear to have derived ultimately from Mexican smithing, either in silver or in iron.

Navajo silver jewelry became jointly an indicator of status and a reserve financial account. The wearing of jewelry on special occasions was a means of advertising one's prestige and wealth, and the jewelry could serve as collateral for loans from trading posts and, later, pawn shops.

The Navajo share the northern part of the Southwest with the various Pueblo tribes, such as the Zuni, Isleta, and Hopi. These latter tribes are distinct tribal entities but share great numbers of cultural traits with one another, enough so that rituals presented by one Pueblo tribe may be attended and participated in by members of another Pueblo tribe. (The Navajo, on the other hand, have very different cultural traits and represent a very different cultural tradition.) Some of the Pueblo peoples adopted the use of the naja from the Navajo and used it in personal adornment, at least in part for similar purposes. Some of the najas in use by the Zuni and Hopi were traded from the Navajo, and others were made by themselves.

By 1930 or so, Indian silverworking entered a new phase. At this point, major marketing efforts brought this jewelry to the non-Indian public, and the more traditional forms began changing in response to the demands of the market. Although najas continue to be made today, the collection presented for your assignment predates the 1930 watershed.

All of the najas in the collection described are sand-cast of silver. That is, they were made by pouring molten silver into sand molds, making each piece unique. The piece, after removal from the mold, would be smoothed with abrasive. Surface decoration could be produced by stamping (hammering a steel stamp into the surface of the silver), filing (using the tip of a file to cut a pattern into the surface), rocker stamping (using the end of a curved, sharp iron tool to rock along the surface, creating a zigzag line indented into the surface), or inlaying (setting stones, usually turquoise, into recesses in the silver). The piece could be further modified by soldering other pieces of silver to it. When fully formed and decorated, the naja would be smoothed and polished and ready for wearing.

BIBLIOGRAPHY ON TYPOLOGY

Adair, John. 1944. *The Navajo and Pueblo Silversmiths.* University of Oklahoma Press, Norman, Oklahoma. Classic work on the subject.

Frank, Larry. 1978. *Indian Silver Jewelry of the Southwest, 1868-1930.* New York Graphic Society, New York. Excellent, well-illustrated treatment of silver jewelry in this time and region.

TABLE 13-1 Information on the najas.

SPECIMEN NUMBER	DATE	TRIBE	USE	COMMENTS
26L	1875	Navajo	pendant	soldered loop
26R	1875	Navajo	pendant	soldered loop
27R	1875	Navajo	pendant	soldered loop
27L	1880	Navajo	pendant	flat; soldered loop
195	1880	Navajo	necklace	cast loop; stamping on loop
222	1880	Navajo	necklace	soldered loop; stamped circles on hands; filed lines at wrists
82	1885	Pueblo	necklace	soldered loop
128B	1885	Navajo	pendant	cast loop; turquoise centerpiece and terminals
128T	1885	Navajo	pendant	soldered loop
160	1885	Navajo	necklace	cast loop; filed and rocker-stamped designs near terminals
192	1885	Navajo	necklace	soldered loop; curved surface
227	1885	Navajo	bridle	filed designs on crescents; turquoise drop
24R	1890	Navajo	necklace	soldered loop; buttons soldered on as terminals
27C	1890	Navajo	pendant	flat; cast loop
83	1890	Pueblo	necklace	soldered loop
95R	1890	Navajo	necklace	cast loop; flat; stamped designs
186	1890	Navajo	necklace	soldered loop; soldered buttons as terminals
217	1890	Navajo	necklace	cast loop; turquoise inset in top piece
210L	1895	Pueblo	necklace	soldered loop; chisel-stamped designs near terminals
25T	1900	Navajo	necklace	soldered loop; crescents soldered together; inset turquoise at drop and terminals
96T	1900	Navajo	necklace	cast loop
197	1900	Pueblo	necklace	soldered loop also holds together crescents; filed designs on loop; soldered disk terminals
95L	1905	Navajo	necklace	soldered loop; stamped designs; crescents soldered together
99L	1905	Pueblo	necklace	loop, drop, and terminals soldered
25R	1910	Navajo	necklace	cast loop with file-cut designs
84	1910	Navajo	necklace	cast loop; file-cut designs
96L	1910	Navajo	necklace	cast loop; turquoise inset at terminals; cross added later
216	1910	Navajo	necklace	cast loop; turquoise inset at terminals and top piece

(continued)

TABLE 13-1 Information on the najas, *continued.*

SPECIMEN NUMBER	DATE	TRIBE	USE	COMMENTS
218	1910	Navajo	necklace	cast loop; turquoise inset in loop, two-piece drop, and terminals
117	1915	Navajo	bridle	soldered loop
172	1915	Navajo	necklace	soldered loop; stamped designs on outer crescent; filed designs on loop; squash blossom drop may be later
196	1915		necklace	soldered loop; turquoise inset at terminals and drop
215	1915	Navajo	necklace	soldered loop; turquoise inset at loop
25L	1920	Navajo	pendant	soldered loop; turquoise inset at drop and terminals
73	1920	Navajo	necklace	cast loop; stamped design on loop and terminals
100L	1920	Navajo	necklace	soldered drop; turquoise inset at terminals and drop
100R	1920	Navajo	necklace	cast loop; turquoise inset at terminals (4), drop, shoulders, and loop
158	1920	Navajo	necklace	cast loop; stamped design at terminals
162	1920	Navajo	necklace	soldered loop; turquoise inset at terminals, drop, and top piece; filed designs on finial projections
173	1920	Navajo	necklace	soldered loop; turquoise inset at terminals (4) and top piece
191	1920	Navajo	necklace	soldered loop; turquoise inset at loop and terminals
95T	1925	Navajo	necklace	soldered loop; thin; stamped designs; soldered drop
98L	1925	Navajo	necklace	cast loop; turquoise drop
98R	1925	Navajo	necklace	soldered loop; soldered drop with turquoise inset
99R	1925	Navajo	necklace	soldered loop; turquoise insets in drop and terminals
100C	1925	Navajo	necklace	soldered loop; turquoise inset at terminals (3 apiece), drop, shoulders, loop, and top of crescents
159	1925	Navajo	necklace	cast loop; stamped arrow designs on crescents; turquoise inset at wrists of terminals
210R	1925	Pueblo	necklace	cast loop; turquoise inset at loop, terminals, and shoulders of crescent
95B	1930	Navajo	necklace	soldered loop; stamped designs; filed designs at terminals
97	1930	Navajo	necklace	soldered loop

117

215

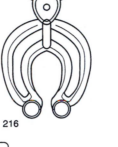
172

218

25L

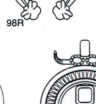
216

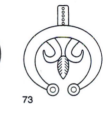
173

100R

98R

158

73

196

162

191

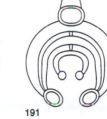

95T

98L

100 L

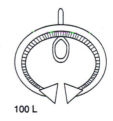

FIGURE 13-2 Najas

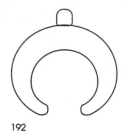

192

25T

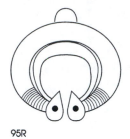

95R

25R

186

227

84

197

96T

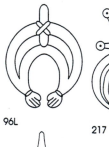

96L

217

24R

83

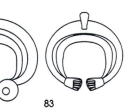

96L

210L

95L

27C

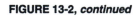

FIGURE 13-2, *continued*

144

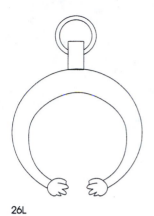

26L

195

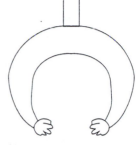

26R

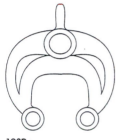

128B

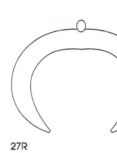

27R

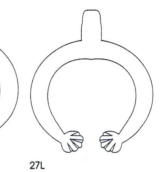

27L

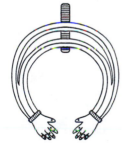

222

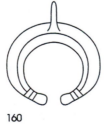

82

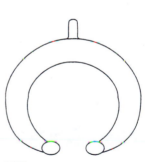

128T

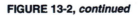

160

FIGURE 13-2, *continued*

99R

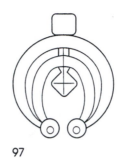

97

210R

95B

159

100C

FIGURE 13-2, *continued*

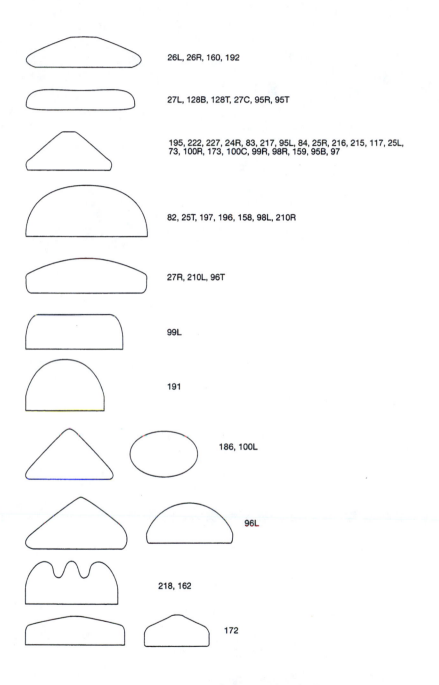

26L, 26R, 160, 192

27L, 128B, 128T, 27C, 95R, 95T

195, 222, 227, 24R, 83, 217, 95L, 84, 25R, 216, 215, 117, 25L, 73, 100R, 173, 100C, 99R, 98R, 159, 95B, 97

82, 25T, 197, 196, 158, 98L, 210R

27R, 210L, 96T

99L

191

186, 100L

96L

218, 162

172

FIGURE 13-3 Cross-sections of najas.

— EXERCISE 14 —
PIPESTEM DATING

OVERVIEW

Pipestems, a seemingly innocuous class of artifact, are the basis of one of the more widely used methods of artifact dating in historic sites. This exercise asks you to use the method to date a series of deposits in New York.

BACKGROUND

Dating is of obvious importance to archaeologists, and they have devoted considerable attention to dating on the basis of pipestems. Pipestems meet most of the criteria of an excellent subject for archaeological dating. They are moderately fragile, so their use life span was short and they were likely to make their way into an archaeological deposit shortly after their manufacture. Although easily breakable, they preserve well in the ground. The pipes from which they came were inexpensive and widely used, so pipestems occur on various types of sites at various periods, regardless of the wealth or poverty of the occupants. Finally, they vary over time in such a way that they can be dated moderately precisely.

It is understandable that any artifact with such potential for dating should have received considerable attention from archaeologists. The major approaches to dating pipestems were formulated by Harrington (1954), Binford (1961), and Hanson (1971), although there have been other archaeologists who have offered refinements on these pioneering efforts. The details of the Harrington, Binford, and Hanson approaches are presented below.

The pipestems being discussed here are of white clay, often incorrectly called "kaolin." They come from any of several types of smoking pipes that were in common use in Europe, North America, West Africa, Australia, and elsewhere from the early seventeenth century onward, right into the twentieth century. These pipes were mass produced in factories, particularly in England, Scotland, and Holland. While there was considerable variation in the shape of the bowl and the length of the stem, the critical attribute for the dating methods discussed here is the diameter of the bore (the hole through which smoke was drawn into the mouth). The bore was formed by molding the wet clay around a metal wire before firing, and the diameter of that wire and the resulting bore changed over time. The Harrington, Binford, and Hanson methods of calculating dates are all based on the bore diameter.

The Harrington Method

J. C. Harrington studied the artifactual remains from Jamestown, Virginia, in great detail, and he realized that the bore diameter of pipestems from there tended to be greater in earlier specimens, lesser in later ones. Harrington based his study on a sample of 330 pipestems from five well-dated contexts, and all of the pipestems were of English manufacture. He measured the bore diameters to the nearest sixty-fourth of an inch with commercial drill bits and recorded the results per period. He found that his impression was accurate, and Figure 14-1 shows the result of his study.

To date an assemblage of pipestems using Harrington's method, an archaeologist measures the bore diameters of the pipestems, converts the data to percentages, and matches the percentages as best as possible with those in Figure 14-1. Harrington specifically avoided any statistical approach, arguing that the data don't demand it.

The Binford Method

Lewis Binford based his dating method entirely on Harrington's data and simply produced another means of calculation. He found that samples of pipestems he analyzed rarely fell precisely into the 30- to 50-year spans into which Harrington divided his data. When the date of a deposit fell near the break between two of Harrington's periods (*e.g.,* 1682) or when its span cut across two periods (*e.g.,* 1670-1700), it was difficult to estimate a precise span for it; some assemblages simply failed to match the ideal distributions Harrington presented. Accordingly, Binford used Harrington's data to perform a statistical operation called *regression*. Regression calculates a formula that makes the best prediction of one variable on the basis of another. In this case, Binford wanted to be able to calculate date on the basis of bore diameter, so he calculated a formula that would produce the best estimate, based on the data from Harrington's 330 pipestems. Another way to look at regression, if it still seems mysterious, is to think of a graph with date on the x-axis (the horizontal one) and bore diameter on the y-axis (the vertical one); each pipestem is a dot that is located on the basis of its date and bore diameter, and the regression line is the straight line that best summarizes the cloud of data points. The regression line can be summarized by a formula, and that formula is the calculation formula. Fig. 14-2 graphically shows this relationship.

Binford's regression produced the following formula:

$$y = 1931.85 - 38.26x$$

where y is the date one is wishing to calculate and x is the mean bore diameter (in sixty-fourths of an inch) for the assemblage of pipestems. To date a pipestem assemblage using the Binford formula, simply substitute the mean bore diameter for x in the formula; simple arithmetic provides the best regression estimate for the date of the assemblage. Binford and others have found that the relationship breaks down fairly badly after 1780.

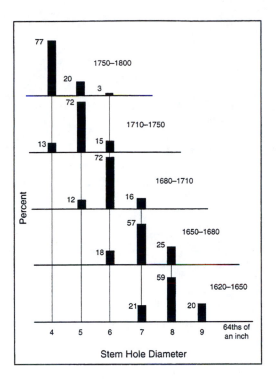

FIGURE 14-1

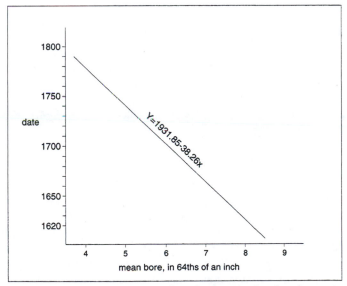

Figure 14-2. Regression of pipestem bore diameters by date, based on Binford's regression.

For example, assume that the mean bore diameter for an assemblage is 7.30 sixty-fourths of an inch. To estimate the date of deposition, simply replace x with 7.30 in Binford's formula, yielding:

$$y = 1931.85 - (38.26 \times 7.30)$$
$$y = 1931.85 - 279.30$$
$$y = 1652.55$$

1652.55 is the estimated date for that assemblage.

It is important to remember that Binford's method of calculating pipestem dates, in common with the others discussed here, is applicable only to *assemblages* of pipestems, not to individual specimens. In any given year, pipestems of two or three bore diameters were produced, and there is no way of telling the exact date of a particular specimen. The mix of diameters for specimens produced and used in a year, however, was distinctive, and all of these methods take advantage of this fact.

The Hanson Method

Lee Hanson, Jr., while examining Harrington's pipestem data, noted that the rate at which bore diameters decreased was considerably greater in the earlier period (1620-1725) than it was later on. Looked at another way, if one were drawing a graph relating dates to mean bore diameter, the mass of dots (one for each pipestem) would form a curved line with a greater slope in the earlier period than in the later period. This means, Hanson recognized, that the relationship was not linear (as Binford has assumed with his linear regression) but rather was curvilinear.

There are statistical methods for producing equations for curvilinear regression, but Hanson decided to take another tack instead. He produced a series of formulas, each specific to a particular period. Each formula approximates the curve of the regression line in the relevant chronological portion of the overall curve; while each formula is inapplicable to most of the span, Hanson argues, it produces a better approximation of reality for its own segment than does the Binford formula.

To use the Hanson formulas, you must have an approximation of what period your assemblage is from. You can make this estimation with Hanson's formula #7 and the mean bore diameter of your assemblage, or you can use the Harrington date span estimate and the distribution of bore diameters in your assemblage. Then, you select the appropriate formula from Hanson's collection, trying to use the one whose time range most narrowly matches that of your assemblage, preferably centering your estimated date within the range of the formula; in some cases there may be more than one formula that seems equally appropriate. Finally, you enter the mean bore diameter for your assemblage into the formula, just as with the Binford formula.

The Hanson formulas are:

#1. [1620-1680]	y	=	1891.64	-	32.90x
#2. [1620-1710]	y	=	1880.92	-	30.70x
#3. [1650-1710]	y	=	1869.31	-	28.88x
#4. [1620-1750]	y	=	1887.99	-	31.66x
#5. [1650-1750]	y	=	1888.06	-	31.67x
#6. [1680-1750]	y	=	1894.88	-	32.98x
#7. [1620-1800]	y	=	1919.10	-	36.06x
#8. [1650-1800]	y	=	1930.24	-	38.23x
#9. [1680-1800]	y	=	1959.33	-	44.32x
#10. [1710-1800]	y	=	2026.12	-	58.97x

where the numbers in brackets are the applicable time span, y is the estimated date of the assemblage, and x is the mean bore diameter of the assemblage.

For example, with an assemblage of unknown date and mean bore diameter of 5.5 sixty-fourths of an inch, one would begin with formula #7, the formula covering the entire span. Feeding 5.5 into the formula yields an estimated date of 1919.10 - (36.06 x 5.5) = 1720.8. Then, one would use that estimate to select the Hanson formula with the narrowest range that fits that estimate, in this case, #6 (1680-1750). Finally, the mean bore diameter is fed into this formula, yielding a refined estimate of 1894.88 - (32.98 x 5.5) = 1713.5.

Hanson's method, like Binford's, is based on Harrington's data. As a formula dating method, it shares virtues and suffers similar limitations with Binford's method. Its only claim is that it will be more accurate than the Binford method. (Hanson cites minor miscalculations, minor in effect, in the derivation of Binford's formula and corrects them in his own calculations.)

LIMITATIONS OF THE METHODS

All methods have limitations, and, if mindlessly applied without considering these limitations, they can give ridiculous results. Limitations on the accuracy of pipestem dating stem from the nature of Harrington's original sample, the adequacy and nature of an archaeological assemblage to be dated, the problems of summarizing a date span with a single figure, and errors inherent in regressions.

All three methods are based on the same data set: that collected by J. C. Harrington back in the 1950s. That sample was moderately small (330 pipestems), and a larger sample would be less likely to distort the true pattern. Beyond that, the sample was composed exclusively of English pipestems. So long as the methods are applied to more English pipestems, all is well; but a pattern derived for English pipestems might bear little relation to Dutch or French patterns in pipestem bore diameters. Unfortunately, not all analysts can be scrupulously sure that their pipestem assemblage has only English pipestems in it; indeed, some researchers knowingly use the methods on Dutch or French pipestems in hopes that they will be appropriate.

The assemblage to be dated should have a reasonable size; archaeological usage has settled on 30 as a reasonable sample size, although the size of a representative sample will vary depending on the inherent diversity in the population of items sampled. If one applies these methods to small assemblages, there is an increased chance that a sample may have an atypical bore diameter average and may yield quite inaccurate dates.

Similarly, assemblages must be quite pure; that is, there should be little chance that pipestems from other periods have found their way into a deposit. Such contamination often will become obvious when applying the Harrington method, since the distribution of different bore diameters in the sample to be dated will be unlike any of the ideal distributions. The formula methods, however, will yield results and give the analyst no hint that there may be problems.

The formula methods of Binford and Harrington will yield confusing results with pipestem assemblages that accumulated over a long span. Since they are based on the mean bore diameter only, they cannot discriminate between a deposit that formed continuously between 1620 and 1800 and one that formed on August 1, 1710; so long as the mean bore diameter is the same, the mean date estimate will be the same. Consequently, the analyst will have to be alert to recognizing assemblages that formed potentially over long periods. Fortunately, a check of the distribution of bore diameters in the assemblage against the Harrington distributions usually will help recognize such cases.

Finally, Hanson has recognized that the regression line between date and bore diameter really is curvilinear. In other words, the best regression line follows a curve, rather than the straight line that both the Binford and Hanson equations are based on. This means that Binford's formula (and, to a lesser extent, Hanson's formulas) will produce systematic errors in some periods. Fortunately, these errors seem to be small, and the Hanson method reduces them to a point where they are of little consequence.

YOUR ASSIGNMENT

The indomitable Prof. Leslie Squarkmuffin has been conducting test excavations in Rhinekill, a small town along the lower Hudson River in Dutchester County, New York. His fieldwork has been largely exploratory, providing data to formulate a detailed research design, but he is interested in charting the changes that have taken place in the economic history of Rhinekill during its 350 years or so of existence. Accordingly, the dates of the sites he has been testing are particularly important. He has already published a brief progress report in which he gave date estimates based on pottery types, but that dating was attacked by Prof. A. Twitt, from Temblor University in California. Squark-muffin wants to marshall his data and reply to Twitt, so he is arranging for the dating of the sites by a variety of techniques. As his graduate student and research assistant, you have been given the task of calculating the dates on the basis of pipestem bore diameters. Tables 14-1 through 14-8 present your measurements of the bore diameters from each site, and now your task is to calculate date estimates for the assemblages, using the Harrington, Binford, and Hanson methods. (Your instructor may substitute one or more pipestem assemblages for you to measure and date.)

Your report should include summaries of your data in tables or histograms (like Figure 14-1), the dates estimated by the three methods, and a brief discussion of any problems or complications in interpretation and their possible causes.

The Data Sets

Tables 14-1 through 14-8 present data on bore diameters for the eight assemblages of pipestems. All measurements are in sixty-fourths of an inch.

Rhinekill was founded in 1644, primarily by fishermen who sold their catches locally and in New York City. While most of the fishermen were of English extraction, some were Dutch, Swedish, and even French. The community remained small, never exceeding 1,000 inhabitants until the twentieth century, but it gradually developed a variety of other economic bases. Farming became prominent early, and by 1670 there were several businesses geared to selling goods to farmers or marketing their crops. Service industries developed primarily in the nineteenth century. The following notes briefly characterize the deposits from which the pipestem assemblages were recovered.

The Jonah Farque site is a habitation of a middle-class farmer. The deposit from which the pipestems came is a lens of trash behind a barn.

The Squiggledunk site is the site of a periodic fair, held annually after the autumn harvest. The particular deposit from which the pipestems came was a circular, packed earthen floor. Structural remains at the deposit are ambiguous, and the nature of the structure surrounding the floor is unclear.

The Sweeney Todd Barbershop is a building, originally used as a barbershop until the mysterious disappearance of its proprietor. After that, it was used as a residence. The deposit where the pipestems were found was formed along the front of the building, probably under and around a porch.

The Widow Noyes Walkway was a trample level formed on a dirt path between the street and the kitchen door of a house owned and tenanted by the Widow Noyes.

Bishop's Landing was the site of a small dock on the Hudson River, from which fishing and oystering boats departed. The deposit from which the pipestems came was formed along the side of a building.

The Primrose Privy was an outdoor toilet; it is unclear whose house it was associated with. The privy pit is particularly deep, and it has several levels, each separated from its neighbors by a layer of sterile sand, apparently purposefully added for hygienic reasons. The site designation (33-7-31) refers to a district of low-class housing.

The Eli Samoulderin house was the residence of a well-to-do business-man and his family. The deposit where the pipestems were recovered was formed in a hollow in the back yard and appears to have received miscellane-ous trash.

The Famosa Midden is a large dump, probably used communally by several families in the district of Rhinekill that was known locally as "Famosa." The midden has a very complicated stratigraphy, and distinctions between levels are not always clear. Further, the midden apparently had a sizable colony of rats that appreciated the organic refuse dumped there and thrived, creating a network of warrens and burrows throughout the midden.

Measuring Pipestem Bore Diameters

If you are measuring the bore diameters of pipestems yourself, you need to know a few standard procedures. The standard device for measuring pipestem bores is an inexpensive set of drill bits. Drill bits are available at hardware stores and discount stores. In the United States and some other parts of the world, the standard interval between bit sizes is one sixty-fourth of an inch; a bit's diameter is stamped on its shank (the smooth end) with a numeral representing its diameter in sixty-fourths of an inch. To measure a diameter, always use the shank end of the bit, the smooth end that normally would be inserted into the drill chuck. Slide it into the bore gently, never forcing it. If it fits snugly, record the diameter of the bit as that of the bore. If it is loose, try the next larger bit; if the next larger will not fit in, record the first diameter. Avoid taking diameters at the original tip of the pipe (the end that would have gone into the smoker's mouth), since that bore occasionally was somewhat enlarged by sloppy removal of the wire during pipe manufacture. If your pipestems have dirt in their bores, you will have to remove that gently with a dry brush or a brush and water; your instructor should show you how to do this.

TABLE 14-1   Pipestem data, Jonah Farque site.

SPECIMEN NUMBER	BORE DIAMETER, SIXTY-FOURTHS OF AN INCH
1	7
2	7
3	8
4	8
5	8
6	7
7	9
8	7
9	8
10	7
11	9
12	7
13	7
14	8
15	7
16	9
17	7
18	8
19	7
20	9
21	8
22	9
23	9
24	9
25	8
26	8
27	8
28	8
29	8
30	8
31	8
32	8
33	8
34	8
35	8
36	9
37	8
38	8
39	8
40	8
41	9
42	8
43	8
44	8
45	8
46	8
47	8
48	9
49	8
50	8

TABLE 14-2   Pipestem data, Floor 1, Squiggledunk site.

SPECIMEN NUMBER	BORE DIAMETER, SIXTY-FOURTHS OF AN INCH
1	7
2	7
3	6
4	6
5	8
6	7
7	6
8	7
9	8
10	7
11	6
12	7
13	7
14	8
15	7
16	6
17	7
18	8
19	7
20	6
21	7
22	6
23	6
24	6
25	7
26	8
27	8
28	7
29	7
30	7
31	7
32	7
33	8
34	7
35	8
36	7
37	8
38	8
39	7
40	7
41	6
42	7
43	7
44	8
45	7
46	7
47	8
48	6
49	8
50	8

TABLE 14-3 Pipestem data, Sweeney Todd Barbershop.

SPECIMEN NUMBER	BORE DIAMETER, SIXTY-FOURTHS OF AN INCH
1	7
2	7
3	6
4	6
5	6
6	8
7	6
8	7
9	6
10	8
11	7
12	5
13	6
14	6
15	6
16	7
17	6
18	8
19	7
20	6
21	8
22	6
23	7
24	6
25	8
26	7
27	5
28	6
29	7
30	7
31	6
32	5
33	5
34	8
35	7
36	8
37	6
38	8
39	6
40	7
41	6
42	6
43	8
44	6
45	7
46	6
47	7
48	6
49	6
50	8

TABLE 14-4   Pipestem data, Widow Noyes Walkway.

SPECIMEN NUMBER	BORE DIAMETER, SIXTY-FOURTHS OF AN INCH
1	8
2	8
3	8
4	7
5	8
6	8
7	7
8	7
9	8
10	7
11	7
12	6
13	6
14	6
15	8
16	7
17	6
18	6
19	6
20	6
21	7
22	7
23	7
24	7
25	6
26	6
27	6
28	6
29	8
30	6
31	7
32	6
33	6
34	7
35	6
36	6
37	6
38	6
39	7
40	7
41	6
42	6
43	6
44	6
45	7
46	6
47	6
48	6
49	6
50	7

TABLE 14-5 Pipestem data, Bishop's Landing site.

SPECIMEN NUMBER	BORE DIAMETER, SIXTY-FOURTHS OF AN INCH
1	7
2	5
3	5
4	8
5	8
6	7
7	6
8	7
9	5
10	7
11	4
12	7
13	7
14	6
15	8
16	6
17	7
18	5
19	7
20	7
21	9
22	6
23	7
24	7
25	5
26	6
27	6
28	5
29	7
30	7
31	7
32	7
33	8
34	7
35	5
36	5
37	5
38	6
39	5
40	5
41	6
42	5
43	5
44	5
45	7
46	7
47	6
48	6
49	5
50	6

TABLE 14-6   Pipestem data, Level 3, Primrose Privy, Site 33-7-31.

SPECIMEN NUMBER	BORE DIAMETER, SIXTY-FOURTHS OF AN INCH
1	5
2	5
3	5
4	7
5	5
6	5
7	7
8	4
9	5
10	5
11	5
12	6
13	5
14	5
15	5
16	5
17	6
18	5
19	5
20	6
21	7
22	6
23	5
24	5
25	5
26	5
27	5
28	5
29	4
30	5
31	4
32	5
33	5
34	5
35	5
36	6
37	5
38	5
39	5
40	6
41	5
42	5
43	5
44	6
45	5
46	5
47	5
48	5
49	5
50	4

TABLE 14-7   Pipestem data, Eli Samoulderin house.

SPECIMEN NUMBER	BORE DIAMETER, SIXTY-FOURTHS OF AN INCH
1	5
2	5
3	5
4	5
5	5
6	6
7	5
8	6
9	6
10	6
11	7
12	7
13	7
14	6
15	6
16	6
17	6
18	6
19	6
20	6
21	6
22	6
23	6
24	6
25	6
26	6
27	6
28	6
29	6
30	8
31	6
32	6
33	6
34	6
35	6
36	6
37	6
38	7
39	7
40	7
41	6
42	6
43	6
44	7
45	7
46	6
47	6
48	6
49	7
50	6

TABLE 14-8   Pipestem data, Level 6, Famosa midden.

SPECIMEN NUMBER	BORE DIAMETER, SIXTY-FOURTHS OF AN INCH
1	4
2	4
3	4
4	4
5	4
6	6
7	4
8	4
9	4
10	6
11	7
12	7
13	7
14	4
15	4
16	4
17	4
18	4
19	4
20	9
21	9
22	9
23	9
24	9
25	4
26	4
27	4
28	4
29	9
30	9
31	9
32	4
33	4
34	4
35	9
36	9
37	4
38	9
39	4
40	4
41	4
42	4
43	4
44	7
45	7
46	6
47	6
48	6
49	7
50	4

BIBLIOGRAPHY ON PIPESTEM DATING

Binford, Lewis R. 1969. A new method of calculating dates from kaolin pipe stem samples. *Southeastern Archaeological Conference Newsletter* 9(1):19-21. This article has been reprinted in several anthologies.

Hanson, Lee H., Jr. 1971. Kaolin pipe stems—boring in on a fallacy. *The Conference on Historic Site Archeology Papers* 4(1):2-15. Institute of Archaeology and Anthropology, University of South Carolina, Columbia, South Carolina.

Harrington, J. C. 1954. Dating stem fragments of seventeenth and eighteenth century clay tobacco pipes. *Quarterly Bulletin of the Archaeological Society of Virginia* 9(1):9-13. This article also has been reprinted in several anthologies.

— EXERCISE 15 —
MEAN CERAMIC DATING

OVERVIEW

Mean ceramic dating is a method of dating a deposit through a formula applied to the frequencies of the different pottery types found in it. This exercise asks you to use the method to date a series of deposits in Virginia and South Carolina.

MEAN CERAMIC DATING

Dating is one of the basic tasks of historical archaeology, and without it research will provide few insights into the past. Stanley South has argued that it is possible to generate formulas that will allow archaeologists to simply plug in values from an archaeological deposit and calculate the date when it was formed. Pipestem dating (Exercise 14) is based on such formulas, as is mean ceramic dating, devised by South.

Artifacts, South (1972, 1974, 1977) argues, change in frequency in a predictable pattern: They initially are rare, rise to numerical prominence, then decline to rarity and finally disappearance. (This assumption is held in common with frequency seriation, discussed in Exercise 18.) Consequently, South argues, at any given moment, the assemblage in use is a mix of the individual trajectories of the several artifact types that make it up. This means that it should be possible to calculate a quite accurate date for a deposit by averaging the dates of manufacture for the artifact types within it, adjusting so that more frequently occurring artifacts have a greater impact on the calculation. This is the basis of his *mean ceramic dating*.

Mean ceramic dating is a method of calculating the date of a deposit on the basis of the ceramic (pottery) types found within it. A wide variety of types have been assigned *median manufacture dates*, dates that approximate the average dates of manufacture for those types. (In more technical usage, a median date is the date before which half of the vessels of that type were manufactured and after which half were manufactured.) These dates have been approximated on the basis of archaeological experience, based on occurrences of ceramic types in dated contexts. The most useful series of median dates so far are for English ceramics in the Mid-Atlantic states and for Spanish majolica in the northern part of Spanish America.

To calculate a mean ceramic date, one uses the following formula:

$$\text{mean ceramic date } \frac{\Sigma(d_1 f_1)}{\Sigma f_1}$$

where d_1 = median manufacture date of type i and f_1 = the frequency of type i. Stated in other terms, one calculates the mean ceramic date for a deposit by:

1. multiplying the frequency of each type by the median manufacture date for that type,
2. adding these products together, and
3. dividing this sum by the sum of the frequencies of the individual types.

In essence, this produces some sort of average date for the specimens in the assemblage. Ideally, frequencies will be expressed in terms of numbers of vessels, but counts of sherds (broken pieces of pottery) often are used.

For example, let's examine a fictitious late twentieth-century ceramic assemblage from a short-term deposit in Santa Moneda, a well-to-do town in coastal southern California. The assemblage and its relevant characteristics are:

TYPE	NUMBER OF SHERDS	MEDIAN MANUFACTURE DATE
terminal American Grotesque ware	11	1991
Beverly Hills artware	22	1983
crystalware	33	1967
black vitreous ware	44	1986
Total	110	

To calculate the mean ceramic date, multiply the number of sherds for each type times the median manufacture date for that type (11 X 1991 = 21,901; 22 X 1983 = 43,626; 33 X 1967 = 64,911; 44 X 1986 = 87,384); add these products together (21,901 + 43,626 + 64,911 + 87,384 = 217,822); and divide that sum by the total number of sherds (217,822 / 110 = 1980.2). The mean ceramic date for the Santa Moneda deposit, therefore, is 1980.2.

A mean ceramic date supplies a single date to summarize a deposit's age. It is a precise date that can be calculated easily and can be reproduced independently by different analysts. By using a mechanical procedure, every analyst should derive about the same date for the deposit, unlike the results obtained with more impressionistic dating methods. These latter approaches to dating call on an analyst to examine the artifacts in a deposit and produce a date that is reasonable in light of the overall assemblage. In the hands of a knowledgeable and experienced analyst, impressionistic dating may provide accurate and useful dates, but choosing between conflicting results produced by different analysts can be difficult, often devolving to the reputations of the analysts. Mean ceramic dating, for better or worse, reduces the impact of the analyst's knowledge and experience.

Limitations of Mean Ceramic Dating

Every method has limitations that must be weighed against its advantages. Mean ceramic dating's primary limitations are seven.

1. Obviously, mean ceramic dating is usable only where median manufacture dates have been approximated on enough common ceramic types so that most of the specimens in any assemblage can enter into the calculation. Consequently, the method has been most successful along the eighteenth-century southern coastal areas of British North America (Maryland to South Carolina) and in sixteenth- and seventeenth-century Spanish America, where the median manufacture dates have been most thoroughly estimated.

2. Differences between the median dates of manufacture and the median dates of discard can distort mean ceramic dating. If, for example, a particular ceramic was typically produced in 1750 but typically was broken and discarded in 1790, that 40-year lag will cause mean ceramic dates to be too early. Some archaeologists have criticized the method on this account, but South has presented a series of examples where the mean ceramic dates accord well with documentary dates for deposits, with an average deviation between three and four years. Also, it could be argued that the manner of calculating median manufacture dates is based largely on when sherds most frequently occur in the archaeological record, suggesting that perhaps these index dates should be considered "median discard dates."

3. Related to the last issue is the problem of an assemblage with a few items that were very old at the time of their disposal. A single antique, for example, could have a major effect on a mean ceramic date, especially in a small sample. For example, a deposit formed in 1800 with a single vessel from 1700 and four from 1800 will have a mean ceramic date of 1780, fully 20 years too early. This process where some items are preserved by their owners and make their way into the archaeological record considerably after their manufacture is called the *curation effect*.

4. If a deposit forms over a long period of time, no single date will be an adequate summary of its age. If a deposit formed continuously from 1750 to 1840, a mean ceramic date of 1795 is hardly the only critical chronological information about that deposit. Under these circumstances, the analyst must be aware of the range of artifacts occurring on the site—including whether some of the earlier types had ceased being manufactured before some of the later ones had been developed. Using this line of thinking, an alert analyst usually will be able to get a good idea whether a deposit was formed over a long or short span.

5. The function of a site may affect how well mean ceramic dating works. South is convinced that mainstream and frontier sites along the southern Atlantic coast of North America received goods from Britain essentially at the same time. (He refers to this phenomenon as a *horizon*, where items of a particular type appear over a broad area rapidly.) While this may be true there, it may not be true everywhere else that mean ceramic dating could be applied. Also, industrial sites or domestic sites of the poor may show consistent patterns of misdating, perhaps as a result of using secondhand or handed-down items.

6. Calculating mean ceramic dates with sherd counts may not produce as accurate results as calculating them with vessel counts. Given the assumptions behind mean ceramic dating, vessel counts are the logical way to quantify ceramics. Unfortunately, ceramics usually occur archaeologically as sherds. There are ways to calculate minimum numbers of vessels from a ceramic assemblage, but they can be time-consuming, and the results are not always satisfactory. Consequently, sherd counts usually are used for mean ceramic dating. This means that sherds from a vessel that was smashed into tiny but identifiable fragments will have a greater impact on the mean ceramic date than one that was split neatly into only three pieces.

7. Small sample sizes can produce distorted mean ceramic dates. If you have a large sample of ceramics, the oddball sherd has only a minor effect. The effects of a single curated specimen (or even a piece that was carried into the deposit by a rodent after the rest of the deposit was formed) will be overwhelmed by the combined effects of large numbers of other, more typical specimens. With a small sample, however, the likelihood of a few oddballs affecting the calculated date in a significant way becomes greater. There are no fixed rules about how large a sample must be to avoid this problem, although there is a piece of archaeological folklore that suggests that a sample of 30 will usually be adequate. South and others sometimes have used mean ceramic dating on samples under ten and with apparent success, but such small samples should inspire concern in the heart of the analyst.

YOUR ASSIGNMENT

In the early 1970s, Dr. Cecilia Bump excavated and analyzed the remains from a series of deposits in Virginia, North Carolina, and South Carolina. All the deposits were from habitations in the British-American tradition. At the time of Bump's work, mean ceramic analysis was new and was not so widely used as it would become later, and she used a more impressionistic method for dating the deposits. Today, you are an undergraduate at Miskatonic University, studying under Leslie Squarkmuffin. You are completing a senior honors thesis in historical archaeology, and part of it involves seeing whether you can refine the Bump dates using mean ceramic dating. Bump's published description of the materials, using the same typology that South used in his method, is in the library, and Squarkmuffin has agreed to contact Bump to get additional information, if you need it. The ceramic assemblages from five of Bump's deposits are summarized in Tables 15-1 through 15-5, using standard type numbers. The type numbers, type names, median manufacture dates, and manufacture date ranges from South (1977) are given in Table 15-6.

Your assignment is to calculate mean ceramic dates for the five archaeological deposits excavated and described by Bump. Your report should include a general introduction and, for each deposit, the mean ceramic date you have calculated and any appropriate discussion about its probable accuracy.

TABLE 15-1   Ceramic assemblage, Feature 2, Haviland House, Norfolk News, Virginia.

TYPE	NUMBER OF SHERDS
16	21
26	4
29	49
37	6
39	7
43	23
48	24
54	6
56	7
61	1
Total	148

TABLE 15-2   Ceramic assemblage, Feature 7, Haviland House, Norfolk News, Virginia.

TYPE	NUMBER OF SHERDS
16	12
26	14
29	14
37	19
39	12
43	19
48	12
54	17
56	21
61	2
Total	142

TABLE 15-3   Ceramic assemblage, Hoag Dump site, Pocoteague, Virginia.

TYPE	NUMBER OF SHERDS
2	22
3	9
4	14
5	6
7	2
31	1
36	14
56	52
58	7
59	3
Total	130

TABLE 15-4   Ceramic assemblage, Upper Level, midden, Fort Jasper, South Carolina.

TYPE	NUMBER OF SHERDS
2	4
69	1
Total	5

TABLE 15-5   Ceramic assemblage, Lower Level, midden, Fort Jasper, South Carolina.

TYPE	NUMBER OF SHERDS
2	44
5	1
22	23
69	1
Total	69

TABLE 15-6 Relevant ceramic types, type numbers, median manufacture dates, and ranges of manufacture dates, excerpted from South (1977).

TYPE NUMBER	TYPE	MEDIAN MANUFACTURE DATE	RANGE OF KNOWN MANUFACTURE DATES
2	whiteware	1860	1820-1900+
3	ironstone and granite china	1857	1813-1900
4	underglaze polychrome pearlware	1830	1820-1840
5	Canton porcelain	1815	1800-1830
7	overglaze enameled Chinese trade porcelain	1808	1790-1825
16	molded white salt-glazed stoneware	1753	1740-1765
22	creamware	1791	1762-1820
26	overglaze enameled Chinese export porcelain	1730	1660-1800
29	Jackfield ware	1760	1740-1780
31	English porcelain	1770	1745-1795
36	"clouded" wares	1755	1740-1770
37	refined red stoneware	1733	1690-1775
39	underglaze blue Chinese porcelain	1730	1660-1800
43	white salt-glazed stoneware plates	1758	1740-1775
48	slip-dipped white salt-glazed stoneware	1745	1715-1775
54	British brown stoneware	1733	1690-1775
56	lead-glazed slipware	1733	1670-1795
57	plain delft wash basin	1775	1750-1800
58	blue decorated Rhenish stoneware	1668	1650-1725
59	embellished Hohr gray Rhenish stoneware	1700	1690-1710
61	North Devon gravel-tempered ware	1713	1650-1775
69	late Ming Chinese porcelain	1609	1574-1644

BIBLIOGRAPHY ON MEAN CERAMIC DATING

South, Stanley. 1972. Evolution and horizon as revealed in ceramic analysis in historical archaeology. *The Conference on Historic Site Archeology Papers* 6:71-116. Institute of Archeology and
Anthropology, University of South Carolina, Columbia, South Carolina. The original
statement on mean ceramic dating.

————. 1974. The horizon concept revealed in the application of the mean ceramic date formula
to Spanish majolica in the New World. *The Conference on Historic Site Archeology Papers*
7:96-122. Institute of Archeology and Anthropology, University of South Carolina, Columbia, South Carolina. The basic paper on the use of mean ceramic dating for Spanish majolica
(a class of pottery).

————. 1977. *Method and Theory in Historical Archaeology*. Academic Press, New York. This general
work contains a chapter on formula dating that presents the logic of the method, revises
the presentation on British ceramic type dates in South (1972), and summarizes the majolica
applications of South (1974).

— EXERCISE 16 —
SIMILIARY SERIATION

OVERVIEW

Similiary seriation is a dating method based on the presumed gradual changes in form for artifacts of a particular class. This exercise asks you to examine a set of pictorial flasks, a fancy kind of American whiskey bottle of the nineteenth century, and to place them in a sequence.

BACKGROUND ON SIMILIARY SERIATION

Among the great variety of artifact classes that are recovered archaeologically, only a limited number are mentioned in sufficient detail in documents so that they can be dated on that evidence. Others can be dated on the basis of similar materials having been found in contexts that can be dated by documents or other means. But that still leaves a large number of artifact classes that cannot be dated well, and archaeologists are always trying to find ways to date them.

In 1849, Sir John Evans developed a method for establishing a sequence of just such items. This method continues in use today and has come to be known as *similiary seriation* (or sometimes as *stylistic seriation* or *developmental seriation*). Similiary seriation is based on the idea that, over time, the traits that characterize artifacts change gradually. For example, the face on a coin might gradually develop a larger nose and larger eyes. These gradual changes will make a coin from 1066 be very like one from 1076, which in turn will be very like one from 1086; ultimately, a coin from 1366 may be very different from a 1066 coin, but the intermediate stages all differ from their immediate predecessors and successors only by small degrees. Accordingly, an archaeologist faced with a series of items from the same class can order them in a sequence that minimizes the degree of difference between any adjacent members of the series, and this is presumed to be a good approximation of the correct chronological sequence. Of course, the archaeologist won't know which end of the sequence is early and which is late, but other information or assumptions may help there.

This common-sense approach to developing artifact sequences has seen considerable success, for example, with coins, amphorae (Mediterranean oil jars), and other classes of artifacts. There are limitations, however. Sometimes artifacts change in big jumps rather than small modifications, and similiary seriation is unable to cope with this. Also, sometimes a nice, gradual sequence is derived, but the sequence may not represent change over time; the archaeologist may have developed a sequence that represents a continuum of rich-to-poor, urban-to-rural, or some other variable other than time. For a seriation to be usable as a reliable chronological sequence, it must be tested against chronological data.

(A separate method for establishing sequences is "frequency seriation." This method, treated in Exercise 18, uses somewhat different assumptions about the nature of change in material culture.)

YOUR ASSIGNMENT

Last summer, Prof. Wendell Bodfish, a colleague of Leslie Squarkmuffin at Miskatonic University, conducted a series of excavations at dumps associated with taverns around the town of Crumpet, West Virginia. This research was directed toward examining economic and spatial distribution patterns in liquor consumption. He was surprised to find dozens of intact pictorial flasks, particularly 25 with American eagle motifs on them. He plans to extend his excavations next season to include other tavern dumps, and he expects to find more eagle flasks.

Bodfish has a hunch that the eagle flasks are delicate chronological indicators, and he hopes to use them as one means of dating his deposits. Unfortunately, no one yet has worked out fully the chronology for eagle flasks. Since Bodfish believes that the flasks evolve by tiny increments, he feels that similiary seriation would be an appropriate approach.

As his graduate student, working with him on the Crumpet sites, you have been assigned the task of actually doing the similiary seriation. Figure 16-1 shows illustrations of the flasks, and Table 16-1 summarizes additional information about them. Most of the dating of the Crumpet sites will be going on at the same time you are doing the seriation, so you won't have other dating information to test or refine your seriation until after it is completed. You do know, however, that documentary, mean ceramic, and pipestem dating all suggest the Coal Hollow Tavern to be the earliest site in the group, dating to around 1824.

Your task, then, is to complete a similiary seriation based on the pictorial flasks illustrated in Figure 16-1 and described in Table 16-1. Your report should place the individual specimens in a sequence based on their characteristics and explain what characteristics you focused on to produce your sequence, describing the trends from its beginning to its end.

Remember that your grade in this exercise will not be based on how well your sequence reflects chronology. No archaeologist can guarantee that the results of a similiary seriation will produce a usable chronological sequence.

Rather, your success in the exercise will be judged on how well you justify your reasoning in establishing a sequence and how well you evaluate it.

Background on Pictorial Flasks

Whiskey was an incredibly popular drink in nineteenth-century America, and it was sold in a variety of bottles. One bottle type was the *flask*, a flattened glass bottle, usually sold in pint and half-pint sizes and rarely in quart size. These flasks were manufactured by blowing molten glass into two-piece molds, and, beginning around 1816, the molds often were decorated with designs and emblems. By the 1820s, these pictorial flasks had attained tremendous popularity, popularity that would last most of the nineteenth century. Among the most popular of the designs were ones with political symbolism: portraits of presidents, the female personification of Liberty, and a variety of others. Sometimes flasks adopted economic themes (*e.g.*, the expansion of the railroad) or entertainment themes (*e.g.*, the spectacularly successful singing tour of Jenny Lind, the Swedish Nightingale).

Pictorial flasks were turned out by the thousands from several glass manufacturing houses, particularly in New England, New York, New Jersey, Maryland, Pennsylvania, Ohio, Kentucky, and that part of Virginia that now is West Virginia. (West Virginia separated from the rest of Virginia in 1861, when its inhabitants chose to remain in the Union during the Civil War.) Documentary evidence shows that the products from these different glasshouses were shipped widely, and apparently most products were available nearly anywhere in the East. Still, the majority of flasks in any locale probably came from manufacturers relatively nearby.

The molds for the designs on flasks could be purchased from professional mold makers, but some bottle makers employed mold makers of their own. The greater mechanization of glassmaking after the mid-century led to a greater similarity of pictorial flasks made after that date.

American eagles appeared on many flasks, forming the most common emblem. Often the eagle was the only emblem, but sometimes another emblem appeared on the other side of the flask (frequently a president or presidential candidate). The eagle often was shown with an olive branch in its right talon and a thunderbolt in its left, as on the Great Seal of the United States. During some periods, however, the order was reversed, symbolically placing power before peace; occasionally, the olive branch would be replaced with thunderbolts, emphasizing the martial aspect of the eagle that typifies so many of its representations. Many of the eagle emblems resemble designs on contemporaneous coinage closely enough to lead some scholars to believe that coins were used as models. Only rarely does the eagle emblem on a flask closely resemble the Great Seal itself.

The flasks were produced in a wide variety of colors. Most common were the colors natural to glass (browns, greens, and aquamarines), but they also appeared in colors that required the addition of colorants (blues, yellows, reds, and purples). These colors apparently were in response to consumer demand, and all these colors apparently were available by the 1820s and were in use for the remainder of the period of popularity for pictorial flasks.

Pictorial flasks are very popular with bottle collectors, and many historic archaeological sites have been looted solely to procure these bottles. This fact, along with the fact that their beauty kept many pictorial flasks from the discard pile after they were empty, has made them a relatively uncommon artifact in archaeological assemblages.

BIBLIOGRAPHY ON SIMILIARY SERIATION AND PICTORIAL FLASKS

McKearin, George S., and Helen McKearin. 1948. *American Glass.* Crown Publishing Co., New York. Includes a major section on pictorial flasks.

Rouse, Irving. 1967. Seriation in archaeology. *In* Carroll L. Riley and Walter W. Taylor (eds.), *American Historical Anthropology: Essays in Honor of Leslie Spier,* Southern Illinois University Press, Carbondale, Illinois, pp. 153-195. Covers both frequency and similiary ("developmental") seriation.

Tables and figures for this chapter follow.

II-37

River Road House

GII-40   II-48

Heinz Heit Tavern

GII-11

The Virginian Tavern

II-47

Paul McCutcheon's Inn

II-58   II-57   GIV-15

Mingo Public House

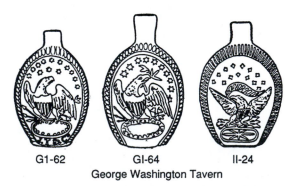

G1-62   GI-64   II-24

George Washington Tavern

Figure 16-1 Pictorial flasks from the Crumpet sités, West Virginia

GI-117 GI-118 GI-119 GI-65 II-22

Coal Hollow Tavern

Dutchman's Inn

II-62 GII-39 II-63 II-65

Hiram Price Inn,
Level 2

Hiram Price Inn,
Level 3

Hiram Price Inn,
Level 5

II-66 GI-6

Union Tavern The Old Tavern

GII-1 GII-2 II-55

John Dys Tavern

TABLE 16-1   Other data on the eagle flasks from the tavern sites around Crumpet, West Virginia.

SITE	SPECIMEN NUMBER	COLOR	SIZE
Coal Hollow Tavern	I-117	aquamarine	pint
	I-118	aquamarine	half-pint
	I-119	blue	pint
Hiram Price Inn			
Level 2	II-62	deep green	pint
Level 3	II-39	aquamarine	pint
	II-63	amber	half-pint
Level 5	II-65	red-amber	half-pint
Dutchman's Inn	I-65	green-blue	pint
	II-22	aquamarine	pint
Union Tavern	II-66	deep green	quart
The Old Tavern	I-6	clear	pint
John Dys Tavern	II-1	yellow-olive	pint
	II-2	aquamarine	pint
	II-55	amber	quart
River Road House	II-37	yellow-olive	pint
Heinz Heit Tavern	II-40	gold-amber	pint
	II-48	blue	quart
The Virginian Tavern	I-11	green	half-pint
Paul McCutcheon's Inn	II-47	aquamarine	quart
Mingo Public House	II-57	amber	pint
	II-58	amber	half-pint
	IV-15	pale green	pint
George Washington Tavern	I-62	aquamarine	pint
	I-64	aquamarine	pint
	II-24	blue	pint

— EXERCISE 17 —
FUNCTIONAL ANALYSIS

OVERVIEW

Not every artifact has an obvious or unambiguous use. This exercise asks you to infer the most likely function of a series of enigmatic notched iron bars from an ironworks in Ohio.

BACKGROUND

In general, historical archaeologists do not have the same problems that prehistorians have in trying to assign a use (function) to an artifact. Since they usually have neither documentary nor pictorial evidence to aid them, prehistoric archaeologists must infer the way an artifact might have been used. Historical archaeologists, however, frequently have a picture of a similar item in use, a name for the item that indicates its use, a textual reference, or informant evidence that clarifies its purpose. Further, the comparative recency of most historical archaeology means that researchers may know the use of an item from their own experience.

Sometimes, however, such evidence is absent. Certain artifacts may go unmentioned because they were so common that everyone knew their use, because they dealt with tasks that polite people wouldn't write about, or because they were used primarily by people that literate recorders didn't find worth writing about. When this happens, historical archaeologists must turn to the methods that prehistorians have devised to deal with similar problems.

Some of these methods are experimental, where replicas of artifacts are made or used to evaluate their efficiency at various tasks; others involve *ethnoarchaeology*, the observation of use of similar artifacts by modern peoples. Finally, archaeologists can infer the probable use of an artifact by intrinsic analysis of the artifact itself. While all of these approaches have been successful in historical archaeology, this exercise focuses on the intrinsic analysis of the artifact itself. This kind of analysis bases its inferences on function primarily on form, material, context, wear, and residues.

Form is the size, shape, and nature of an artifact. Form always has to be considered when inferring function, since certain forms simply are impractical or impossible for certain functions. A shallow ceramic saucer, for example, could never be used to store wine or to reinforce a piece of riveted leather.

While form places limits on the possible functions of an artifact, it often is unjustified to draw a conclusion about function on the basis of form alone. A pair of shears might be for clipping sheep, for snipping semi-molten glass in the blowing of bottles, for trimming hedges, or for some other function. The archaeologist must use additional evidence to base a conclusion.

Material refers simply to the stuff of which an artifact is made. Different materials obviously have different qualities that would make them more or less suitable for a particular use, and it is assumed that the makers and users of an artifact took this factor into consideration. At the ludicrous level, for example, a lumbering axe never will be made of felt, and clothing is unlikely to be made of mahogany. Finer differences in material also were taken into consideration, as with choices between cast iron or wrought iron for axes or among copper, brass, and bronze for straight pins. Of course, sometimes limitations on availability of materials, limited expertise in their working, or expense of optimal materials will cause items to be made of non-optimum materials, as when a frontier blacksmith hammered iron to form a scalpel that better would be made of rolled steel. Finally, a failed experiment or error of judgment on the part of its maker sometimes will find its way into the archaeological record.

Context is the setting, both physical and cultural, in which one finds an artifact in a site. A bolt, for example, might be found in place in a sewing machine, in a bunch of construction rubble, in the basement of a machinist's shop, or alone along the side of a path; each of these contexts suggests a somewhat different set of possible functions for that particular bolt. The functional possibilities for the shears discussed above probably could be reduced to a single interpretation through the consideration of context. Sometimes, of course, context will add little to an analysis, as when the artifact comes from a general dump, but often the context will be more specific and telling.

Using an artifact usually produces some form of alteration in the item itself, and this *wear* can help establish its function. The abrasion of a surface indicates that the surface was in contact with something and rubbed against it; the presence of scratches indicates that the material was moderately hard, and the direction of the scratches can show the dominant direction of movement; polishing of surfaces can indicate rubbing against a material softer than the artifact; bending or deformation can indicate long-term tension on an item; and so forth. These generalizations hold true for artifacts of most materials, and there are many other patterns that apply only to specific materials.

The final category, *residues*, is found on a relatively small percentage of archaeological remains. Residues are small amounts of material that adhere to an artifact or are contained in it, material that indicates the use of the artifact. A pair of shears with tiny wisps of glass adhering to it, for example, would be interpreted differently than one with a few strands of raw wool snagged on it. When residues occur, they often are in minuscule amounts, and, unfortunately, overzealous cleaning of artifacts in the laboratory can destroy these vestiges.

In practice, the archaeologist trying to establish the function of an artifact almost always will begin with form and material, since they immediately eliminate so many possibilities. If context is available, it usually will then be integrated into the inference. Often wear and residues, the types of evidence that require more labor in collecting and interpreting, are not used unless difficulties remain in interpreting the artifact. Nonetheless, even in cases where the function of an artifact appears clear, they can add their part to the interpretation. For example, a green glass wine bottle from the mid-seventeenth century might appear to have only a single interpretation, but examination of the wear on its base could refine an interpretation. Light wear implies use as a wine container, while heavy wear implies subsequent (and repeated) reuse, typically as a water bottle.

In the end, a conclusion derived by these methods is an interpretation, not a fact. It may be well supported, but it always is subject to possible error and reinterpretation. Experimental archaeology often is used to refine or evaluate conclusions derived by intrinsic analysis of an artifact.

YOUR ASSIGNMENT

Dr. Vitas Gingivaitis, an expert in ironworking, is a visiting professor from Lithuania, spending two years at Miskatonic University under the sponsorship of Leslie Squarkmuffin. Gingivaitis has been conducting excavations at the Faithwell Furnace, an iron-producing site in Ohio, and he has found 31 specimens of an enigmatic artifact category termed *notched bars*. Most of these notched bars are fragments, but a few are complete. Gingivaitis is unsure what the function of these artifacts was, but he has some ideas. You are an intern at the Greater Ohio Prehistoric and Historic Evidence Research Center (the GOPHER Center), where Gingivaitis is conducting the laboratory portion of his research; he has assigned you to examine the notched bars and figure out their function. Using the information that follows, conclude what the probable use of the notched bars was. Gingivaitis has given you a set of possible functions, and your task is to see which (if any) is consistent with the characteristics of the notched bars themselves. Your report should draw a conclusion, stress the logic and evidence behind your conclusion, and recommend whether further study is warranted; if you recommend further study, describe what needs to be done and why.

The Notched Bars

While 31 specimens of notched bars have been recovered, only one is whole and another can be reconstructed (glued together from pieces to produce a complete specimen).

Form: Gingivaitis has studied the notched bars and decided that they should be classified into two descriptive types. Type A is about 28 inches long with a more or less square cross-section of about 1 inch to a side. One end of a Type A notched bar has an unnotched section about 8 inches long. The notches themselves are along one side of the bar only, running from the end of the unnotched area to the end of the bar. Each notch is formed by a triangular projection, and each triangle projects about 1/2 inch outward from the bar; each triangle is equilateral. Type B is a bit shorter (about 25 inches) and less heavy (about 3/4 inch in each dimension). Type B notched bars have notches running on one side of their entire length. The notches are formed by equilateral triangles, but they have indentations running down each side of each notch from the top to the bar itself. Type B notched bars taper as the notches become progressively smaller nearer the ends. Of the 31 specimens, 19 are of Type A and 12 are of Type B. Examples of Types A and B are shown in Figure 17-1.

Notched bars similar to both Types A and B have been found at the Hopewell Furnace (Pennsylvania), the Cornwall Furnace (Pennsylvania), and the Saugus Ironworks (Massachusetts); known dates for these notched bars

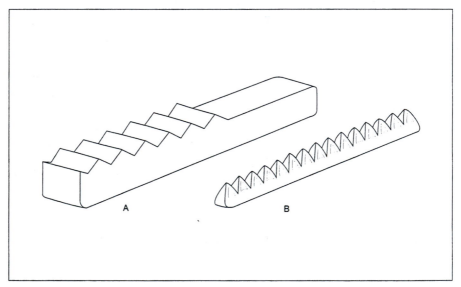

Figure 17-1.

range from mid-seventeenth to early nineteenth century. They have not been reported from other sites.

Material: All of the notched bars are made of cast iron; that is, they were made by pouring molten iron into molds made to the shape desired. Cast iron is less pure than wrought (hammered) iron, since it has a higher percentage of silica slag incorporated into it. Consequently, it is a bit softer and more brittle in most uses; it also is considerably less expensive to make, since it can be mass produced and requires no work from a skilled blacksmith.

Context: The majority of the specimens (21 of 31), including the whole and the reconstructible specimens, were found around the blast furnace, where casting would have taken place. None of these specimens was found in direct association with any piece of machinery. Seven of the remaining ten specimens were found in deposits of broken waste iron. The final three specimens were found in a pathway, in the basement of the ironmaster's house, and in a deposit of general trash. There were no recognized differences in the patterning of the distribution of the two types of notched bars.

Wear: Recognizable wear was found on 24 of the notched bar specimens. Thirteen of the 19 Type A specimens show wear on the corners of the notches along one side; on pieces that include part of the unnotched area, the wear is on the right side (if the notches are upward and the unnotched area is held toward the viewer). The wear consists of heavy abrasion and a bit of "smearing" as the metal has been pushed slightly over the corner. Striations seem to be visible, but the rusted nature of the surface makes it difficult to be sure. The Type B specimens have wear similar to that on the Type A specimens, but it extends further down the side of the bars (including the indentations along the notches) and it appears on both edges of the notches. The heaviest wear on Type B notched bars is in the central area, away from the ends. The wear on both types is essentially continuous along the edges of the pieces. Figure 17-2 shows typical wear.

Breakage often is an aspect of wear. The fragments broken from the notched bars vary considerably in length, averaging 3.4 inches and ranging from 1.1 to 9.6 inches. There is no evidence of impact at the breakage points.

Residues: All of the bars have been examined under magnification to see whether residues remain, but none have been found. There are high-technology tests to see whether minuscule traces of materials are embedded in the fibers of the worn iron, but Gingivaitis is reluctant to spend his dwindling analysis funds for these tests unless they clearly are needed.

Gingivaitis thus far has been unable to find any documentary mention or illustration of these notched bars.

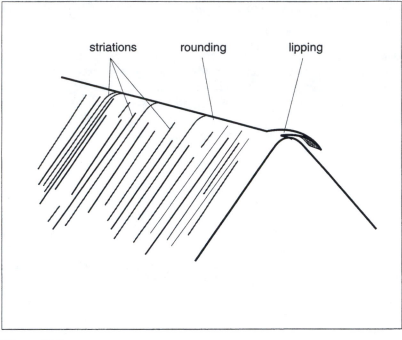

Figure 17-2.

The Faithwell Furnace and Ironworking There

Gingivaitis has completed one season of excavation at the Faithwell Furnace, located about 15 miles outside Dakron, Ohio. The Faithwell Furnace operated for only six years, between 1811 and 1817. The site was away from any sizable settlements, probably accounting for difficulties in distributing the finished products, leading to the demise of the operation. There was a small cluster of workers' housing about half a mile from the iron furnace, but the smell and soot from the plant discouraged settlement nearer. While Gingivaitis has excavated in the housing area, no notched bar has been found there.

The Faithwell operations consisted of an iron furnace, a power forge, and a rolling and slitting mill. Ore was mined about 30 miles away and brought to Faithwell by canal. It was reduced to raw iron in the furnace; further removal of impurities could take place in the power forge, and iron from there could be rolled into bars or slit into wire.

The furnace consisted of a mortared-stone structure built into a hill. A wooden walkway allowed cartloads of ore to be dumped down the top of the furnace, where it would be mixed with limestone and charcoal. A waterwheel, powered by a channelized stream running down the slope, provided power to run a power bellows. The bellows provided enough air to allow efficient combustion of the charcoal, which burned at a high temperature. The limestone acted as a flux, making the iron ore melt at a lower temperature than otherwise. After a few hours, the iron had separated from the other materials in the ore; because of differences in density, the iron sank to the bottom and the impurities rose to the top of the mixture. At this point, a clay plug that stoppered the *casting hole* (an opening in the bottom of the furnace) was removed, and the iron was drawn out from the bottom of the liquid mixture; when the level was lowered to a point that the impurities were beginning to flow through the casting hole, they were permitted to flow onto the ground and harden into slag, which was discarded.

The iron that flowed through the casting hole was used for two main purposes. First, troughs would be scraped into the sand floor at the base of the furnace. The iron that flowed into the main troughs leading from the furnace would harden into "sows," and the iron that hardened in the troughs leading off the main ones would be called "pigs." Hence, the iron ingots that came directly from the furnace came to be known generically as "pig iron." Second, wooden frames were packed with wet sand that had been impressed with molds of shapes for desired objects, such as pots, stove parts, and even notched bars. These sand molds were usable only once but were easy and inexpensive to make. Cast iron objects made by this method have a *seam* (a slight raised ridge between the two halves of the mold) and a *sprue* (a tab or plug of metal that projects from the cast object at the point where the molten iron was poured in through a hole in the mold).

The cast iron that formed both the ingots and the cast objects described above was relatively high in impurities. This meant that it was relatively soft and brittle. If a more durable iron was desired, ingots would be taken to the power forge. Here they would be heated till red hot (but still solid) and moved onto a large anvil, where a 600-pound hammer was operated by another water wheel. The hammer would beat the hot ingot and literally force impurities out of it, making it more pure, harder, less brittle, and more fibrous. This iron was known as "wrought iron."

Much of the iron from the power forge was sent to the rolling and slitting mill, where another water-powered apparatus would press the hot iron between rollers either to produce flat bars or to cut it into wire. At this point, the iron had gone through all the stages possible at Faithwell, and it could be shipped to blacksmiths and others who would work it further.

Most of these operations required few hand tools, and virtually all of those tools were made of wrought iron. At the furnace, there were shovels and hoes for making casting troughs and for moving sand for molding. In addition, there were a series of tongs for lifting iron and scraping tools for removing the burned clay from the casting hole and cleaning the casting hole itself. A small number of blacksmithing tools (hammers, tongs, files, etc.) were found in the power forge area, presumably for the making of wrought iron tools to be used at the site. The small quantity of tools and smithing debris indicates that there was never any sizable commercial smithing operation at Faithwell.

As at most ironworks, the quantity of scrap metal is smaller than one might expect, presumably because scrap iron was simply dumped back into the furnace and melted into the next batch. Slag and some scrap metal were carted off to the south end of the site, where they were dumped.

Ore was taken more or less directly from the canal barges to the furnace, and there appear to have been no major storage areas for ore. Limestone was locally quarried, and there are storage piles remaining near the furnace. There is some mystery over the source of the charcoal to fuel the furnace, since neither charcoal-making tools nor remains of charcoal furnaces or storage heaps have been found; Gingivaitis believes that such remains are at the site but have not yet been located.

Gingivaitis's Ideas on the Function of the Notched Bars

Gingivaitis believes that the notched bars are somehow related to ironmaking, particularly because the only places that similar artifacts have been found are at other iron furnaces. He has developed the following ideas for possible functions:

1. a pull hook. This is a tool to pull hardened pigs out of their troughs to cool further. He believes that possibly the notches could be used to catch the edge of a pig and lever it up.
2. a casting hole rasp. The casting hole needs periodic cleaning to remove bits of burned clay and hardened iron or slag. He believes that the notches could have been used for this purpose. Other tools are known to have been used for this task.
3. a sprue rasp. The sprue is broken from cast artifacts with pliers, but this leaves a roughened area or even a slight projection. Gingivaitis believes that maybe the notched bars served as coarse rasps for the removal of these roughened areas and the seams that form by small amounts of iron squeezing between the pieces of a mold.
4. a bark rasp. If charcoal were made at the site, Gingivaitis believes, perhaps these notched bars were used to remove the bark from the wood prior to igniting then smothering the wood to produce charcoal.
5. a trammel. A trammel is a support with notches in it to permit a pot to be held over a fire at different heights. The bail or handle of the pot is simply hooked over the right notch. Gingivaitis believes that possibly it has some use in the power forge or rolling and slitting mill.

A Note on Industrial Archaeology

This exercise is an example of *industrial archaeology*, the study of industry and industrial processes. Industrial archaeology largely is consumed with the documentation of past technological and industrial processes. Consequently, much industrial archaeology demands considerable knowledge of science and the history of technology, and the methods and techniques used in it may include exotic analyses. A study of a nineteenth-century paint factory, for example, might require a large battery of chemical tests to ascertain the nature of the pigments, solvents, and other components of the paint.

There is, however, a growing and healthy concern with the study of the social consequences of the industrial revolution. Studies of this sort use the same methods as other historical archaeology and focus on the culture and behavior of mill towns and mill neighborhoods. Many of these studies have made substantial contributions to the understanding of the social side of industrialization.

BIBLIOGRAPHY ON FUNCTIONAL ANALYSIS AND IRONWORKING

Bining, Arthur Cecil. 1973. *Pennsylvania Iron Manufacturing in the Eighteenth Century*. Pennsylvania Historical and Museum Commission, Harrisburg, Pennsylvania. Basic treatment of iron technology and organization in this period.

Gilbert, R. I., and J. H. Mielke (eds.). 1985. *The Analysis of Prehistoric Diets*. Academic Press, New York. Includes some treatment of residues analysis.

Hudson, Kenneth. 1979. *World Industrial Archaeology*. Cambridge University Press, Cambridge, England. Introduction to industrial archaeology with a section on ironmaking, including case studies, maps, and illustrations.

Schubert, H. R. 1958. Extraction and production of metals: iron and steel. *In* Charles Singer, E. J. Holmyard, A. R. Hall, and Trevor I. Williams (eds.), *A History of Technology*, vol. IV ("The Industrial Revolution, c. 1750 to c. 1850"), Oxford University Press, Oxford, England, pp. 99-117. The classic, though technical, account of ironworking in this period.

Semenov, S. A. 1964. *Prehistoric Technology*. Translated by M. W. Thompson. Adams and Dart, Bath, England. Originally published in the Soviet Union in 1957. The classic source on wear pattern analysis. While it has been surpassed by more recent works dealing with stone tools, it is current regarding metal tools.

PART FIVE

Cemetery Studies

T HE EXERCISES IN THIS PART differ from the others in that they require you to go into the field, collect data, and analyze them. They all focus on cemeteries, sometimes considering grave markers as artifacts and sometimes as documents. Because you must design your research and tailor your activities both to the cemetery you are studying and to your objectives, you will need to know a bit about cemeteries in general. This introduction attempts to provide that information and prepare you for fieldwork and data analysis.

CEMETERIES AS HISTORIC SITES

Disposal of the dead is an unavoidable part of human existence, but cemeteries are not. They arise when a community feels the need for a special area to practice the distinctive activities that they hold appropriate for commemorating or otherwise dealing with the dead. Cemeteries may provide a dignified place of rest for the dead, but that is in some sense secondary to their primary function: They provide a setting for the activities of the living in relation to the dead.

Cemeteries, therefore, contain a wealth of information about past and present attitudes toward the dead and their proper treatment. If approached imaginatively, they can provide a rich data set for analysis by the various social science disciplines.

In a sense, cemeteries are a microcosm of historical sites as a whole. They contain artifacts in the form of grave markers, and these can be used for most of the sorts of studies that can be performed on other artifacts. In addition, the markers often have inscriptions that allow for various types of textual analysis. The layout of the graves is amenable to many of the methods of spatial analysis. And the mourning and other activities that go on in active cemeteries add a dimension unknown at most archaeological sites. Finally, the graves often can be dated quite accurately, resolving a major problem in archaeology.

TYPES OF CEMETERIES

There are eight basic types of cemeteries in the United States.

1. The church cemetery. This cemetery may be adjacent to a church, in which case it may be known as a "churchyard." Alternatively, it may be separate from the church. The cemetery is owned by the church and is private property, though normally it is open to all. Burial costs typically are low to moderate in this type of cemetery.

2. The public cemetery. This cemetery is owned by a governmental unit, usually a town, city, or county. By law, public cemeteries must be open to the public, although there may be limitations designed to discourage abusers. Burial costs typically are low in public cemeteries.

3. The customary cemetery. This type of cemetery is simply a plot used by neighbors as a burying place. It has no formal or legal status, so there is no sexton or sexton's records, unless an individual decided to keep records as a public service. Customary cemeteries usually are cared for by the survivors of those buried within; sometimes they are scarcely cared for at all. Customary cemeteries are most common in rural areas. Often they are not legal, but they usually are tolerated well. Customary cemeteries have few or no burial costs.

4. The private cemetery. This type of cemetery is owned by a corporation and (in most states) must post information to that effect at the gate. It is run as a for-profit corporation and often has quite restrictive rules for markers and offerings, rules that usually are designed to cut maintenance costs. Burial costs at private cemeteries usually run from moderate to high.

5. The lodge cemetery. These cemeteries are owned and operated by lodges or other fraternal organizations, especially the Masons or Oddfellows. These cemeteries sometimes are restricted to members of the organization, but often others can purchase plots. Many of these organizations were founded in part to provide burial insurance, and they often were inexpensive for members.

6. The ethnic cemetery. To a certain extent, this category overlaps with some of the others, since an ethnic group may also be a religious group (*e.g.*, Russians and the Russian Orthodox Church). An ethnic cemetery can be public (*e.g.*, one owned by an Indian tribe), private, or customary. This category is especially useful for cemeteries that otherwise would be difficult to classify.

7. The family cemetery. This type of cemetery remains legal in most states, and at one time there were many thousands of them in the United States. This is a plot of land, owned by a family and given over to the burial of its family members. Close friends occasionally also are included. Most families with family cemeteries had large amounts of rural land and could afford to allocate some of it to this purpose. There were, of course, few or no burial costs.

8. The mass grave. The victims of disasters sometimes are buried in a common grave. Often a memorial is erected to their memory afterward. The Earthquake Cemetery in Lone Pine, California, for example, is the mass grave of the victims of a major earthquake in 1872.

SITE FORMATION PROCESSES AT CEMETERIES

Archaeologists refer to the complex set of processes that produce an archaeological site as *site formation processes*. They are divided into *c-transforms* (cultural processes), and *n-transforms* (natural processes). Any thoughtful investigation of an archaeological site must consider these processes in order to assess how the various features of a site developed and what they mean. In addition, the study of site formation processes can help the archaeologist become aware of the changes that may have befallen a site between the date of its formation and the date of its study. The special set of site formation processes relevant to cemeteries warrants consideration.

C-transforms

1. The construction and marking of the grave itself, as well as subsequent offerings and plantings at the grave. These may have been designed by the deceased's survivors or may have been purchased "off the shelf" from a funeral home.

2. Limitations of grave marking. Many cemeteries, especially private ones, place strong limitations on the possible grave markings allowed, frequently effectively eliminating traditional folk marker styles and limiting the marker to a horizontal granite or bronze slab.

3. Cemetery cleanups. Run-down parts of most cemeteries are periodically cleaned up. Wooden crosses and other structures are very vulnerable to disrepair, and often it is easier to remove or replace them than to repair them, especially if the years since their construction have seen the aging, death, or emigration of the deceased's family. Cleanups can be conducted by a family, a crew hired by the cemetery, a community group, or an individual.

4. Vandalism. Cemeteries frequently have been the target for various forms of vandalism and looting. Isolated cemeteries may be dug into to rob the dead of jewelry or watches, or even to remove skulls for curios or sale. Grave markers are vulnerable, especially if there are photographs set into them. Tall markers may be toppled and may break in their falls. Jewish and

black markers especially are vulnerable to anti-Semitic and other racist attack, and recent years have seen some spread of this phenomenon to other groups, *e.g.*, Arabs and Iranians.

5. Mowing damage. Power lawn mowers take a heavy toll on grave markers. If left upright, older markers may be chipped around their bases as the mowers crowd against them. Often they are set flat into the ground to permit the passage of a mower over them, and a mower blade set too low can chip away artwork and inscriptions in a single mowing.

6. Removal or moving of graves. The laws regarding the moving of graves within a cemetery are arcane, and sometimes a cemetery will move graves (both markers and bodies) to make room for a new lane or section of plots. In some cases, cemeteries have the option to remove markers altogether for convenience. Sometimes, the cemetery will be relocated to make way for development, in which case the graves usually will be moved elsewhere with their markers.

N-transforms

1. Surface erosion of markers. The surfaces of markers, with their inscriptions and bas-reliefs, tend to erode relatively rapidly. Paint erodes most rapidly from wood or stone, although it may impede the erosion of the wood surface beneath it to the point that a raised rendition of the inscription may be read many years later. Carved surfaces of wood can erode to a point of unrecognizability in only a few years, depending on the environment. The surface of marble, slate, or sandstone can erode fairly rapidly, especially in the desert (where windborne sand is so abrasive) or in the city (where acid air and rain attack marble surfaces).

2. Deeper marker breakup. This is particularly serious with wood and concrete markers, but slate and sandstone also are vulnerable. Only after considerable erosion will marble be in structural danger, and granite and bronze are quite durable.

3. Fires. Wooden markers and other grave architecture are vulnerable to wildfires whose paths can include cemeteries.

4. Seasonal variations in weather. Blazing sun and frigid cold each can be hard on grave markers, but their alternation with the seasons can be especially damaging. Dry summer heat can cause cracking in many materials used for grave markers, and water seeping into cracks can expand when freezing, resulting in splitting.

5. Rodent and ant excavations. The soil that is disturbed by digging a grave pit and then perhaps softened by frequent watering of lawn or plantings is particularly attractive to ants and rodents as places for burrows and nests. For the most part, these are merely unsightly and a hazard for those walking through a cemetery (the ground can be weakened to the point where an

unwary walker can sink into it). Occasionally, however, they will undermine a marker, leading to its breakage or removal.

CEMETERY TERMS

There is a special terminology for describing cemeteries, and you may find this useful in your research. A glossary of these terms is provided as Appendix E.

THE CEMETERY EXERCISES

The cemetery exercises treat a variety of topics. Exercise 18 uses dated grave markers to test the assumptions underlying frequency seriation, a technique of dating archaeological remains. Exercise 19 asks you to use information from inscriptions on markers to study the population structure of the community that produced the cemetery you are studying. Exercise 20 investigates the archaeological estimation of social status on the basis of grave markers, offerings, or both. And Exercise 21 asks you to interpret both art and inscriptions on grave markers to infer something of the ideology of the people buried there. All of these methods are extensible to types of archaeological data other than cemeteries.

Efficiently Collecting Data for the Cemetery Exercises

The following hints may assist you in planning and executing the fieldwork necessary for these exercises.

1. Read any exercise before going to the cemetery. That way you will be able to think through your strategy and be prepared for your cemetery visit.

2. Before trying to collect any information, spend a bit of time getting acquainted with the cemetery, just wandering through it and getting an idea of its nature, condition, and size. You probably will have to do this before you finalize your strategy for data collection.

3. Many students find it useful to make forms for data collection. Collecting data can be fatiguing. Heat, cold, wind, or mosquitoes can come to dominate your thoughts, and a form can prevent you from forgetting some of the data you had meant to collect. Make sure to bring a few more forms than you anticipate needing, and be sure to bring a clipboard or similar writing surface. If the equipment is available to you, you may wish to place the form in a laptop or other portable computer, but remember that even a few pounds can become tiring over time.

4. Be prepared to visit the cemetery more than once. It would be wonderful if your planning were so perfect that you could gather all the information you need, go home, and write it up. Unfortunately, reviewing your information at home may give you new and better ideas of something

you want to consider, and you may have to return to the cemetery to collect additional information.

5. If you and other students are planning to coordinate your efforts in data collection and pool your data, plan early. First, be sure that this is acceptable to your instructor. Then, allow for possible miscommunications and even a possible shirker.

6. If you will be working in a cemetery where grave inscriptions are in a language with which you are familiar but not fluent, bring along a pocket dictionary for translation. Regardless of what language they are written in, folk inscriptions may have idiosyncratic or phonetic spellings, so be ready to be imaginative in your interpretations.

Proper Conduct in Cemeteries

While cemeteries are historic sites in one sense, they also are active loci of current activity and are accessible to the scholar really only at the pleasure of the people to whose lives they form a vital part. Consequently, the scholar has a moral and ethical obligation not to be offensive in his or her use of these sites; practically speaking, this is more than "merely" an obligation, since offending parties can be expelled from cemeteries for their behavior.

The following dozen rules of behavior really are mostly common sense, but you should read them and abide by them as you visit cemeteries to collect data for the exercises in this part of the manual, as well as at any other time you visit a cemetery.

1. Be generally respectful and unobtrusive. The people who use a cemetery usually have strong religious feelings; you may not share these feelings, but you still have an obligation to avoid interfering with their ability to perform activities as they wish.

2. Avoid loud talk, raucous laughter, or horsing around. These are highly disturbing to mourners and others using cemeteries.

3. Don't interrupt or disrupt funerals, burials, mourning, or other cemetery activities. Not all such activities will be immediately obvious, so be cautious. A group of Chicano men in their twenties may drink beer at a grave in California, then pour the rest on the grave as an offering to a dead friend—an unthoughtful observer might take this for a profane activity and not respect it for the ritual it is.

4. If cemetery rules are posted, obey them, even if they seem silly or overblown.

5. Never enter a closed cemetery. Many cemeteries remain open somewhat later than their posted hours, and they signal this by leaving their gates open. If the gates are closed, don't go in.

6. Don't enter ethnic cemeteries where you have reason to believe your presence will be unwelcome unless you have permission to do so. American Indians often are particularly sensitive to this issue, probably because many

of their cemeteries (especially prehistoric ones) have been studied and excavated by archaeologists in ways that have not always been sensitive to their concerns. Consequently, non-Indians in a cemetery often are viewed with suspicion.

7. Don't bring pets into cemeteries. Many cemeteries explicitly prohibit this, and none like it. Even if Spot really won't dig a hole, the people in the cemetery don't know this. They have good reason to be concerned.

8. Be very careful with motorcycles. Many cemeteries have had bad experiences with vandals on motorcycles and have generalized their concerns to all motorcyclists. Even the most considerate motorcyclist, it must be conceded, can be a bit disruptive to the quiet of a cemetery.

9. Don't walk directly on graves. Many traditions hold this to be disrespectful. In some folk cemeteries it is almost impossible to avoid walking on graves amid the jumble of them, but do the best you can.

10. Don't take offerings from graves. This may be especially tempting in Asian cemeteries, where there is a strong tradition of food offerings or in Hispanic cemeteries, where unopened bottles of beer sometimes are left on graves. Yes, the food will be eaten by squirrels and kids may steal the beer. But your obligation is to leave it where it was placed with good intentions by the devotee. It is a good practice to disturb nothing at a grave, since a seemingly insignificant object may have tremendous significance. Pebbles on Jewish gravestones, for example, are placed there by loved ones as tangible symbols of their love for the deceased ("Jewish calling cards"); removing these is a desecration.

11. Never disturb the soil. The kind of archaeology for these exercises is done aboveground and is non-destructive. Many people will be very distrustful if they hear that an archaeologist wants to do research in a cemetery where their relatives are buried. Most people have little inkling that archaeologists aren't always digging up bodies. Don't fuel their misconceptions.

12. Be mindful of approaching people you meet in a cemetery. Many will be mourning and probably will be in no mood for exchanging pleasantries or (even worse) being grilled by an insensitive anthropologist or oral historian. There certainly is nothing wrong with chatting with the caretaker or sexton if you have a specific question, but even here you should be aware that this person has other duties and may not be able to spend as much time with you as you might desire.

GENERAL BIBLIOGRAPHY ON CEMETERIES AND GRAVE MARKERS

Barba, Preston A. 1953. *Pennsylvania German Tombstones: A Study in Folk Art*. Pennsylvania German Folklore Society, Allentown, Pennsylvania. Largely art historic/folkloric.

Benes, Peter (ed.). 1977. *Puritan Gravestone Art*. (The Dublin Seminar for New England Folklife, Annual Proceedings, 1976.) Boston University, Boston, Massachusetts. A collection of essays on Puritan gravestone art.

————. 1979. *Puritan Gravestone Art II*. (The Dublin Seminar for New England Folklife, Annual Proceedings, 1978.) Boston University, Boston, Massachusetts. A further collection of essays on Puritan gravestone art.

Combs, Diana Williams. 1986. *Early Gravestone Art in Georgia and South Carolina*. University of Georgia Press, Athens, Georgia. Particularly treats the colonial period.

Hanks, Carol. 1974. *Early Ontario Gravestones*. McGraw-Hill, Ryerson, Toronto. One of the few book-length treatments of Canadian grave markers.

Hanks, Patrick, and Flavia Hodges. 1989. *A Dictionary of Surnames*. Oxford University Press, Oxford, England. A major resource treating English, Jewish, Portuguese, and Spanish names in the English-speaking world. Over 70,000 entries identified to ethnicity/nationality; much other information given, also.

Jean, Donald G. 1969. The traditional upland south cemetery. *Landscape* 18:39-41. The defining statement on the most common sort of American southern white cemetery.

————. 1978. The upland south cemetery: an American type. *Journal of Popular Culture* 11:895-903. Refinement and expansion of his earlier statement.

Jordan, Terry. 1982. *Texas Graveyards: A Cultural Legacy*. University of Texas Press, Austin, Texas. An excellent geographical treatment of Texas cemeteries, including sections on Mexican and German cemeteries.

Kniffen, Fred B. 1967. Necrogeography in the United States. *The Geographical Review* 57:426-427. The initial statement on the geographical study of cemeteries.

Markers. The annual periodical of the Association for Gravestone Studies. Presents essays in various aspects of cemetery and gravestone studies, especially in the United States and Canada.

Meyer, Richard E. (ed.). 1989. *Cemeteries and Gravemarkers: Voices of American Culture*. UMI Press, Ann Arbor, Michigan. An excellent collection of essays on various aspects of cemeteries and grave markers. Includes a quite thorough topical bibliography.

————. *Ethnicity and the American Cemetery*. Bowling Green State University Popular Press, Bowling Green, Ohio. A collection of essays focusing on ethnicity and cemeteries as seen from historical archaeology, folklore, landscape architecture, and other disciplines.

Smith, Elsdon C. 1973. *New Dictionary of American Family Names*. Harper and Row, New York. While not quite so compendious as its title suggests, this work identifies a wide variety of names to nationality or ethnic group.

Vlach, John Michael. 1978. *The Afro-American Tradition in Decorative Arts*. Cleveland Museum of Art, Cleveland, Ohio. (Reprinted in 1990 by the University of Georgia Press, Athens, Georgia.) Contains an eight-page section on graveyard decoration.

Other references are given under particular cemetery exercises where they seem most appropriate.

— EXERCISE 18 —
FREQUENCY SERIATION
WITH GRAVE MARKER DATA

OVERVIEW

Frequency seriation is a method of dating archaeological assemblages on the basis of the frequencies of the types, attributes, or attribute clusters within them. This exercise asks you to apply it to grave markers of known dates to examine its accuracy.

BACKGROUND

Over the years, scholars have had various ideas about how material culture changes. These different conceptions have led to different methods of interpreting material culture in attempts to use it for dating archaeological deposits.

To discuss these ideas and methods, it is necessary to define a bit of terminology first. An *attribute* or *trait* is a minimal kind of characteristic of an artifact, such as having a disk-shaped body, having red color, or having an incised line around the rim. *Dimension* is the category into which a series of traits can be grouped: Red, green, and blue are traits, but color is the dimension. The traits of a dimension should be such that any individual specimen has one and only one trait per dimension. If several traits consistently cluster together in artifacts, then they are said to define a *type*. Intermediate between the single trait and the cluster of traits at the artifact level (the type) is the *trait cluster* or *mode*: a set of traits that regularly occur together and characterize some portion of an artifact, such as a handle, a lip, or a blade. A trigger handle on a mug, for example, is composed of several traits (round finger holes, three finger holes, vertical arrangement, etc.) and is a trait cluster. (These terms are discussed further in Exercise 13.)

One major conception of material culture change can be termed *gradualist*. According to this conception, an individual trait, trait cluster, or type gradually modifies into a new form. For examples, the green color of wine bottles gets gradually deeper and browner and eventually becomes brown (trait modification), the wings of an angel represented on a coin gradually become thinner and turn into laurel branches flanking or encircling a head (trait cluster modification), or the sixteenth-century horseshoe gradually becomes the nineteenth-century horseshoe through a series of accumulated changes of various traits (type modification). Central to this conception is the notion that a time sequence of artifacts will show a gradual change from one form to another, with small modifications producing few abrupt changes. This conception of material culture change supports similiary seriation as a dating technique. (Similiary seriation is discussed in detail in Exercise 16.)

In contrast to the gradualist conception, the *punctualist* conception of change in material culture maintains that older types, traits, and trait clusters are used, essentially unmodified, until they are rejected outright and replaced with new ones that may be totally different. With this conception, there are no intermediate steps, as with the gradualist conception; instead, each type, trait, or trait cluster remains intact until it is replaced, not modified. The standard metaphor is the old woman at the edge of the plaza, continuing to make her pots in the old form; when she dies, the number of pots of that form declines; when all of the old women who make that form die, it becomes extinct. In the meantime, new forms are being developed by the younger women and are growing in popularity. This conception is based on the assumption that individuals tend to continue making and using the artifact types to which they are accustomed.

The greatest proponent of the punctualist conception was James Ford, an American prehistoric archaeologist who developed *frequency seriation,* the focus of this exercise. (Sir W. N. Flinders Petrie developed "sequence dating" in the late nineteenth century, but, while that method was based on assumptions similar to Ford's, it was cumbersome and never attained such widespread use.) Using the punctualist assumptions, Ford (1962) argued that each type, trait, or trait cluster has a distinct trajectory, as it arises, becomes popular, and finally trails off to extinction. Viewed graphically, using bars of different widths to represent different levels of popularity, the earliest period at the bottom of a chart has a narrow bar, as does the latest period at the top, while the middle periods have wide bars; this shape was dubbed "lensatic" or "battleship-shaped" for the shape of its graphic representation.

Ford maintained that if you consider a large number of types (or traits or trait clusters), each following this pattern, you will see a composite pattern that characterizes material culture change. Each date will have a predictable mix of percentage popularity of the various types under consideration. Ford argued that an assemblage of unknown date could be assigned a place in a sequence simply by slipping it in between assemblages whose patterns of percentage popularity for the various types were similar. In fact, Ford argued that a series of assemblages of unknown date could be put into chronological order ("seriated") using only this approach. He took deposits of unknown dates, calculated percentages of different pottery types, converted those percentages into bars of different widths, and physically shuffled them into different orders until he came upon an ordering that would produce a series of reasonable approximations of lensatic distributions. Since then, statistics and computer programs have been devised to produce the optimum sequence without the tedium of shuffling scraps of paper.

Ford devised this method of frequency seriation in the 1940s, before the era of radiocarbon dating, and it was quite successful, especially in regions such as the prehistoric Lower Mississippi Valley, where stratified sites were rare and stratigraphy couldn't be used to establish a relative sequence. It was a major means of archaeological dating before the advent of radiocarbon dating and other methods. It still is used sometimes, and, although it no longer is a major means of dating deposits, the conceptions of culture change that underlie it are important.

But a basic question remains: Is the assumption that cultures change in this manner generally warranted? The fact that frequency seriation has achieved significant successes in the prehistoric Lower Mississippi Valley does not mean that the assumptions that underlie it are valid everywhere and in all cases.

In a classic series of studies of colonial and early federal period grave-stones in New England, James Deetz and Edwin Dethlefsen examined the assumptions underlying frequency seriation (Deetz and Dethlefsen 1965, 1967; Dethlefsen and Deetz 1966). They collected data on various traits, using the dates on gravestones as the dates of manufacture. Then, they constructed charts of the sort one could construct with frequency seriation. The difference was that, in a sense, they were turning the process on its head. In frequency seriation, the true sequence is unknown and one uses the frequency of traits and assumptions about lensatic distributions to try to reconstruct the true sequence. In contrast, Deetz and Dethlefsen knew the true sequence and were using the frequency of traits to see whether they fell into lensatic distributions over time. Their studies concluded that gravestones during the periods they studied truly were characterized by the lensatic distribution and the notions of cultural change that it represented; they also were able to suggest some other factors that refined the conception of cultural change.

YOUR ASSIGNMENT

The fact that Deetz and Dethlefsen were successful in supporting the punctu-alist conception of cultural change in colonial and early federalist New Eng-land does not necessarily mean that we should conclude that this pattern of change is universal. Your task is to further test this general conception of material culture change.

Your first step is to select a data set of grave marker data. Your data can come from any place and period, so long as it is not New England between 1630 and 1820—you want your data set to be different from that of Deetz and Dethlefsen.

Your write-up should consist of a brief statement of the problem and your methods; a list of the dimensions and traits you used, including definitions of traits; a copy of your data sheets (these don't have to be pretty, just functional); your graphs; and your conclusions. An example of the sort of graph you should produce is given in Figure 18-1.

Hints

You will need to select several dimensions to use, since the results of any single one will not be convincing. Probably three to six dimensions is a good range, since this should give you an adequate data set from which to draw conclusions without demanding too much time in data collection and analysis. The dimensions you select can be technological (*e.g.*, materials from which markers are made, techniques of rendering inscriptions), formal (*e.g.*, the shapes of markers, the symbols and motifs put on them), stylistic (*e.g.*, the organization of the different elements of the markers, the dominance of curvilinear or rectilinear elements), or linguistic (*e.g.*, the contents of inscriptions, the languages used). Feel free to choose dimensions from any or all of these various classes of dimensions. Use your creativity to select interesting dimensions that may provide stimulating data. Your best results probably will be obtained if you select dimensions whose traits are neither too rare (so that your numbers will be too small to permit recognizing any clear pattern) or too common (so that you may get the same pattern for the entire period of the cemetery).

You probably will have to visit your cemetery to decide which dimensions to use. Wandering around and looking at markers should provide you with ideas, and a bit more wandering and looking should help you decide whether a dimension is promising. While at the cemetery, try to get a list of the traits to expect under each dimension you will use. Then, at home, you probably will want to make up a form that will list each dimension and the traits within it (and spaces for others that you didn't anticipate), as well as a space to record the date of the grave. Going into the field to seriously collect data before this point probably will lead to problems.

The date of the marker is best approximated by the death date given in the inscription. Some markers, of course, will have been set some years after the burial, and others may be replacements for damaged markers. These, of course, will hurt your results, but there is little you can do about it, except trying to recognize the most blatant cases and exclude them from your analysis. You also will have to decide how to deal with markers that have no death dates.

Ultimately, you will be summarizing your data into periods. You want to be sure that your periods are long enough that you have enough cases in each one to potentially show a clear pattern, yet not so long that significant changes might take place within them and be obscured. Most students find ten-year periods best, but you will have to decide what is best for your data

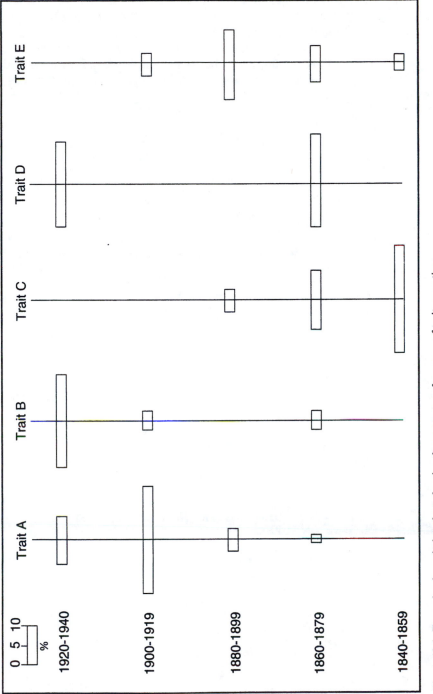

Figure 18-1. Example of a seriation chart showing the percentage frequency of traits over time.

set. Accordingly, you should take down exact dates, since you will be able to change and experiment with the periods you use without having to go back into the field and regather the data.

When you have collected your data, you are ready to analyze it. In this case, you should follow the approach that Deetz and Dethlefsen used. This involves making graphs that summarize your findings. There are three basic steps to making each graph:

1. Set up your graph. By convention, time is measured on the vertical axis, with earlier dates toward the bottom. Each graph will treat a single dimension, and each trait on that dimension will have a horizontal bar for its occurrence at a particular period. It is conventional to draw a vertical line where the horizontal bars for a trait will be drawn and to center those bars on that line.
2. Convert your raw data to percentages for the traits of each dimension in each period. For example, you may have 20 graves within the period 1880-1890, 7 of white marble, 11 of red granite, and 2 of black granite. Percentages per period for the dimension of material will be 35% white marble, 55% red granite, and 10% black granite. If you didn't take this step, your graph would be badly distorted by the effects of greater and lesser numbers of graves in the different periods you are using.
3. Plot the percentages. You will need to establish a scale, perhaps 1 inch = 25%. Simply draw a horizontal line of the proper length in the appropriate place for each trait and period. If you find that your graph is getting too large, you have some options: (a) use a different scale and redraw the graph, (b) tape several sheets together and use these with your write-up, or (c) make a reduced photocopy for inclusion in your write-up.

The aesthetic quality of your graphs is not critical, but you should take basic care to be clear and accurate.

Once you have your graphs, you are in a position to see whether they support or refute the gradualist conception of culture change. This evaluation may be quick and simple (if the results are clear) or difficult (if they are ambiguous).

BIBLIOGRAPHY ON FREQUENCY SERIATION AND GRAVESTONE ANALYSIS

Deetz, James, and Edwin S. Dethlefsen. 1965. The Doppler effect and archaeology: A consideration of the spatial effects of seriation. *Southwestern Journal of Anthropology* (now *Journal of Anthropological Research*) 21:196-206. An elaboration on the interpretation of the patterns observed in the 1966 article.

———. 1967. Death's head, cherub, urn and willow. *Natural History Magazine* (March), pp. 30-37. Less technical treatment than most of their articles; emphasis on ideological meaning.

Dethlefsen, Edwin S., and James Deetz. 1966. Death's heads, cherubs, and willow trees: Experimental archaeology in colonial cemeteries. *American Antiquity* 31(4):502-510. The basic analysis on which this exercise is patterned.

Ford, James A. 1962. *A Quantitative Method for Deriving Cultural Chronology.* (Technical Manual 1.) Pan American Union, Washington, D.C. The basic statement of the frequency seriation model.

Marquadt, William H. 1978. Advances in archaeological seriation. *In* Michael B. Schiffer (ed.), *Advances in Archaeological Method and Theory*, vol. 1, pp. 257-314. Academic Press, New York. Leads the beginner to an advanced understanding of frequency seriation.

Rouse, Irving. 1967. Seriation in archaeology. In Carroll L. Riley and Walter W. Taylor (eds.), *American Historical Anthropology: Essays in Honor of Leslie Spier*, Southern Illinois University Press, Carbondale, Illinois, pp. 153-195. Covers both frequency and similiary ("developmental") seriation.

— EXERCISE 19 —
CEMETERY DEMOGRAPHY

OVERVIEW

Cemeteries are one of several sources of information that can support the study of the population structures of past communities. This exercise asks you to collect cemetery information and analyze it for demographic insights.

BACKGROUND

Demography is the study of population in the broadest sense, including both modern populations and historic or prehistoric ones. Demographic studies typically treat the number of persons in a community; the distribution of that population into different groups by age, gender, class, occupation, and other categories; life expectancy for those categories; changes that are taking place or have taken place in the demographic structure; and many other issues. In addition, demographers often deal with spatial and economic factors as they affect population. Demography looks for population patterns (descriptive demography) and tries to explain those patterns (explanatory demography).

Studying modern populations, while difficult because of the vast amounts of data usually involved, often is easier than studying past populations. Modern censuses are relatively thorough and accurate; and as a last resort, a demographer could go out and count people to get certain types of data. The historical demographer, on the other hand, has to rely on records already collected in the past, and those may or may not be particularly reliable or enlightening. Many of those records will be conventional documents, and a great deal of demographic detail can be collected there. Censuses, probate documents, obituaries, death records, and other documentary sources can provide a wealth of critical information to historical demography. Sometimes, however, conventional documents do not contain the whole picture, and historical archaeologists then may turn to cemeteries.

Cemeteries can provide data for historical demography in two ways. First, they contain the remains of human bodies, and forensic anthropologists are very skilled at reconstructing details of the person whose remains are recovered. Some of the sorts of information that often can be obtained from the analysis of skeletal remains include:

- age at death;
- sex;
- race;
- approximate number of children to which a woman has given birth;
- degree of muscular development;
- nutritional status;
- diseases from which a person suffered;
- injuries a person has suffered; and
- cause of death.

With such information, a detailed demographic profile of a community sometimes can be obtained, providing the excavated remains are representative of the community as a whole. This kind of study, however, is quite uncommon in historical archaeology because of the ethical considerations involved. Usually such studies are made only when a cemetery is in the path of development and is excavated before relocation of the remains of those buried there.

Far more common are demographic studies based on documentary records of a cemetery. Cemeteries can have two kinds of these records, and they usually contain different types of information. The *sexton's records* are the conventional documents the cemetery maintains on each person buried there. Not all types of cemeteries are required by law in all states to maintain sexton's records, but most American cemeteries in the last 50 years (and many before that) have done so. What is maintained in the sexton's records will vary greatly from cemetery to cemetery but often will be consistent from grave to grave within a cemetery. Typical information includes name of the person interred, date of death, age at death, owner of the cemetery lot, and location of the lot and grave.

The second kind of document in a cemetery consists of the inscriptions on the grave markers themselves. The information given will vary greatly from grave to grave, primarily because the survivors of the deceased typically decide what will be included in an inscription. Most historic cemeteries have had no regulations about what is included on a marker (although some more recent cemeteries have been concerned to see that inscriptions are neither frivolous nor obscene), and the survivors could include as much as they could afford to have carved or otherwise recorded. Most graves have the deceased's name and birth and death dates (or death date and age); other information can include ancestors, survivors, spouses, occupational information, information alleged to describe the deceased's personality, place of birth, place of death, military service, religious convictions, noteworthy achievements, membership in lodges and fraternal orders, scriptural quotations, and various verses. Much of this information can be of use to the demographer.

There are many descriptive analyses that a historical demographer can undertake using cemetery data, but this exercise will focus on life expectancy and related issues of mortality.

Life expectancy is the average number of years people born in a given year will live. If you examine subsets of the people born in a given year (*e.g.*, different genders, ethnicities, and classes), you often will find different life expectancies for those different groups. To calculate life expectancy, organize your data according to year of birth, and simply average the ages at death for the individuals born in that year; if you want to examine subsets, recalculate the average age at death for the members of each subset. (This method of calculating life expectancy will work only if all the people born in a year under consideration have died. If you take a recent year, perhaps ten years ago, all those who appear in the cemetery necessarily will have died under the age of ten, giving you a highly misleading life expectancy estimate. Demographers use a different estimation procedure when forecasting life expectancy for those born in recent years, basing estimates on current threats to life at each age.)

Infant mortality refers to how many infants out of 1,000 births die. (The United Nations considers "infancy" to end at 1 year of age, though some scholars prefer to consider it to last until 2 years of age.) *Child mortality* refers to the number of deaths per 1,000 births of children in the ages between 1 (or 2) years and 12 years of age. To calculate either rate for a given year, determine the number of deaths in the relevant age group during the year, divide by the number of people who were in that age group during that year (including those who died), and multiply times 1,000. Increases in infant mortality have a large effect on life expectancy, much as one failing grade will pull down an otherwise solid A average.

The *crude death rate* (CDR) is simply the number of deaths in a year divided by the mid-year population for that year, then multiplied times 1,000. The CDR is measured in deaths per thousand, as are infant and child mortality. As the name implies, it is a crude measure, since a large number of deaths in an elderly population (such as Palm Beach, Florida or Hemet, California) does not necessarily mean that life expectancy is low.

A sudden and short-lived increase in death rates is known as a *mortality spike*. If the crude death rate for a community typically runs in the range of 10 to 15 deaths per thousand, a year where the CDR runs 35 or 40 deaths per thousand is definitely a mortality spike. Mortality spikes most often result from a local disaster of some sort, usually an epidemic, but sometimes war, natural disaster, or famine. As one might expect, mortality spikes may cut across all of a community or may be confined largely to one or more subsets within it.

Segments of communities typically will have differing demographic patterns that can be described by these (and other) measures. The reasons that lie behind these differences stem from a variety of sociocultural and other factors. Poor people, for example, are more likely to die younger, because they may have less access to medical treatment, or they might have poorer nutrition, or they might be less well educated in terms of hygienic life styles. Women are subjected to different health risks, particularly because of the health risks associated with childbirth; there might also be cultural reasons for gender differences in mortality, such as differing access to food during hard times, differing typical occupations (miners or soldiers might be at higher risk than schoolteachers), or differential exposure to disease (men often have spent more time outside the house than women). Ethnic and religious differences might have demographic effects if they are mirrored in significantly differing patterns of behavior. If one ethnic group, for example, suffers from educational or employment discrimination that results in lower incomes, this probably will be reflected in mortality rates. Similarly, ethnic eating habits that include vast quantities of fatty and salty foods probably will have a deleterious effect on mortality for that group, compared to another group with a healthier diet. Demographers must search for reasons behind the differences they see in mortality patterns for different groups.

Unfortunately, some of the differences they see may result from problems with the methods used to calculate the mortality measures. This, alas, is particularly true with cemetery data. First of all, not everyone in a community will be buried in the local cemetery. Some people will be returned to their place of birth or to a town where they formerly resided and purchased a cemetery plot. A few will be lost at sea or in a mining disaster and will never be buried anywhere; they may or may not be memorialized with a marker in a cemetery. Some people in a cemetery will have immigrated to the community only a very short while before, and their status as part of the community otherwise represented by the cemetery is suspect: Their lives have not been shaped by the same forces as their necrological neighbors. Further, poorer people might typically have less permanent markers than richer ones, so the differential destruction of markers or inscriptions by time may skew the sample toward the wealthier members of the community. The same skewing might occur between members of different ethnic or religious groups, one favoring wood markers and the other favoring stone ones. These methodological considerations must be considered whenever one is basing demographic interpretation on grave inscription data. Wise researchers will be concerned over these issues but will not allow themselves to be crippled by them.

YOUR ASSIGNMENT

Your assignment is to collect data from a cemetery and to investigate the patterning of mortality. You will need to complete either Task 1 or Task 2.

Task 1: For Task 1, you should investigate a single period and compare subsets of the community to one another within that period. Gender, ethnic, or religious subsets are obvious possibilities to consider. Gender and ethnicity can be determined by names, though there will be some errors; religion may be assessed by names in some communities, although religious symbols (*e.g.*, crosses versus stars of David) may be more useful. Some cemeteries have particular sections devoted to members of certain religions. (Status level also is a possible factor by which subsets can be defined, and you may already have subsets based on status distinctions if you have completed Exercise 20.) Some cemeteries have only a single ethnicity within them, and if you are studying one of these and wish to make a comparison by ethnic group, you probably will have to find a research partner to pool data with. An example of demographic measures for the United States as a whole is included in Tables 19-1 through 19-3 to provide values to which you can compare your results.

Task 2:   For Task 2, you should examine a single community and chart its demographic changes over time. If your cemetery has little diversity in terms of ethnicity and economic status, you have a greater likelihood of seeing simple patterns, since these variables will not intervene. You may wish to restrict your study to a single ethnic community within a cemetery, if the cemetery is large enough to permit this.

   With either task, once you have described the demography of your necrological (dead) community, you have to try to explain it. Why was life expectancy increasing or decreasing over time? Why might a mortality spike have occurred at two cemeteries or among one economic class and not another? Why did one ethnic group have higher mortality rates than another, particularly in terms of infant mortality? Why was life expectancy lower for women than men in one ethnic group, while the opposite pattern was true in another? You may not be able to truly answer these questions without a good deal of further research, but you at least can suggest reasonable possibilities.

   Your report should include an introduction explaining the question you are examining and the data base, a section describing the mortality pattern(s) you examined, a section describing how you calculated the measures you used, and a section suggesting explanations of selected aspects of the pattern(s). Remember that tables or graphs can save a lot of text in the descriptive sections.

Hints

   1.   Be sure that your periods are of appropriate length. If they are too short, there is a risk that a mortality spike will affect your measures inordinately. A one-year epidemic would severely impact a five-year period. Probably 10- to 25-year periods are optimal in most cases.

   2.   In your comparisons, try to control for extraneous variables as much as possible. If you want to compare the first decade of the twentieth century with the second, try to use comparable samples. If one sample has 80% women

TABLE 19-1 Life expectancies for residents of the United States.*

Year of Birth	WHITES		NON-WHITES	
	Males	Females	Males	Females
1850	38.3	40.5	***	***
1890	42.5	44.5	***	***
1900-1902	48.2	51.1	32.5	35.0
1909-1911	50.2	53.6	34.1	37.7
1919-1921	56.3	58.6	47.1	46.9
1929-1931	59.1	62.7	47.6	49.5
1939-1941	62.8	67.3	52.3	55.5
1949-1951	66.3	72.0	58.9	62.7
1959-1969	67.5	74.2	61.5	66.5
1969-1971	67.9	75.5	61.0	69.1
1979-1981	70.8	78.2	65.5	74.0
1984	71.8	78.8	67.2	75.2

*These figures have been calculated by a technique different from that described in this exercise, but the figures can be used for comparison. Triple asterisks indicate that figures are not available from U.S. census data for these periods and groups.

TABLE 19-2 Infant mortality rates for residents of the United States, in numbers of deaths before the age of 1 year per 1,000 live births.*

Year	Whites	Non-Whites
1915	98.6	181.2
1920	82.1	131.7
1930	60.1	99.9
1940	43.2	73.8
1950	26.8	44.5
1960	22.9	43.2
1970	17.8	30.9

*Nationwide statistics are unavailable before 1915.

TABLE 19-3   Crude death rates for residents of the United States, in deaths per 1,000 living persons during the calendar year.*

| Year | WHITE | | NON-WHITE | |
	Male	Female	Male	Female
1900	17.7	16.3	25.7	24.4
1910	15.4	13.6	22.3	21.0
1920	13.0	12.1	17.8	17.5
1930	11.7	9.8	17.4	15.3
1940	11.6	9.2	15.1	12.6
1950	10.9	8.0	12.5	9.9
1960	11.0	8.0	11.5	8.7
1970	10.9	8.1	11.2	7.8

*Statistics before 1900 are unavailable. Tables 19-1, 19-2, and 19-3 were compiled principally from two publications: U.S. Bureau of the Census, 1975, *Historical Statistics of the United States, Colonial Times to 1970*, two parts, Washington, D.C., and U.S. Bureau of the Census, 1979, *The Social and Economic Status of the Black Population in the United States: An Historical View, 1790-1978*, Washington, D.C.

and the other has 20% women, you really are comparing mortality at different periods *and* mortality of different sexes. Try to be sure that your samples for different periods are comparable in terms of other variables that might affect the results.

3.   Whichever task you are working on, you will need to collect data representing the entire community at your cemetery, at least for the period(s) you plan to analyze. This means that you will need to study either a small community or sample a larger one. As always, sampling will require some thought. If you were to examine only one side of a cemetery, for example, your sample might by chance include mostly rich people from an early period and mostly poor people from a later period, perhaps giving an erroneous impression that life expectancy was falling. (See Appendix B for some pointers on sampling.)

4.   As with other cemetery exercises, team data collecting might reduce the time needed to successfully collect the required data.

5.   It is important to calculate all the measures described in this exercise for each data set or subset you are studying. It may be, however, that your interpretation and conclusions will focus on certain telling measures and not deal in depth with others.

6.   Assessing the causes of demographic patterns is not easy. You may find, for example, that women are dying younger than men in your sample. In all probability, you will not be able to prove the reason why, at least not without a great deal of outside research. Consequently, your conclusions probably will focus on possible causes for the patterns.

BIBLIOGRAPHY ON CEMETERY DEMOGRAPHY

Barclay, George W. 1958. *Techniques of Population Analysis.* John Wiley and Sons, New York. A widely used text in the techniques of population study. Although theory has changed in the intervening period, the techniques described here remain current.

Bogue, Donald J. 1969. *Principles of Demography.* John Wiley and Sons, New York. A classic text in sociological demography, designed to take the beginning student all the way to a substantial knowledge of the field.

Dethlefsen, Edwin S., and James Deetz. 1967. Eighteenth-century cemeteries: A demographic view. *Historical Archaeology* 1:40-42. A brief note citing the value of cemeteries for historic demographic data from the viewpoint of historical archaeology.

Hollingsworth, T. H. 1969. *Historical Demography.* Cornell University Press, Ithaca, New York. Only a brief treatment of the use of cemetery data, with a general treatment of the field.

Howell, Nancy. 1986. Demographic anthropology. *Annual Review of Anthropology* 15:219-246. A review of current and significant literature of the field, with excellent bibliography.

Swedlund, Alan, and George Armelagos. 1976. *Demographic Anthropology.* William C. Brown Publishers, Dubuque, Iowa. Largely concerned with methods, which have changed little since this treatment.

Weiss, Kenneth M. 1973. *Demographic Models for Anthropology.* Society for American Archaeology, Memoir #27. A general treatment of use to archaeology, emphasizing life tables.

Willigan, Dennis J., and K. Lynch. 1982. *Sources and Methods of Historical Demography.* Academic Press, New York. A basic text in the field.

In addition, most states have compilations of vital statistics that present historical demographic patterns, often calculated for separate genders and ethnic groups.

— EXERCISE 20 —
ESTIMATION OF SOCIAL STATUS
WITH CEMETERY DATA

OVERVIEW

Cemeteries provide data that can be used to assess the degree of personal worth that an individual had in life. This exercise asks you to collect and use data on grave markers and post-interment offerings from a cemetery to evaluate individuals' status.

ARCHAEOLOGICAL ESTIMATION OF STATUS

Archaeologists frequently wish to estimate the status of an individual. Strictly speaking, they usually are dealing with *socioeconomic status* (a measure of an individual's access to wealth, goods, and prestige), rather than simply *social status* (a measure of how highly an individual is regarded in his or her community). Often, however, archaeologists use the term "social status" or simply "status" as a sort of shorthand.

There are two basic categories of ways that archaeologists estimate social status, and the two have many similarities. First, one can examine the artifacts or other remains directly associated with individuals' lives, *e.g.*, the foundations of their residences, ceramics in their refuse-disposal areas, or food remains in their refuse-disposal areas. The more expensive the items, the higher an individual's socioeconomic status.

This general approach is reasonable, since the remains are presumed to have been procured and used by the individual in question. In practice, however, distortions may arise from inaccurate identification of remains with a particular individual (the historical archaeologist misreads documents and erroneously identifies a house as that of S. Frost, when it really was that of R. Sepulveda); from blurring of patterns as a result of individuals, usually from the same household, sharing a refuse-disposal area (rich Uncle Harry lived his last years with relatives of modest means, or slave and slaveholder refuse are commingled); from blurring of patterns as a result of various other mechanisms (someone disposes of trash in a neighbor's area, a house and its dump change hands, a house burns down and its cellarhole becomes a dump for other families, etc.); and from charitable gifts of hand-me-downs from the rich to the poor (Black Lucy is impoverished but receives gifts of partial sets of fancy china from rich people).

Second, the archaeologist can examine items associated with an individual's death, grave offerings in the broad sense, to estimate socioeconomic status. Since these items typically will be found with the person's remains and often include personalized inscriptions, most of the problems discussed above disappear. Of course, other sources of potential distortion replace them. Since offerings usually are purchased by survivors, they sometimes indicate more about the affection for the deceased than about the deceased's socioeconomic status. Also, some individuals or cultures (*e.g.*, Mennonites) discourage ostentatious grave offerings, while others (*e.g.*, Italians) value them highly and may encourage survivors to spend beyond their means to come up to expectations. In addition, a family's financial situation may change over time, as when the nineteenth-century death of a husband and loss of his income often would reduce the circumstances of a widow and her children, a fact reflected in grave offerings. Finally, those at the lowest end of the socioeconomic ladder may have no marker whatsoever and may be archaeologically invisible. These potential difficulties don't invalidate the approach, but they must be kept in mind as limitations. It is this second approach to estimating status that you are asked to explore in this exercise.

GRAVE OFFERINGS

There are three major categories of offerings that occur at graves. First, *interment offerings* are items that are included with the body when it is placed in the ground. Some of these goods are conventional within a society (*e.g.*, a coffin in Anglo-American society), although there can be considerable differences in the nature and cost of these conventional goods; the inclusion of other goods, such as a wedding ring, favorite book, or piece of religious paraphernalia, often is optional. Obviously, these offerings can be made only at the time of the burial. Second, there is the *grave marker* itself and any associated architecture. These items usually are placed moderately soon after the interment itself, although there can be lags or replacements. Third, there are *post-interment offerings*, items that are placed on the surface of the grave (or perhaps within an aboveground tomb) after the burial. These items may be placed at any time, although they are most commonly placed on holidays and anniversaries of the deceased's birth, death, and perhaps marriage or other significant life events. Depending on the cultural tradition, post-interment offerings may consist of flowers, candles, food, drink, toys, shoes, money, glass, or any variety of other items. Post-interment offerings typically are temporary, intended to remain on the grave only for a limited time.

From the point of view of the survivor who is placing the offerings, there are very real economic differences among the kinds of offerings. An interment offering requires that the item be available for inclusion in the grave immediately, since burial must be soon after death. Offering a cherished object belonging to the deceased usually produces no financial hardship. But for expensive purchased items, especially coffins, a shortage of immediate funds can mean that the survivor must settle for a lesser item than that desired. (Of course, credit can alter this situation, and some ethnically based credit unions have special "funeral loans" to finance a funeral and associated offerings that otherwise would be financially beyond the reach of a family. Also, some fraternal organizations in the last decades of the nineteenth century and the first few decades of the twentieth century had primary functions as burial societies, assisting members in the financing of their funerals and burials; this was particularly true of the Woodmen of the World.)

The grave marker, like the coffin, often is an expensive item. In contrast, however, it is a simple matter to defer the placing of the marker in most cemeteries, using the time between the burial and the placement of the marker to save the funds required. (Some cemeteries, especially private cemeteries that have their own monument sales, have strict rules that the marker must be placed within a specified, short interval after the burial.) Some families have the best intention of purchasing a grave marker but never are able to save sufficient funds, leaving the grave marked with the typical white-metal tag that is placed as a temporary marker by many funeral homes or cemeteries (often known as a "pauper's marker").

Post-interment offerings differ from the other types of offerings in that they typically are small items, costing relatively little. Consequently, they are within the financial reach of a far greater proportion of the survivors than are the other types. A family that may never be able to save $2,000 for a granite marker may place a floral arrangement on a grave twice a month for ten years, for a total expenditure of $2,400; the difference is not in the total amount of money expended but in the timing of that expenditure.

PRICE INDEXES

In order to establish what individual has the greatest expenditure for a grave marker (or ceramic vessels or anything else), the archaeologist needs to have some way of estimating relative costs of items. One way to do this, of course, would be to conduct the extensive documentary work that would establish prices for the item or items in question. A new scale would be necessary for each period, and some fancy calculations would need to be performed to compensate for the changing value of currency over the years.

An alternative approach to this problem has been pioneered by George L. Miller (1980) for nineteenth-century American ceramics, and the same approach can be (and has been) applied to a variety of other commodities. Rather than calculating exact prices, Miller's ceramic price scaling index gives relative prices. One ceramic type (it doesn't matter which one) is assigned a cost of 1.00, and others are given index values in relation to that one. In 1870, if Type X cost twice as much as the baseline type, its index would be 2.00; if Type Y cost half as much, its index would be 0.50. By 1880, the baseline type still is given an index of 1.00, regardless of how much its price might have changed from 1870; if Type X now costs one and one-half times as much as the baseline type, its index is 1.50; if Type Y now costs two-thirds as much as the baseline type, its index is 0.67. In this manner, a matrix of price indexes for different items and different periods can be produced. While the index values cannot be converted directly into dollars, they provide a common measure of the cost of these items at different times, independent of fluctuations of the value of currency and other economic factors.

Price scaling indexes can be established for different regions, in recognition of different market, production, and transportation factors. Sometimes, of course, exact prices are not available, but reasonable estimates of the costs or relative costs of items usually are known in historical periods. In practice, the archaeologist may have to make some assumptions about the cost of an item on the basis of its size, its fanciness, the rareness of its materials, the quality of artistic expression, the amount of labor required to produce it, or the distance from its point of origin or manufacture.

This price-index approach has been used widely in recent historical archaeology. Tables 20-1 and 20-2 present price-index information for grave markers and typical post-interment grave offerings. The grave marker indexes are modified from work by Clark (1987). Instructions for their use are given in the captions to the tables. These are only approximate guides, and ideally local factors would be considered before using them. Nonetheless, they will help you establish relative costs of grave markers and offerings.

YOUR ASSIGNMENT

Your assignment is to analyze socioeconomic status as evidenced by the grave markers and other offerings at a cemetery. The assignment has two component tasks, which can be completed individually or together.

Task 1:   Which social groups have generally higher or lower social status than others, as evidenced by grave markers? For this task, you will need to select two social groups, such as men versus women, Jews versus Gentiles, or Irish versus Germans. Then, using the price indexes presented above, calculate the relative expenditure for each grave marker and the mean expenditure per social group. Your report should include a statement on your methodology, your data, your calculations, your conclusions, and an evaluation of what factors may have distorted the analysis in your case.

TABLE 20-1   Price-index figures for grave markers, 1850-present, by region of North America.*

		REGION				
Period	Material	Northeast	Southeast	Midwest	Southwest	Northwest
1970-	gray granite	1.00	1.00	1.00	1.00	1.00
present	black granite	1.65	1.60	1.60	1.50	1.50
	red granite	1.50	1.40	1.40	1.30	1.30
	green granite	2.00	1.85	1.85	1.75	1.75
	white marble	1.00	1.00	1.00	1.00	1.00
	gray marble	N/A	N/A	N/A	N/A	N/A
	other marble	3.50	3.50	3.60	3.70	3.70
	white bronze	N/A	N/A	N/A	N/A	N/A
	yellow bronze	1.35	1.30	1.30	1.20	1.20
	slate	2.00	2.00	2.00	2.00	2.00
	concrete	0.25	0.20	0.20	0.15	0.15
1910-1969	gray granite	1.00	1.00	1.00	1.00	1.00
	black granite	1.85	1.80	1.80	1.70	1.70
	red granite	1.50	1.40	1.40	1.30	1.30
	green granite	2.00	2.00	2.00	2.00	2.00
	white marble	0.50	0.50	0.60	0.60	0.60
	gray marble	0.35	0.30	0.35	0.40	0.40
	other marble	3.40	3.50	3.50	3.50	3.50
	white bronze	1.35	1.25	1.00	1.25	1.25
	yellow bronze	1.40	1.40	1.40	1.40	1.40
	slate	N/A	N/A	N/A	N/A	N/A
	concrete	0.25	0.20	0.20	0.15	0.15
1850-1909	gray granite	1.00	1.00	1.00	1.00	1.00
	black granite	1.90	1.85	1.85	1.80	1.80
	red granite	1.50	1.40	1.40	1.30	1.30
	green granite	2.00	2.00	2.00	2.00	2.00
	white marble	0.50	0.50	0.60	0.60	0.60
	gray marble	0.35	0.30	0.35	0.40	0.40
	other marble	3.40	3.50	3.50	3.50	3.50
	white bronze	1.25	1.20	1.00	1.20	1.20
	yellow bronze	N/A	N/A	N/A	N/A	N/A
	slate	0.75	0.75	0.85	1.00	1.00
	concrete	0.25	0.20	0.20	0.15	0.15

*Since these figures are for monuments of equal size, they must be multiplied times the volume of the marker. To estimate volume, multiply height times depth times width; in cases of irregular shapes, calculate the volume of the smallest rectangular prism that would enclose the marker. Ledger stones, set flush with the ground surface, should be calculated as six inches thick. While the amount of engraving affects cost, that has not been figured into these indexes.

N/A = material not available.

TABLE 20-2   Price index figures for typical post-interment offerings, as of the late twentieth century.*

OFFERING	PRICE INDEX
real roses (per rose)	1.0
real lilies (per lily)	0.8
real other flowers (per flower)	0.5
plastic flowers (per arrangement)	1.0
silk flowers (per arrangement)	1.6
wreath of real flowers	4.5
wreath of plastic flowers	2.0
other wreath	2.5
potted plant	1.6
bottle/can of beer	0.7
bottle/can of soda	0.5
plate of food	3.0
hell money (per bundle)	0.7
tennis racquet	12.0
baseball glove	15.0
baseball cap	10.0
small toy	4.0
glass vase	1.5
ceramic vase	1.8
candle	1.0
holy statue	6.0
shells	0.1

*These indexes apply to all regions of the United States and Canada.

Task 2: Do grave markers and post-interment offerings produce the same estimates of status? For this task, you should take ten recent graves. Using grave markers and the price index given above, calculate their relative costs and place the graves in order of cost of their markers. Then collect data on post-interment offerings at the same graves and produce another ordering of the graves. Compare the two sets of orderings you have derived. Your report should include a statement on your methodology, your data on the grave markers and post-interment offerings, your calculations, and your resulting orderings of graves. In addition, you should explore any differences in the two sets of status rankings, answering such questions as:

• What financial or other circumstances on the part of the deceased's survivors might account for these discrepancies?

- If you are looking at two cultural traditions, are there consistent differences between the patterns?
- Considering the differing preservability of the different types of offerings, what distortions of interpretation might develop if only archaeological information were available?

Hints and suggestions for these tasks are given in the following sections.

Hints and Suggestions: Task 1

1. Stick to a single, short period. Since your goal is to compare two social groups, don't confuse the matter by also studying different periods. If you can restrict yourself to a decade or two, that will be best.

2. It is important to have enough graves so that your patterns are meaningful and not produced by chance, but you do not want so large a sample that data collection becomes your life's work. Probably about 25 graves per social group is best.

3. Remember that it is unlikely that any pattern will be absolute, with everyone in one ethnicity or gender being high status and everyone in another being low status. Accordingly, you probably will have to use some simple quantitative methods (*e.g.*, percentages or averages) to make your comparisons. If you have statistical skills, feel free to use them.

Hints and Suggestions: Task 2

1. You will need a set of graves to monitor for post-interment offerings. These should be moderately recent graves, since post-interment offerings will trail off over time, as friends and relatives die or move away, or even as grief fades among the survivors. One way to determine how long after death post-interment offerings continue to be made in your cemetery is to simply look around it, noting death dates on markers and presence or absence of recent offerings.

2. If you have completed Task 1 and some of those graves fit the requirements for Task 2, feel free to reuse the data and calculations from them.

3. Be sure that the graves you select have some diversity in terms of status level as evaluated by grave markers. This is a good way to increase the probability that you will have enough variability to make the exercise meaningful.

4. A major variable affecting the differential emphasis given to different types of offerings is ethnicity. So, you may want to select all graves from a single cultural tradition and keep the number of variables low.

5. To monitor the graves, you must set up a schedule of visits to the graves, at which time you will record the post-interment offerings present on the grave. You will want enough detail on the offerings so that you can estimate their cost and so that you can recognize any that might be carried

over from your last monitoring visit. You will need to visit each grave at least once a week, preferably twice a week.

6.   How long should you monitor post-interment offerings? The longer the better. Probably a full year would be ideal, but that clearly is not feasible. Although longer would be better, a few weeks of observation probably will allow you to draw some conclusions, providing you realize the limitations of your data set.

7.   Be aware of the impact of holidays on your results. For example, if you are comparing offerings on Jewish and Christian graves, Easter might have a great impact on the number of offerings for one set of graves and not for the other. Be sure to note in your report what relevant holidays (if any) fell within the span of your data collection.

8.   Watch out for cleanup days at the cemetery. Most public cemeteries in urban areas have a designated day when all offerings are removed and thrown away. Usually that information is posted on a sign, but sometimes you will have to ask the groundskeeper. It is worth your time to find this out, since a schedule that calls for checking offerings every Friday morning is going to be fruitless if Thursday afternoon is cleanup day. In some rural cemeteries there are informal cleanups by families, and those usually take place on weekends.

9.   Be especially aware of ethical considerations. Your observation of offerings and offering behavior should be as unintrusive as possible. In your write-up, you should avoid identifying individuals in such a way that a reader could make value judgments regarding the sincerity or depth of emotion felt by survivors; because of this, some students will decide to identify graves with fictitious names or with numbers.

A Note on the Relevance to Archaeology

Some of the older definitions of archaeology stress the antiquity of remains. Clearly, historical archaeology as a discipline quarrels with such definitions, since so many of its remains are so recent. But some archaeology students might wonder whether observing post-interment offerings, as you are required to do in Task 2, is still the province of archaeology.

Many archaeologists argue that archaeology is a set of concerns, theories, and methods that relate behavior and material remains, and that the age of the material remains is irrelevant. Following this line of thinking, this assignment reasons about people on the basis of physical remains and is simply archaeological in nature.

Alternatively, one can view studies such as that in Task 2 as *ethnoarchaeology*, the study of contemporary cases to help calibrate archaeological methods for use in interpreting archaeological remains from the past. In this latter sense, the assignment can inform the archaeologist about the subtleties of methods of estimating status archaeologically, particularly the use of grave markers for inferences of socioeconomic status.

Your conception of the task, either as modern archaeology or ethnoarchaeology, may color the conclusions you draw from your investigation.

BIBLIOGRAPHY ON THE ESTIMATION OF STATUS FROM CEMETERY DATA

Brown, James A. (ed.). 1971. *Approaches to the Social Dimensions of Mortuary Practices*, Society for American Archaeology, Memoir #25 (published as *American Antiquity* 36(3), part 2). Several of the articles in this collection treat the use of mortuary data for the estimation of social status.

Clark, Lynn. 1987. Gravestones: Reflectors of ethnicity or class? *In* Suzanne Spencer-Wood (1987), cited below, pp. 383-395. A treatment that involves constructing a consumer price index for some grave markers.

Miller, George L. 1980. Classification and economic scaling of 19th century ceramics. *Historical Archaeology* 14:1-41.

Spencer-Wood, Suzanne (ed.). 1987. *Consumer Choice in Historical Archaeology*. Plenum Press, New York. A collection of essays on consumer choice, many of which deal with price indexes and the estimation of status.

— EXERCISE 21 —
INFERRING IDEOLOGY
FROM GRAVE MARKERS

OVERVIEW

Scholars commonly assume that symbolic art and inscriptions on grave markers reflect ideas about the world, death, and religion. This exercise asks you to collect data from a cemetery and examine this idea.

THE ISSUE

Many scholars who study gravestones, especially those of colonial New England, assume that typical epitaphs and artistic motifs reflect a period's ideology or idea system. Gravestones bearing depictions of skulls and verses like "My body, soon to be decay'd/Into the mould'ring grave is laid," they argue, indicate a period that dwells on the sorrows and fears of death, as did Calvinism; when the stones are adorned with angels and have lines like "She has gone to a better world above," this is a period that looks forward to the expected joys of heaven after death. Some scholars have gone so far as to characterize periods of colonial history as "morbid" or "hopeful" on the basis of gravestone art and inscriptions. They find support for this idea also in contemporaneous religious writings.

It is an open question, however, whether or not gravestone art and inscriptions are direct reflections of religious philosophy in places and times other than colonial New England. This exercise takes a first step toward examining this idea.

YOUR ASSIGNMENT

Your assignment is to examine the grave marker art and inscriptions at a cemetery and to make some interpretation of the religious ideology they may reflect. Do the inscriptions and art on gravestones encapsulate the ideology of the religion whose members are buried beneath them? Do the symbols, images, and messages on the marker reveal the group's attitudes toward death, the afterlife, and other relevant issues? You can use a cemetery of any period or region *except* colonial New England. Your report should present your goal, evidence, discussion, and conclusion.

Hints for Success

It will be best to choose a single religious group to study during a single period. If possible, select a religion whose ideology is familiar to you; if not, you will have to do a bit of reading to gain some familiarity with its ideas. If possible, the time period you select should be characterized by a general consistency of ideas. If members of the religion you are examining were very traditional in the 1920s, were in turmoil in the 1930s, and became very progressive by the 1940s, a period from 1910 to 1950 would span a variety of viewpoints and would make a poor and confusing unit of analysis. One way to help ensure a consistent period is to limit it to a decade or two.

Examine both epitaphs and artistic motifs. If the assumption that gravestone imagery reflects ideology is valid generally, they should carry similar messages. You will want to focus your attention on symbols and meanings that seem relevant to the group you have selected to study. For Quakers, peace symbolism might be critical; for the Penitente Catholics of northern New Mexico, Christ's passion and suffering might be more important.

One of the more difficult tasks in this assignment is figuring out what the message of a particular epitaph or motif might be. For the epitaphs, consider them as you would poems. What is the theme? If you had to restate the author's main point in everyday language, how would you do so? Try to reduce each epitaph to a single kernel.

For the art motifs, you will have to look a bit more deeply. A sheaf of reaped wheat symbolizes one's life, as does a dead bird. (A particular bird, however, can have a different meaning, as a dove can symbolize peace or the Holy Spirit of Christianity.) A weeping willow indicates the sorrows ("weeping") of death. Sometimes similar symbols can have radically different meanings; a cut flower symbolizes death, while a living one symbolizes life or resurrection. Additional trickiness is introduced by the fact that the same image can have different meanings in different traditions, as when a lotus symbolizes indolence and self-gratification in Christian ideology, yet the same image symbolizes religious enlightenment in most Buddhist traditions. This symbolism can be difficult, but fortunately you have various reference works on the subject, some of which are listed in the bibliography of this exercise. You may also be able to get assistance for especially difficult symbols from a clergyman of the religion you are studying.

Sometimes you will not be able to find any symbolic interpretation in your sources for an artistic motif. In this case, you may be able to make a reasonable guess about its meaning by considering how symbols work. A symbolic image always shares something with that which it represents. Daffodils represent resurrection, because they are the first flowers (in some areas) that arise from their "death" at the end of winter and begin blooming. A lamb or flower bud can represent a child, because neither has reached maturity. A butterfly in flight may represent a soul ascending to heaven, since both "fly" upward. By considering the characteristics of the object depicted, you may be able to mount an argument for its symbolic meaning. Of course, some symbols make sense only with additional information, as when Protestants symbolize religious faith with an anchor, symbolism that makes sense only if one knows the hymn that celebrates "the anchor of faith." There is nothing wrong with suggesting a possible interpretation for a symbol whose meaning you are unable to find, but you must be careful to explain the reasoning behind your suggestion and recognize its possible fallibility. The fewer documented symbols in your evidence, the less faith you can have in your interpretation.

Remember that you have to look at all the graves in your period; alternatively, you can devise an appropriate sampling scheme, following the ideas presented in Appendix B. In any case, you shouldn't just "cherry pick" the cases that support your own viewpoint.

BIBLIOGRAPHY ON INFERRING IDEOLOGY FROM GRAVE MARKERS

Abrahams, Israel. 1921. Symbolism (Jewish). *In* James Hastings (ed.), *Encyclopaedia of Religion and Ethics,* Charles Scribner's Sons, New York, vol. 12, pp. 143-145. Brief treatment of Jewish symbols.

Appleton, LeRoy H., and Stephen Bridges. 1959. *Symbolism in Liturgical Art.* Charles Scribner's Sons, New York. A brief compendium of Christian symbols.

Barber, Allen H. 1989. *Celestial Symbols: Symbolism in Doctrine, Religious Traditions, and Temple Architecture.* Horizon Publishers, Bountiful, Utah. A non-academic treatment of religious symbols in Mormonism.

Benes, Peter. 1977. *The Masks of Orthodoxy: Folk Gravestone Carving in Plymouth County, Massachusetts, 1689-1805.* University of Massachusetts Press, Amherst, Massachusetts. Revisionist treatment of Puritan gravestone art and its symbolism.

Ferguson, George Wells. 1959. *Signs and Symbols in Christian Art.* Oxford University Press, Oxford, England. Moderately thorough compendium of symbols from Christian art.

Fleming, Daniel Johnson. 1940. *Christian Symbols in a World Community.* Friendship Press, New York. Valuable in its treatment of Christian symbols as modified in India, China, Japan, and Africa.

Hall, James. 1974. *Dictionary of Subjects and Symbols in Art.* Harper & Row, New York. Discusses many symbols from classical mythology and Christianity.

Ludwig, Allan I. 1966. *Graven Images: New England Stonecarving and Its Symbols, 1650-1815.* Wesleyan University Press, Middleton, Connecticut. Treatment of Puritan gravestone symbolism.

Preston, Percy. 1983. *A Dictionary of Pictorial Subjects from Classical Literature: A Guide to Their Identification in Works of Art.* Charles Scribner's Sons, New York. Useful in deciphering many neoclassical art motifs.

Réau, Louis. 1955. *Iconographie de l'Arte Chrétien.* Presses Universitaires de France, Paris. A compendious, multi-volume guide to the symbolism of European Christianity; in French.

Sill, Gertrude Grace. 1975. *A Handbook of Symbols in Christian Art.* Macmillan Publishing Co., New York. Excellent guide to Old Testament, New Testament, and customary Christian symbolism. The symbols discussed under "Miscellaneous Objects" are especially far-ranging.

Tashjian, Dickran, and Ann Tashjian. 1974. *Memorials for Children of Change: The Art of Early New England Stonecarving.* Wesleyan University Press, Middleton, Connecticut. Pioneering study of symbolic reflections of Puritan ideology in gravestone art.

— APPENDIX A —
PLANNING YOUR RESEARCH

Several of these exercises ask you to decide how to use the data presented to come to a conclusion; others ask you to collect the data and use them to reach a conclusion. Since these are tasks you may not have been asked to do before, a few words on how to go about them are in order.

You will need to develop a *research strategy*. That is, you will need to get straight in your mind exactly what it is that you wish to learn, what information you will need, and how you will interpret that information. This sounds childishly simple, but it can be terribly difficult in execution.

The first step, deciding your goal, may have been taken partly for you in the assignment, but it still remains for you to figure out the details. For example, the assignment may ask you to compare social status for two social groups in a cemetery (Exercise 20); you need to figure out which groups you will be comparing. Keeping this goal in mind is paramount to successful research.

The second step, figuring out which data to collect, is a bit harder. For this, you must consider what sorts of information could support the achievement of your goal, as well as what sorts of information may be available and feasibly collected. There is no point in collecting data just because they are readily available, even though they don't help you achieve your objective. Conversely, there is no point in worrying about some set of data that doesn't exist or that you can't collect. If your data are provided by the exercise, of course, you don't need to consider whether they are available, but you certainly do if you will be collecting them yourself. Even if data are provided in the exercise, it is up to you to decide which data are relevant to the task at hand.

The third and final step in planning research is to decide how to interpret the data. You must already have developed some idea, or the data would not have survived your examination for relevance in the second step. Now, you must make sure that you really can use these data to support a conclusion. In some cases, it may be wise to establish criteria for supporting one or another conclusion before you actually begin the analysis, so that your subconscious urge to have the results come out as you wish will not color your conclusion.

Most historical archaeologists produce *research designs* before they begin their research. The research design is a written version of the research strategy, usually with a fair amount of detail and a summary of the relevant research to date. Research designs take a bit of time to complete well, but they can be quite helpful in formulating your ideas and presenting them to others in order to get criticism. They also usually are required in applying for grant support for a project or for archaeological permits, required in many places for fieldwork.

Collecting data, as you are required to do in Exercise 3 and all the exercises in Part Five, should take place only after you have your research strategy clear. It is wise to go into the field only when you have established exactly what you want to collect; efforts before that often lead to having to repeat the collection process to fill in gaps or clarify data. Many students find forms or checklists useful to remind them of the data they need.

If your instructor approves, you may be able to pool your efforts in data collection for some of the exercises. The cemetery exercises, in particular, require a fair amount of effort in the collection of data, and you may be able to reduce your time commitment without diminishing the educational value of the exercise. For example, three or four students examining a cemetery might want to divide it into sections, assign each student a section to investigate, then share the data. Remember, of course, that you will have to standardize your data collection procedures ahead of time. Also remember that you have to trust your partners' skills and diligence; select your partners accordingly. There are few things more frustrating than completing an analysis of data you suspect are faulty and wondering if your conclusions (or lack thereof) are valid. If you do opt for sharing data this way, be sure that each partner has a large enough chunk of data to collect so that he or she gets a good "feel" for the data and the job of collecting them; this can be an important part of the educational experience of these exercises.

Most of these exercises should be able to be completed without major consultation of outside sources. Your class discussions and readings, as well as the exercises themselves, normally will provide adequate background, but there may be cases where you will need to consult some of the sources listed in the bibliographies. If you missed a class discussion or if your instructor has decided not to cover a particular topic in class or readings, you may need to do outside reading to complete an exercise. You may, of course, simply want to enrich your knowledge of a particular method or topic, in which case the bibliographies also should be helpful.

A few of the exercises, however, will demand that you consult reference works for certain pieces of information. The source analysis (Exercise 1) will demand that you use dictionaries to find eighteenth-century meanings of unusual words and to search for anachronisms; the toponymy exercise (Exercise 2) will require that you search out place names for transfer names; the faunal analysis (Exercise 10) will require that you consult outside sources to determine the approximate sizes of the animals whose meat was consumed at the sites; and the grave-marker symbolism exercise (Exercise 21) will require researching the meanings of particular symbols.

For some of the exercises, you may need to use simple statistics or quantitative measures. Appendix C can assist you with some very simple quantitative measures.

Finally, be especially aware of ethical considerations for any exercise requiring fieldwork. It is important to remember that you are collecting information at the pleasure of those individuals into whose life you are intruding. Consequently, it is imperative to be concerned that your intrusion is only minimally disruptive. This is especially true for the cemetery exercises, where it would be possible for an insensitive investigator to wound people's feelings at a fragile time.

— APPENDIX B —
SAMPLING

In the ideal world, sampling would be unnecessary. If a researcher wanted to know public opinion on the next presidential election, pollsters would scurry over the nation, asking every registered voter. This presumably would produce a fine reflection of opinion, but there is an obvious practical problem with this approach. In much the same manner—and for much the same reasons—historical archaeologists and other researchers need to come up with some way to look at a manageable portion of something and to learn about the entire thing. This is the heart of sampling.

Sampling is the methodology of examining a subset of something to draw conclusions about the whole. In the terminology of sampling, the whole is called the *population* and the subset is called the *sample*. The *sample fraction* is the percentage (or proportion) of the population that is comprised of the sample; the *sample size* is the number of items in the sample. For example, assume there are 22,000 grave markers in a cemetery, and you want to take a sample of 220. Your population is all 22,000 grave markers, your sample size is 220, and your sample fraction is 1%.

Is this an adequate sample? Without knowing the characteristics of the population as a whole, you can't tell; of course, most of the time you wouldn't bother with a sample if you knew the characteristics of the population, so this isn't much help. There are, however, a couple of rules of thumb that can help you in establishing the size for an adequate sample. First, sample size means more than sample fraction. The 1% sample in the example given above (sample size of 220) is more likely to be adequate than a 25% sample of a cemetery with only 8 grave markers (sample size of 2). Second, the greater the diversity in the population, the larger the sample needs to be to be likely to represent that diversity. A very small sample size might be permissible with a mass-produced product, while a larger sample size might be required for a hand-produced and variable product.

There are several ways to select a sample. A *systematic sample* is drawn by assigning serial numbers to the elements in your population and selecting each whose serial number is evenly divisible by a previously agreed-upon number. For example, if you want a sample fraction of 1/8, include every eighth element. Systematic samples are easy to select, and (so long as you don't doctor your sample by assigning serial numbers in such a way that you overrepresent some subset of the population) they ensure some sort of diversity in your sample. (For example, if all the Japanese graves in a cemetery are in the southwest corner, you are unlikely to get only Japanese graves in a systematic sample.) There are problems, however. If you choose every other grave in line, you could get all men, providing husbands and wives were buried alongside one another, with each gender always on the same side.

Another kind is the *random sample*. A random sample is drawn by assigning serial numbers to all the elements in the population, then using a random number generator (available easily on virtually all computers and on many calculators) to select which numbers will be in the sample. This sample type has considerable advantage for statistical inferences, but it can be time-consuming to use. Further, occasionally the sample will—by chance—underrepresent some segment of the population, such as the Japanese graves mentioned above.

One way around this latter problem is to use a *stratified sample*. Let's assume that you are studying a cemetery whose graves are entirely of Japanese and Mexicans, and you want to compare them. Obviously, you want a sample that will include both in acceptable numbers. You can decide that you want 50% of your sample to come from each group (even if they are not evenly divided in the cemetery population). Each one of these groups is known as a *sample stratum* (not to be confused with a soil stratum), and this type of sampling is stratified sampling. Within each of these strata, you may use any approach to select the sample. Consequently, you could select a "stratified random sample" or a "stratified systematic sample." Stratified sampling may leave you with a sample that has some limits for representing the population as a whole, as when you take a 50% sample of the Japanese graves, although they may comprise only 3% of the whole. Nonetheless, stratified sampling is popular and solves many sampling problems.

Finally, there is *judgmental sampling*. Some researchers object to calling this sampling at all, since it allows the researcher to simply include or reject any element in a sample at will. While there are serious dangers with judgmental sampling, it is a way of selecting a sample and it sometimes is appropriate to use. The greatest danger, of course, is that it gives free reign to the researcher's prejudices: If you expect the Mexican graves to be fancier than the Japanese graves, you might—consciously or unconsciously—choose graves that will help you confirm that pattern.

These various types of sampling can be applied to a wide variety of problems. In addition, researchers modify them as seems desirable. For example, a systematic sample of 1/8 could be taken by including every eighth grave in the rows of a cemetery or by including all the graves in the northeasternmost corner of the cemetery. The important thing in any sampling design is that it make sense in terms of producing a data set that fairly represents the population and can be gathered efficiently.

BIBLIOGRAPHY

Babbie, Earl. 1992. *The Practice of Social Research,* sixth edition. Wadsworth Publishing Co., Belmont, California. This is a standard and widely available text on research methods in the social sciences, and it has a readable and useful section on sampling.

Mueller, James W. 1974. The use of sampling in archaeological surveys. Society of American Archaeology, *Memoirs* 28. This is a widely available reference for sampling in archaeology, though it is very technical and oriented particularly toward field survey.

Thomas, David H. 1986. *Refiguring Anthropology: First Principles of Probability and Statistics.* Waveland Press, Prospect Heights, Illinois. This text has a section on sampling.

There also are brief discussions of sampling in most modern texts on archaeological methods, at least those beyond the introductory level.

— APPENDIX C —
BASIC DESCRIPTIVE STATISTICS
AND OTHER RELEVANT ARITHMETIC

Many of the exercises in this manual require that you summarize data, and you will need to use some mathematics to do so. This appendix reviews some of the simple procedures that may assist you in the exercises.

Statistics, the use of mathematical procedures to analyze data, usually is divided into two categories. *Inferential statistics* is the set of techniques that allow a researcher to make some probabilistic statement about a phenomenon on the basis of a sample. While inferential statistics would have many applications in these exercises, some techniques are fairly complex, and they are beyond the scope of this appendix. All of the exercises in this book can be completed without resorting to inferential statistics.

Descriptive statistics, the set of techniques designed to summarize the characteristics of a set of data, is the other type of statistics. These techniques are more critical to successful completion of these exercises, and most techniques of descriptive statistics are far simpler to use. In fact, many are in common usage.

PROPORTIONS AND PERCENTAGES

Proportions are used to indicate what part of a whole is composed of something. For example, a proportion could be used to indicate what part of an assemblage of sherds is glazed. Proportions are calculated according to the formula

$$\text{proportion} = \frac{x}{n}$$

where n is the total number or measure and x is the number or measure of the subset. If 3 sherds are glazed in an assemblage of 6 sherds, 3/6 or 0.5 are glazed. Proportions always range between 0 and 1.0.

Percentages are very similar to proportions and are used mostly in the same ways. To convert a proportion to a percentage, simply multiply it by 100. A proportion of 0.5 equals 50%.

Occasionally very small proportions are described in terms of other units. Death rates, for example, are often expressed in "deaths per thousand" in order to avoid fractional percentages; similarly, chemical analyses of artifacts to identify their sources of raw material often identify rare elements in "parts per million."

AVERAGES, MEANS, AND SIMILAR MEASURES

"Average" is a general word to refer to any single figure that summarizes a series of figures. In more technical usage, these are called *measures of central tendency*, and there are several of them.

Mean is the most commonly used measure of central tendency. It is calculated according to the formula

$$\text{mean} = \frac{\Sigma x}{n}$$

where Σx is the total of the individual values and n is the number of individual values. For example, if 11, 12, 15, 16, and 16 pipestems were found in the five cellars in a site, the mean would be calculated by adding 11 + 12 + 15 + 16 + 16 (= 70) and dividing the sum by 5 (= 14). The mean is a basic summary of a series of numbers, but it can be misleading if a few of them are very different from the others, dragging the mean up or down. (A simple test to help catch computational errors in deriving a mean is to look at the highest and lowest values being averaged; the mean must lie between these. Often the mean will be more or less centered between these extreme values, but this is by no means universal.)

Median is a measure of central tendency that is largely unaffected by a few extreme values. To calculate the median, place all your values in order; the one that has an equal number of values above and below it is the median. If there is an even number of values and two of them are tied for the middle value, then take the mean of those two values. In the pipestem example given above, the median is 15.

The *mode* is a lesser-used measure of central tendency. It is simply the most common value in a set of values. It is most useful if most of the values are alike and there are a few oddballs. In the pipestem example, the mode is 16.

As another example of how these measures work, consider a case where there are seven pieces of window glass with thicknesses of 0.12, 0.12, 0.12, 0.13, 0.14, 0.22, and 0.27 inch. The mean is 0.16 inch; the median is 0.13 inch; and the mode is 0.12 inch. Each is a valid summary of the series, but each fails to convey some of the information carried by the others.

SUMMATION

Formulas sometimes require that you add things together, and this is represented by Σ, the Greek letter "sigma." This symbol simply means that you should add together the value of each individual for the characteristic that follows the Σ. For example, if d = the diameter of a doughnut's hole, then Σd means the sum of the diameters of the doughnut holes in your sample.

ROUNDING OFF

When working with decimals, you can begin accumulating lots of numbers to the right of the decimal point quickly. For example, multiplying 7.822 times 3.1212 results in 24.4140264, with a numeral in the ten-millionths place. To avoid accumulating unnecessary and potentially misleading numbers to the right of the decimal point, the rule is that the result of multiplication or division can have no more places to the right of the point than any number that went into its calculation. For the example in this paragraph, then, the result could have only three decimal places: 24.414.

Sometimes numbers are rounded off to fewer decimal places for other reasons. When calculating dates by formulas, for example, it is silly to produce a date like 1655.7124; this is equivalent to September 16, 1655, at 9:07 P.M., and no archaeological dating is that precise. Instead such dates usually are rounded off, either to a whole year or tenths of a year, *e.g.*, 1655 or 1655.7.

There are standard rules for rounding off decimals. Always look one decimal place to the right of the place you want your last numeral to be. If the number to the right is 5 or larger, round upward; if it is 4 or smaller, round downward. So, 6.77 rounds upward to 6.8, 81.9 becomes 82, 33.65 becomes 33.7, 2.99 becomes 3.0, and 3.22 becomes 3.2.

BIBLIOGRAPHY

Shennan, Stephen. 1988. *Quantifying Archaeology*. Academic Press, New York. Reprinted with minor corrections in 1990. An excellent treatment of both descriptive and inferential statistics as they relate to archaeological analysis.

Thomas, David H. 1986. *Refiguring Anthropology: First Principles of Probability and Statistics*. Waveland Press, Prospect Heights, Illinois. A widely available text on quantification and statistics, largely devoted to archaeology.

— APPENDIX D —
WRITING YOUR REPORTS

The exercises in this manual are similar to real-world historical archaeological cases. That is, they are complex and have their share of ambiguities and seeming contradictions. Analyzing these problems and writing up your results require skills that may be new to you. This appendix offers a few suggestions to assist you, though your instructor, of course, may choose to modify or override them.

GENERAL POINTS

1. Think through the problem and plan carefully before beginning an exercise. The exercises are sufficiently complex that you will need to develop a strategy before beginning the analysis, much less before writing your report. Appendix A treats this issue in greater depth.

2. Be analytic in your thinking. You must make various decisions in completing the exercises: which data to use, what methods to follow, and the like. Be sure that those decisions are based on rational reasoning, and explain to your reader that reasoning.

3. Explore the issues. Even moderately straightforward exercises, such as Exercises 14 and 15, have factors that could influence your conclusions, and you should be alert to recognize and discuss those factors in your reports.

4. Expect contrary evidence and try to choose between conflicting data rationally. In the real world of archaeology (and in these exercises), it is unlikely that every piece of information will point to the same conclusion. In that case, the analyst must decide which pieces of evidence warrant greater confidence than others. What outside forces might have led to error, distortion, or confusion? Did the writer of the document have a vested interest in making people believe he was poorer than he really was? Were the potsherds in Test Pit 37 possibly brought in by the rodent who dug the burrow in that unit? Did the type of statistical test used in the analysis predispose a particular conclusion? Is one set of evidence only from a single source and overwhelmed by equally good but numerically superior evidence to the contrary?

5. In your concern with presenting a sound argument for your conclusion, don't shortchange contrary evidence. It is all too easy to brush aside such evidence as "too trivial to note," but fight the urge. Sometimes you won't even realize that you are actually suppressing data that weaken your argument, so

remain vigilant. Note contrary evidence fairly; if you feel it is appropriate to do so, dismiss it and tell why. You may be left, however, with niggling bits of contrary evidence that you cannot dismiss in good conscience.

6. Expect that not all conclusions will be absolute. The nature of archaeology is such that critical tests of the sort common in physics and chemistry are rare. Consequently, conclusions often are prefaced with "probably" or "apparently," and they certainly are subject to reassessment with further study. It is perfectly reasonable to state a conclusion with reservations and to explain those reservations.

7. Be sure to include a statement and justification of your methodology. Most of these exercises ask you to devise a way to answer a question, and there are many different ways to do so. You feel that the approach you have selected is reasonable and valid, and you should explain why to your reader. Other analysts may choose different approaches, and you need to argue why your approach is more likely to produce valid results.

8. There are few "correct" answers. For most of these exercises, there are several possible conclusions, depending on how you approach the question and which data you consider most reliable. Consequently, the justification of your reasoning is at least as important (and often more important) than the conclusion you reach.

9. In the real world of research, scholars share ideas and seek criticism before completing a study, and you may want to do the same. It is perfectly reasonable to ask classmates whether such and such an argument makes sense (to anyone other than its creator) or whether they have found an eighteenth-century meaning of "limner" or some other word in a document to be analyzed. There are a couple of cautions, however. Be sure that you are not overwhelmed by a classmate's criticism, whether negative or positive. The most intelligent person sometimes will fail to recognize a good argument or catch a spurious one. You should *consider* your critic's response but not be ruled by it. Also, remember that your exercises ultimately lead to your grade in a course, so your analysis, conclusions, and reports must be essentially your own work.

PRESENTING YOUR REPORTS

1. Be sure that your report addresses the assignment. In the heat of analysis, you may stray from the task originally assigned. Consequently, it is often useful to reread the assignment section of an exercise periodically as you progress.

2. Follow the rules of good writing. Your first task in writing is to communicate. Therefore, be direct and avoid convoluted constructions. Large, scientific-sounding words can have their places in reports, providing they are used properly and assist communication. Misusing them or using them in

such density that they make the writing more confusing or harder to read, however, should be avoided.

3. Organize your reports into labeled sections. Your report doesn't need to flow like a poem, and including headings will make both your writing and your instructor's reading easier.

4. Use tables, graphs, and other devices when they will assist communication. If you have a series of numbers to list, for example, a table probably is appropriate. It will be much more readable than a paragraph stuffed with data, and it will leave your text for discussion and interpretation of the data presented in the table. Always be sure that your text refers to the table at the point when you want your reader to examine the data. If you have more than one table, always number them to be sure there is no confusion. The judicious use of tables and other devices can reduce the size of your report and your effort expended in producing it.

5. Pay attention to the hints included in the individual exercises. These often will guide you, particularly in terms of pitfalls to avoid. Your instructor probably also will present additional hints, suggestions, and cautions.

6. If you use outside reference works, cite them appropriately. Whenever you use data or distinctive ideas that you got from a published source, note the fact. Include a bibliography of the sources you used. For most of the exercises, there is no expectation that you will need to use outside sources, but for some (especially Exercises 1, 2, 10, and 21), you clearly will need to do so. See the note in Appendix A regarding outside references.

7. You will have to decide how long the report for an exercise should be. Never pad your report with fluff because you feel it is too short; instructors are highly skilled at recognizing this technique and will look for substance, not mere volume. Most good reports probably will fall between four and eight typewritten pages.

― APPENDIX E ―
GLOSSARY OF TERMS
USED TO DESCRIBE CEMETERIES
AND GRAVE MARKERS

archaism a conscious return to an older style, no longer current. The term can be used to refer to grave markers or any other form of art. An example is the 1970s revival of slate gravestones with cherubs.

arm the crosspiece of a cross.

backdating the practice of a gravestone carver to date a marker to the date of the deceased's death, although the stone was carved at a later date. Many stones are placed some years after burial, sometimes replacing less permanent markers that have decayed over time.

bas-relief sculpture *see* **sculpture, bas-relief**.

bolster a form of gravestone where a cylinder (usually at least 18 inches in diameter and 36 or more inches long) rests on its side on a footing. Bolsters were most common in the early twentieth century.

bronze an alloy of copper and tin.

—bronze, white a form of bronze used in upright grave markers, especially from the American Midwest in the late nineteenth and early twentieth centuries. White bronze is recognizable by its dusty gray color. It was cast into markers and typically has preserved well.

—bronze, yellow a form of bronze used in many late twentieth-century flat markers. It is recognizable by its brownish-yellow color.

bundle burial *see* **burial, bundle**.

burial 1. grave. 2. the body within the grave. 3. the act of burying a body.

—burial, bundle a burial where the body is tied into a tight mass with cords or fabric. Bundle burial is prominent in some American Indian burial traditions, though it is uncommon in most Western traditions.

—burial, primary a burial where the body is placed in its grave shortly after death, with no prior or temporary burial. Primary burial is the most common form of burial in most modern cemetery traditions. *comp.* **burial, secondary**.

—burial, secondary a burial where the body has spent considerable time (often several years) in a temporary resting place before removal to its final resting place. Secondary burials have been fairly common in various death traditions around the world and persist mostly in traditions that have strong non-Western folk elements. *comp.* **burial, primary**.

—burial, urn the burial of an urn with cremated remains in it.

burial axis the line that follows along the length of the body in a burial; the "length" of the grave. *see* **orientation**.

cairn a pile of rocks. Cairns can be erected over graves as markers, as bases to support crosses or other upright markers, or as protective devices from scavenging animals. *comp.* **mound, rock**.

Celtic cross *see* **cross, Celtic**.

cemetery any place where more than one body has been buried, especially (but not necessarily) with grave markers. Different governmental agencies have slightly different criteria for what legally constitutes a cemetery.

—**cemetery, church** a cemetery owned by and organized by a religious body.

—**cemetery, customary** a cemetery that has developed by custom, as patrons have used an area for a cemetery but have developed no institutional structure to deal with it. Customary cemeteries often have no legal basis.

—**cemetery, ethnic** a cemetery that is dominated by members of one ethnic group. Ethnic cemeteries often are established especially to give members of an ethnic group a place to practice their particular death rituals.

—**cemetery, family** a cemetery where a family uses some of its own land to bury its members. Occasionally a non-family member will be admitted.

—**cemetery, private** a cemetery operating as a for-profit operation, owned by a corporation.

—**cemetery, public** a cemetery owned and operated by a governmental unit for the public use. This type of cemetery can be extremely variable in its nature.

cenotaph a grave where the body is not present; a memorial erected as over a grave, but at a place where the body has not been interred. A cenotaph may look exactly like any other grave in terms of marker and inscription. Cenotaphs often commemorate the deaths of those lost at sea, in war, or by some other means where recovery or transportation of a body would be difficult.

centerpiece a sculpture or other monument, usually in the middle of a cemetery, commemorating no one in particular, but for the benefit of all buried there. Centerpieces usually are religious and are quite prominent in many Catholic traditions, as with the ornate crucifixion scenes of French-Canadian cemeteries and the large crosses of Mexican cemeteries.

cerquita in the Mexican cemetery tradition, a low fence that surrounds a grave or a grave plot. *see* **grave fence**.

chest tomb *see* **tomb, chest**.

chronological layout *see* **layout, chronological**.

church cemetery *see* **cemetery, church**.

coffin a box for holding a body at burial, usually made of wood in folk traditions. Modern coffins are usually made of metal and concrete. *see* **vault2**.

columbarium a building for the housing of cremated remains. *comp.* **mausoleum**. *see* **niche2**.

commercial referring to something that is the product of commerce, something that is sold.

coped stone any stone with a coping, especially one with a peaked (roof-shaped) top. Coped stones were common in the British cemetery tradition from the eighteenth through the early twentieth centuries.

coping a narrow ornamental thickening and overhang of the margin of the top of a gravestone. The term comes from a sort of roof element, and a coping resembles a small, overhanging roof.

cremation the burning of human remains before their disposal. In the United States, some cremated remains are placed in cemeteries or columbaria, while others are strewn over the ocean or retained in survivors' homes.

cross the geometric form produced by the intersection of two (rarely more) lines; the Christian symbol of the crucifixion of Jesus, frequently used as a grave marker. Crosses most frequently are made of wood, stone, or concrete. The parts of the cross are the upright (the central, vertical piece), the arm or arms (the crosspiece or crosspieces that intersect the upright), and the terminals (the ends of the crosspiece or crosspieces and the upper portion of the upright, often ornamented). Most crosses in Western Christianity have a single arm, while many in the Russian, Serbian, Byzantine, and Greek Orthodox churches have two or even three sets of arms. A cross may have a nimbus, a more or less circular or diamond-shaped piece in back of the intersection of the upright and (main) arm, often representing the spirit of Jesus. *see* **arm; nimbus; terminal; upright.**

—**cross, Celtic** a form of cross, particularly associated with Irish and Scottish graves in Ireland, Scotland, and elsewhere. The Celtic cross has a circular nimbus, ornate surface or openwork carving, and frequently arms that expand toward the terminals.

—**cross, rustic** a grave marker of stone or concrete, representing a crude cross made by lashing together two small logs, complete with carving or molding to represent bark and stubs of side branches.

—**cross, slab** a form of grave marker, usually in concrete or stone, but occasionally of wood. The slab cross has a slab section at its base (often, in the Mexican tradition, with a shallow nicho) and is surmounted with a cross; they are made of a single piece of material. Slab crosses are common in the Mexican tradition but occur elsewhere.

crown the central hump in a crowned gravestone. *see* **crowned.**

—**crown, lateral** on a crowned gravestone, one of the (usually lower) humps on the sides. *comp.* **crown.**

crowned referring to a gravestone shape where the top rises in several (usually three) humps, usually with the central one higher than the others. *see* **crown; crown, lateral.**

curb *syn.* **grave curb.**

curbing *syn.* **grave curb.**

customary cemetery *see* **cemetery, customary.**

dressed referring to stone whose surface has been completely smoothed or otherwise finished. *ant.* **undressed.**

emerging stone a type of gravestone where one portion of the stone has been fully carved, while another portion remains undressed or only partially dressed, giving the impression of a stone that has been incompletely carved. The emerging stone was most common in the late nineteenth and early twentieth centuries and symbolized a life partially completed but cut short. Emerging stones are nearly always of granite.

epitaph a brief saying or literary note, inscribed in a grave marker. An epitaph may be standardized (*e.g.*, "memento mori") or unique to the individual (*e.g.*, "Here lies John Brown, lost at sea and never found."). The name, places and dates of birth and death, and other such biographical information that may be part of the inscription are not considered part of the epitaph.

exhumation the removal of a body from a grave.

extended referring to a burial where the body is laid in the ground more or less fully straight, with arms and legs straight and arms by the sides, as when a person lies on a narrow couch. *comp.* **flexed.**

false crypt *syn.* **tomb, false.**

false tomb *see* **tomb, false.**

family cemetery *see* **cemetery, family.**

family-plot layout *see* **layout, family-plot**.

family stone a gravestone that marks the entire family's plot, not a particular individual's grave. In the United States, such stones are most common in the European traditions. Sometimes a family stone also will have the names and dates of the individuals of the family carved on it, but there usually will be separate stones for the individuals.

finial an ornament atop a post or similar element in furniture or other craft. Finials can occur on the posts of grave fences or (less commonly) on grave markers themselves. Finials always have radial symmetry, as if formed on a lathe.

flexed referring to a burial where the body is placed in the ground in a more or less compressed position, on its side with the knees bent and drawn up under the chin and the arms bent accordingly. *comp.* **extended**.

flowerholder a commercial vessel, usually made of bronze, that fits into a recess in the footing of a grave and can be pulled upward to hold flowers.

flowerpot a vessel inset into a concrete footing to hold flowers at a grave. Flowerpots often are parts of homemade grave markers in folk traditions.

folk referring to any tradition that is passed down from generation to generation and is relatively uninfluenced by popular culture. *comp.* **popular; commercial**.

footboard a flat, slab-like wooden grave marker placed at the foot end of a grave. Footboards are used only in conjunction with headboards and usually are considerably smaller and less ornate, often bearing only initials as inscriptions. *see* **headboard**. *comp.* **footstone**.

footing a slab, usually of concrete, that is horizontal and flush with the surface of the ground, on which a grave marker is placed. The footing itself usually is unornamented and considered structural, not a part of the marker itself.

footstone a flat, slab-like stone grave marker placed at the foot end of a grave. Footstones are used only in conjunction with headstones and usually are considerably smaller and less ornate, often bearing only initials as inscriptions. *see* **headstone**. *comp.* **footboard**.

full-round sculpture *see* **sculpture, full-round**.

grave the individual feature where a body (rarely more than one body) is buried in a single pit or its equivalent, including any marker or monument associated with it. *comp.* **plot**.

—**grave, horizontal-flush** *syn.* **ledger stone**.

—**grave, horizontal slab** *syn.* **ledger stone**.

—**grave, mass** a grave where many people are buried together. In most historic societies, mass graves have been expedients for emergencies when death was massive and rapid, as during an epidemic, war, or disaster.

—**grave, multiple** a grave where two or more bodies are buried together. A multiple grave may be a mass grave or simply a grave where members of a family or other social groups are placed upon death. Multiple graves are rather uncommon in recent historic societies.

—**grave, outlying** a grave that is located well away from others. Such graves often are given to members of society deemed unacceptable, *e.g.*, at the San Miguel Cemetery (San Miguel, California), where two outlying graves are for a bank robber and the only Chinese in town. In Catholic cemeteries, outlying graves may be for excommunicates, suicides, and the like.

—**grave, sunken** *syn.* **grave depression**.

—**grave, vertical slab** *syn.* **upright stone**.

grave curb a low border, usually of stone or concrete, surrounding a grave or plot, beginning slightly underground and extending no more than a few inches above the surface of the ground. A grave curb is open in the middle, although the central area may be filled with gravel, scraped earth, or lawn. *comp.* **grave fence; paving**.

grave depression a hollow in the surface of the ground over a grave, brought about by the collapse of a disintegrating coffin. *syn.* **grave, sunken**.

grave fence a fence surrounding a grave or plot completely, usually one or more feet high. A grave fence can be of the most homely materials or of elegant and expensive commercial fencing. *e.g.* **cerquita**. *comp.* **grave curb; grave rail**.

gravehouse a ramada (roof with corner posts supporting it) over a grave, or a shed over a grave. The gravehouse is known especially from the American South. It probably developed there from local Indian usage, but it may have developed from a weaker tradition in England.

grave lamp any type of lighting device placed on a grave, apparently symbolizing eternal light (in the Judeo-Christian tradition). It may be kept lighted or not; it may even be incapable of being lighted, as with a light bulb placed on the surface of a grave, a fairly common grave offering in various parts of the American South.

grave landscaping any modification of the grave area in terms of plantings, gardens, fountains, or the like. Grave landscaping is most prominent with elite graves, such as that of Douglas Fairbanks, Sr., the famous actor. His grave has fountains, reflecting pools, a shrine, and trees. Grave landscaping in America began essentially with the rural cemetery movement of the mid-nineteenth century, beginning in the Northeast.

grave marker any above-ground device or monument to mark a grave. e.g. **gravestone; grave rail**.

grave offering any item sacrificed or donated at a grave. A grave offering may be durable and visible (*e.g.*, shells, jewelry), ephemeral (*e.g.*, wine or beer poured into the ground), or anywhere in between (*e.g.*, flowers). Grave offerings may be conceived as items of use to the deceased in the afterlife, as items to enhance or commemorate the status of the deceased (and his or her survivors), or as simple obligations. A grave offering may be made at the time of burial and included in the coffin or grave pit with the body, or it may be placed on the grave at any time after burial. *e.g.* **libation**.

grave pit the actual hole into which a body is placed, including a filled-in hole.

grave post a simple wooden post used as a grave marker.

grave rail a wooden rail placed along the long side (burial axis) of a grave on the surface as a grave marker. Normally, grave rails form a pair, one on each side of the grave. They are in the British burial tradition and are immediate predecessors to gravestones in England and New England, although they are a simple form and may have been reinvented in different traditions.

gravestone 1. a stone grave marker. 2. more loosely, any grave marker. *syn.* **tombstone**. *comp.* **memorial; monument**.

haka a grave post in the Japanese cemetery tradition. Haka typically are about three feet high and eight inches across, square in cross-section and usually untapered, with a top faceted into a point. Haka frequently are of white-painted wood, though they can be of stone or other materials. They usually bear inscriptions in Japanese.

headboard a flat, slab-like wooden grave marker placed at the head end of a grave. Headboards may be used alone or in conjunction with footboards. *see* **footboard**. *comp.* **headstone**.

headstone a flat, slab-like stone grave marker placed at the head end of a grave. Headstones may be used alone or in conjunction with footstones. *see* **footstone**. *comp.* **headboard**.

hell money paper, sometimes printed to resemble money and sometimes blank. It is burned in Chinese (and some Southeast Asian) offerings to the dead; sometimes it is offered at a grave unburned. It can be purchased in many Asian food markets. *syn.* **joss paper**.

horizontal-flush grave *syn.* **ledger stone**.

horizontal slab grave *syn.* **ledger stone**.

hornito in the Mexican cemetery tradition, a type of relicarito shaped like a cylinder cut in half lengthwise, with the cut surface placed on the surface of the ground. (The overall shape resembles that of a quonset hut.) The hornito is hollow, so flowers, statuary, or other offerings can be placed within it, often semi-permanently. The name comes from the Spanish for "little oven" because of the similarity in shape to the Spanish-American traditional bread oven.

impressed referring to a form of decoration of concrete grave markers. Impressed decoration is made by pressing something against the surface of the concrete while it is wet, then removing it, leaving an impression. This is a fairly common technique in various folk cemetery traditions, with leaves and crucifixes among the more commonly impressed items.

incising the creating of a line by drawing a stylus or similar tool through the surface of a wet material before it hardens. Incising is a common method of making inscriptions or producing artwork on concrete markers, particularly in folk traditions.

inhumation the burial of a body in the ground.

initial stone a gravestone with initials carved at the base as a maker's mark. *see* **maker's mark**.

inscription writing on a grave marker. By convention, this term is used regardless of the technique used to render the writing (*e.g.*, carving, painting, etc.). The inscription usually includes biographical information and the epitaph, if any.

—inscription, relict the traces of an inscription, otherwise destroyed, that may reveal that inscription. For example, although a painted inscription on a wooden slab has worn away completely, the painting may have protected the wood beneath it, so that the lettering remains in subtly raised letters, while the surrounding wood has been eroded slightly away. Appropriate lighting can be very important in recognizing and deciphering relict inscriptions.

inset referring to the placing of objects in the concrete of a grave marker when it was wet. This is particularly common in some folk traditions, including the Mexican folk tradition, where marbles may be inset in the form of a cross or a small crucifix may be inset into a concrete cross.

interment the burial or other disposition of a dead body.

joss paper *syn.* **hell money**.

lateral crown *see* **crown, lateral**.

layout the spatial organization of a cemetery.

—layout, chronological a cemetery layout where graves are arranged by death order, with no consideration of family or other alliances. This layout is typical of the Mexican folk tradition cemetery.

—**layout, family-plot** a cemetery layout where graves are arranged by family affili-
ation, not by death order. This layout is typical of most recent European cemetery
traditions.

ledger stone a grave marker that is placed horizontally, flush with the surface of the
earth. This style marker has become increasingly popular with cemetery maintenance workers because of the ease of mowing grass around and over them.
syn. **horizontal slab grave; horizontal-flush grave.** *comp.* **upright stone.**

libation a special sort of offering consisting of liquid that is poured onto or into the
ground over a grave.

lichgate an arching gate, usually of iron, at the entrance to a cemetery. This comes
from the northern European burial traditions but is considerably more widespread now. The term literally means "corpse-gate." *var. sp.* **lychgate.**

lot an area of a cemetery owned or controlled by an individual or family. Most often,
a lot is owned by a family and will contain their graves, although lots sometimes
are owned by friends, organizations, even motorcycle clubs. Although the notion
seems engrained in most American burial practices, it developed in relatively
recent times. *comp.* **plot.**

lot marker a small marker, usually stone or cement and usually flush with the surface
of the ground, used to demarcate the corner of a cemetery lot.

maker's mark a distinctive mark, usually initials or a name, placed on a gravestone
as an indication of its maker. *see* **initial stone.**

mass grave *see* **grave, mass.**

mausoleum a building for the housing of bodies in separate drawers or compart-
ments. A mausoleum differs from a tomb in that it is owned communally by the
cemetery and patrons purchase rights to a section of it, while a tomb is built,
owned, and used exclusively by a single family or similar group.

memorial a grave marker, usually an ornate one.

monument a grave marker, usually one with some fanciness and size.

motif any more or less standardized artistic theme or representation, such as a rose,
cherub, or urn-and-willow.

mound a pile of earth or similar material erected over a grave as a form of marker.
Earthen mounds are common in many pre-modern societies around the world
(*e.g.*, Adena and Hopewell societies of North American prehistory, Neolithic and
Bronze Age societies of prehistoric Europe, the Jomon culture of prehistoric
Japan, etc.), but earthen mounds are less common in recent burial traditions and
tend to be small when they do occur.

—**mound, grave** a modest earthen mound piled over a grave, whether with or
without an additional grave marker. In the United States, grave mounds tend to
occur mostly in rural folk traditions in the West and South.

—**mound, rock** a low pile of rock, often admixed with earth, erected over a grave. By
convention, "rock mound" refers to an oval or oblong structure that covers the
entire grave area, while "cairn" refers to a circular structure at the head of a grave.
In the United States, rock mounds are most common in the desert cemetery
traditions of the Southwest and California.

multiple grave *see* **grave, multiple.**

neoclassical referring to the art style of the late eighteenth and nineteenth centuries,
where motifs and scenes drawn from classical Greece and Rome (or at least
imagined to be drawn from there) were used in decoration. Urns, draperies,
columns, and certain human poses typify this style.

niche   1. in general, any recess in the surface of something. 2. a compartment in a columbarium or other area for the placement of cremation remains.

nicho   in the Mexican burial tradition, a recessed area in the face of a grave marker (usually of stone or concrete), often receiving a relic of the deceased on earth, a painting or photograph of the deceased, or a holy picture.

nimbus   a halo-like representation in Christian art, especially the representation of such a glow at the intersection of the upright and arm of a cross. In such a position, the nimbus indicates that the cross was that on which Jesus was crucified. The nimbus can be circular, diamond-shaped, oval, jagged, or even square.

obelisk   a gravestone that is tall, slender, square in cross-section, and pointed at the top. Obelisks usually are quite large and imposing, indicating the wealth and stature of the deceased.

offering   *syn.* **grave offering**.

offertory oven   a brick or other oven in a cemetery for the purpose of receiving offerings to be burned. These are most prominent in Chinese-tradition cemeteries. *see* **hell money**.

openwork   carving that cuts entirely through a stone, creating arches, loops, and similar openings.

orientation   the direction of the burial axis of a grave. The direction to which the head points (or at least where the main marker is) is usually considered the orientation. *see* **burial axis**.

outlying grave   *see* **grave, outlying**.

paving   a surface of concrete, brick, or stone placed on the ground over a grave. Pavings often are used in conjunction with grave markers, although some traditions (*e.g.*, Mennonites) typically simply incise the inscription into a concrete paving and provide no other marker.

pillar   a grave marker consisting of a tall, slender, ornate gravestone with a circular cross-section. Pillars give the appearance of being turned on a lathe and actually derive from the British tradition of Georgian furniture. The term usually is not applied to columns that fit the neoclassical tradition.

plot   an area of a cemetery given over to an individual, family, or other social group. The term is more inclusive than "lot," since a lot can occur only in a cemetery with some institutional organization that assigns areas; in contrast, a plot can develop through usage in a customary cemetery. *comp.* **lot**.

popular   referring to something that derives its vogue from mass media or advertising, as opposed to folk tradition. *comp.* **folk**.

primary burial   *see* **burial, primary**.

private cemetery   *see* **cemetery, private**.

public cemetery   *see* **cemetery, public**.

relicarito   in the Mexican cemetery tradition, an elaborate masonry structure over a grave for housing a relic of the deceased when on earth or for presenting flowers, holy statues, and the like. Relicaritos often have several large recesses for these items; they usually are quite ornate. Rarely (particularly in New Mexico), relicaritos will be made of wood. *e.g.* **hornito**.

relict inscription   *see* **inscription, relict**.

rippling   the undulating or ridged marks left on the back side of a hand-carved gravestone by the chisel, as it was used to thin the stone to its slab-like shape.

rock mound   *see* **mound, rock**.

rock outline an enclosure of undressed rocks around the perimeter of a grave. The rocks typically are cobble-sized or smaller. This really is a simple form of curb. *comp.* **grave curb**.

rubbing a means of obtaining a copy of the bas-relief carving on a gravestone or similar object. Rubbings are made by placing rice paper over the surface of the marker, then rubbing gently on the paper with a soft pencil, a crayon, or a similar writing material. Rubbings are quite accurate in their copying of a design, but some cemeteries have had to forbid the making of rubbings, because the activity is slowly wearing away the surface of the stones.

rustic cross *see* **cross, rustic**.

scraped earth *see* **scraping**.

scraping a characteristic of the American Southern burial tradition and others, consisting of scraping away all vegetation and surface soil from graves or from an entire cemetery. In the South, the trait almost certainly derives from West African usage, although it now is prominent among all races in all parts of the South. *syn.* **scraped earth**.

sculpture any carving or other rendering of stone where all three dimensions (including depth) are used.

—sculpture, bas-relief low-relief sculpture, where depth is only slight and the design is worked on a nearly flat surface.

—sculpture, full-round sculpture where the dimension of depth is developed fully, so that the sculpture has proportions similar to its model.

secondary burial *see* **burial, secondary**.

side panel on a gravestone, a decorative strip along one vertical side.

slab any grave marker that is essentially a thin, flat piece. Slabs can be of any material but usually are of stone, concrete, or wood. They may form a rectangle, a rectangle with rounded corners, or more elaborate shapes.

slab cross *see* **cross, slab**.

slope on a gravestone with a convex upper surface, either of the upper surfaces that curve or angle downward from the stone's highest point.

stamping the placing of an inscription in concrete by pressing letter molds into it while wet.

sunken grave *syn.* **grave depression**.

table tomb *see* **tomb, table**.

terminal the ends of the side arms and upright of a cross. The shape of terminals of wooden crosses in the Mexican tradition is distinctive of regional subtraditions.

terrazzo a synthetic material sometimes used for grave markers. Terrazzo consists of chunks of stone, glass, or ceramics mixed into a fine cement. Typically a polished surface is produced, showing the inclusions in the cement.

tomb a building-like burial receptacle, where a body or bodies are stored aboveground in drawers. A tomb may be grand, but it houses the remains of only a few people, usually family members. *syn.* **vault1**. *comp.* **mausoleum**.

—tomb, chest a form of stone grave marker that resembles a rectangular box with a flat upper surface. The chest tomb is rather heavy appearing and requires a fair amount of stone. It is not a true tomb, since the body actually reposes below ground, under the marker.

—tomb, false a type of grave marker where a slab of stone or concrete covers the area of a grave and extends above the ground anywhere from a few inches to a couple of feet. A false tomb most frequently is boxy, but it may be rounded or otherwise embellished. It may have an accompanying gravestone, or it may bear an inscription itself. It is not a true tomb, since the burial is underground.

—**tomb, table** a stone grave marker similar to a chest tomb but differing in that its top is supported by small columns at the corners only.

tombstone *syn.* **gravestone.**

undressed referring to a stone marker that has not had its surface completely smoothed or otherwise finished. *see* **emerging stone.** *ant.* **dressed.**

upright the vertical element of a cross.

upright stone a grave marker that is placed upright, above the surface of the ground. *comp.* **ledger stone.**

urn burial *see* **burial, urn.**

vault 1. a tomb. 2. a modern concrete shell placed over a coffin to prevent sinking of the ground surface in a cemetery.

vertical slab grave *syn.* **upright stone.**

wedge stone a style of grave marker, usually of stone but occasionally of concrete. A wedge stone, not surprisingly, is essentially wedge-shaped, so that the bottom surface lies flat on the ground, the back surface runs more or less vertically, and the top surface (with the inscription) slopes from the top of the stone at its back to ground level at its front. Wedge stones rarely extend more than 18 inches above the ground surface.

white bronze *see* **bronze, white.**

yellow bronze *see* **bronze, yellow.**

ABBREVIATIONS

ant.	antonym; opposite.
comp.	compare; a similar but different term.
e.g.	example.
see	see for further information; reference to a synonym or other entry where the definition appears.
syn.	synonym.
var. sp.	variant spelling; the definition is given at the more common spelling.